Biodiversity Conservation in India

About the Editors

Bidhan Kanti Das is Assistant Professor of Anthropology (Senior Grade) at Institute of Development Studies, Kolkata (IDSK). He was awarded with Gold Medal for First class First in Masters Degree in Anthropology. He worked as UGC-JRF and SRF for five years. He also worked as Protected Area Sociologist at Buxa Tiger Reserve, Department of Forests in West Bengal under World Bank assisted India Eco Development Project from 1998 to 2003. He is engaged in research in current forest conservation policies, livelihood impact on forest dependent people, Forest-Tribal interface for last 15 years. He has published more than 30 research articles in various national and international journals of repute. He has, also, presented papers in many international and national conferences. He taught post graduate students of Anthropology at Vidyasagar University for eight years. E.mail: *bidhand@gmail.com, bidhan@idsk.edu.in*

Ajit Banerjee is Visiting Professor at R.N.Tagore Centre for Human Development Studies (RNTCHDS), Kolkata. He served in the Indian Forest Service for 22 years. He completed his Ph.D. in Forestry at the University of Toronto, Canada. He was also a senior forestry specialist at the World Bank from 1984 to 1995. He also worked in China as a Consultant promoting participatory forestry on behalf of KfW, the German Development Bank. He has published many papers and research reports on social and community forestry in international and national journals of repute. He has also edited a book entitled "*Footprints in the Forests*" published by Nataraj Publishers, New Delhi. His major contribution to forestry was the 'Arabari' experiment which formed the precursor to now famous Joint Forest Management of over 20 million hectares of forests in India. E. mail: *ajitbanerjee2@gmail.com*

Biodiversity Conservation in India

Management Practices, Livelihood Concerns and Future Options

Edited By

Bidhan Kanti Das
Ajit Banerjee

CONCEPT PUBLISHING COMPANY PVT. LTD.
NEW DELHI-110059

ISBN-13: 978-93-5125-053-1

First Published 2014

Published and Printed by

Since 1974

Concept Publishing Company Pvt. Ltd.
A/15-16, Commercial Block, Mohan Garden
New Delhi-110059 (India)
T: 25351460, 25351794, *F*: 091-11-25357109
E: publishing@conceptpub.com, W: www.conceptpub.com
Editorial Office: H-13, Bali Nagar, New Delhi-110 015, India.

Cataloging in Publication Data—*Courtesy:* D.K. Agencies (P) Ltd. <docinfo@dkagencies.com>

'Potential of Diverse Biodiversity Conservation Approaches and Livelihood Concerns in India' (Conference) (2011 : Institute of Development Studies, Kolkata)
Biodiversity conservation in India : management practices, livelihood concerns and future options / edited by Bidhan Kanti Das, Ajit Banerjee.
p. cm.
Includes bibliographical references and index.
ISBN 9789351250531

1. Biodiversity conservation—India—Congresses. 2. Biodiversity conservation—Government policy—India—Congresses. 3. Biodiversity conservation—India—Case studies—Congresses. I. Das, Bidhan Kanti. II. Banerjee, Ajit. III. Title.

DDC 333.95160954 23

Dedication

To the hundreds of Forest dependent communities in India, who are struggling for survival since pre-Independence period

And

To P B Gangopadhyay, who passed away while it was still in preparation.

His paper appears as Chapter 7

Preface

A vast majority of countries all over the globe held that human actions were destroying the Earth's ecosystems, eliminating genes, species and biological traits at an alarming rate in the first Earth Summit. Biodiversity, in terms of species diversity, is rapidly declining and extinction rates are currently estimated to be 100 to 1000 times than normal rate. Globally, three quarters of the habitable area has been disturbed by human actions. One estimate suggests that about 40 per cent of net primary production on land mass was used directly by human activities; co-opted or lost as a result of activities — for consumptive purpose like crops, timber or fish; livestock grazing or other activities like fires or human induced soil erosion. But it is also a fact that rural communities have always been dependent on these bio-resources for their daily needs particularly in developing countries, including India. So conservation of bio-resources is intricately related to the sustainable livelihoods of local populations. Biodiversity conservation is not only important for its aesthetics, ecology or leisure activities, but is also a matter of equality and social justice. For the poor, the importance of bio-diverse resources is immense. It acts as a 'safety net's against increasing risk of uncertainty, shocks and disasters. Wild resources are considered as the most important resources for families facing hardships at the individual or societal level like poverty, sickness, drought, economic crisis etc. Wild food provides a balanced diet for the poor. Wild meat, fish, insects provide much of their proteins, while forest fruits and vegetables are a source of vitamins. In developing countries, 20-30 per cent of total rural people's income comes from wild plants and animals.

For more than last two decades, conservation of bio-resources across the globe is one of the major agendas for international conventions, international environmental NGOs , national and state agencies as well as conservation biologists. To prevent the depletion of bio-resources, various conservation approaches have been initiated. The approaches range from 'fines and fences' or 'fortress conservation' approach, to 'community based conservation' approach to neoliberal approaches like 'payment for ecosystem services' or 'eco-tourism' or 'bio- prospecting'. The present book is an attempt to provide a comprehensive discussion on the best possible conservation approach which may be undertaken in developing countries including India in the context of socio economic realities.

India is one of the twelve mega diversity countries that collectively account for 60-70 percent of the world's biodiversity. This richness of biodiversity is under threat. The rural population particularly tribal population residing in and around forest areas are facing acute poverty. These tribal communities cohabit with the environment, with production and reproduction systems that depend on the biodiversity of forest ecosystems. An estimated 200 millions of people's lives depend on the conservation of biodiversity of forests. Most biodiversity rich zones or biodiversity 'hotspots' are , in fact, social and political 'hotbeds'. These areas are characterized by high levels of poverty, insecure land tenure and landlessness, unstable political systems, and state sponsored repression. The distribution of forests and indigenous population is correlated particularly in India as well as other developing countries. It is worth noting that areas with high biodiversity overlap with areas where traditional communities maintain control over resource management. In India, the 150 poorest districts, constitutionally designated as Schedule V areas, are primarily inhabited by tribals and are also the 'prime tiger districts'. Creation of protected areas(PAs) without human interference is the major approach for conservation of bio-resources all over the globe including India. Interestingly more than half of the PAs of the world are inhabited by local population and two thirds for PAs in India. India contains 668 PAs at present and has the plan to extend the network in future. This 'fortress conservation' model has frequently been criticised for its adverse socio economic impacts. The creation of PAs causes restriction of future land use options with potentially significant economic opportunity costs. The forced relocation from land or resource use cause exacerbation of poverty as well as contravention of legal or human rights. Moreover, it is ethically incorrect to displace communities without their consent. Forced exclusion has actually led to violent protests, rallies, and acts of sabotage against national parks and sanctuaries themselves.

The current approach of conservation is expensive for developing countries. The rehabilitation programme of the forest department (FD) in India is largely ineffective and the FD has been able to relocate only a few families till now. The Tiger Task Force estimated that if FD wants to relocate all the families from the PAs, about 665 crores of rupees would be required as per current compensation rate (one lakh per family). If compensation amount has to increase by ten lakhs per family one can imagine how much money is required. In India, under 'Project Tiger', a flagship programme for conservation of tigers, crores of rupees have been spent in 28 reserves. The central funds are increasing with time, but without any fruitful results. Notably, the reserves where most funds have been invested are not necessarily the best PAs in the country. On the other hand, market driven natural resource use under neo-liberal paradigm seems to be problematic in the Indian context where poor, marginalised tribals who mostly inhabit the rich biodiversity zones , are incapable of handling market forces. This may lead to further marginalisation. In between these two paradigms, a community conservation narrative that includes local people's participation in managing bio-resources has emerged. Evidences suggest that local communities in India are protecting more than 10,000 forest zones, ranging from a few hectares to several hundred thousand hectares, known as 'Community Conserved Areas'. Though creation of PAs is a dominant approach in India, eco-development approach is being implemented in some PAs with the aim of reducing poverty as well as to conserve biodiversity.

It was in this perspective, the Institute of Development Studies Kolkata (IDSK) organised a national conference on '*Potential of Diverse Biodiversity Conservation Approaches and Livelihood Concerns in India*' held at IDSK Auditorium on 11 and 12 March 2011. It was attended by participants representing broad range of interests -ranging from representatives of forest dwellers, academicians from renowned research Institutes , researchers from NGOs , social activists, forest administrators and decision makers from Government agency, and Ex-forest Administrators in India. Considering the complexity in conservation of biodiversity in developing countries like India, the participants in the conference were engaged in intense debate and discussion so as to enrich the collective understanding on how to conserve dwindling bio-resources in the best possible way and promote livelihood, to identify areas and measures to advocate policies and programmatic actions as well as future research options. This book is an outcome of the said conference.

What is evolved from the debates and discussions that active participation of local people in conservation of biodiversity seems to be most feasible and viable option in India considering the huge social and ecological costs of PAs, overlapping nature of rich biodiversity zones and settlements of traditional forest dwelling communities, poor implementation of rehabilitation programmes for forced displacees, and huge costs associated with the compensation package of forced evictions. In addition, some developmental inputs should be undertaken among the forest dependent communities to enhance livelihood status. This will reduce pressure on forest resources and provide positive conservation outcomes. The possible management operation would be zonation of areas like 'core' and 'buffer' or at the 'landscape' level depending on the biogeography of the local areas. Forest managers should recognise local people as co-partners and should act as facilitators in management of forest resources.

Bidhan Kanti Das

Ajit Banerjee

Acknowledgements

At the very outset, we wish to express our gratitude to all our co-authors, whose known expertise and keen interest in the subject of current biodiversity management policies and livelihood issues of the local residents have contributed enormously to the initiative that have led to the production of this volume. The finalisation of this volume has taken much longer time than expected and we would like to thank all our colleagues for their patience and continuous support extended during this period.

Professor Amiya Kumar Bagchi, Former Director of the Institute of Development Studies Kolkata, first proposed a volume on this subject. He constantly inspired and guided us at every step. We owe our gratitude to Professor Bagchi. We are grateful to Professor Achin Chakraborty, Director, IDSK for inspiration and logistic support. This volume would not have come into existence without Dr. Ramkrishna Chatterjee, IDSK who provided us necessary help in every stage of the work. We are grateful to Dr. Chatterjee.

Most of the articles that feature in this anthology were presented at the national conference held at Salt Lake campus of Institute of Development Studies Kolkata on 15-16 March, 2011 on the 'Potential of Diverse Biodiversity Conservation Approaches and Livelihood concerns in India' which brought together anthropologists, geographers, ecologists, wild life biologists, forest managers, activists from all parts of India to share their experience on current conservation policies and programmes and its impact on livelihood of local residents. We acknowledge with thanks, the constant support and inspiration of our colleagues at the Insititute of Development Studies Kolkata for organising this conference. We are grateful to the Institute of Development Studies Kolkata for providing financial assistance in this endeavour.

We express our warmest thanks to our colleagues at Institute of

Development Studies Kolkata particularly Gorky Chakraborty, Subrata Mukherjee and Saswata Ghosh who continuously enquired about the progess of the book.

We recall with gratitude the excellent support we received from our Library personnel, particularly Madhusri Ghosh, Shyam Prasad Ram, and Ashok Patra who helped us to procure relevant literature whenever required. We are also grateful to the entire staff of IDSK for helping generously whenever such help was needed.

Once again many thanks to the contributors for the trust they reposed in us despite the delay. Finally, we take the opportunity to express our gratitude to Mr. Ashok Kumar Mittal of Concept for undertaking the publication of the volume. Our thanks are due to the editorial team at Concept Publishing Company Pvt. Ltd., New Delhi for adding value to this manuscript.

June 2013
Institute of Development Studies Kolkata

Bidhan Kanti Das,
Ajit Banerjee

Contents

Part - III
CASE STUDIES

List of Tables

List of Figures and Maps

Figures

Maps

List of Contributors

Adrian Lopes is a Ph.D. Student at the Charles H. Dyson School of Applied Economics and Management, Cornell University, Ithaca

Anirban Ganguly is a Faculty at The Energy and Resources Institute (TERI), New Delhi.

Asish Ghosh is the Director, Centre for Environment and Development, Kolkata and Visiting Faculty at School of Environmental Sciences and School of Oceanography, Jadavpur University; Department of Human Rights, University of Calcutta. He has served as a member of the National Biodiversity Authority, Government of India (2003-2010), and also as a Member of the Working Group for the Eleventh Five Year Plan on Environment & Biodiversity, Planning Commission, Government of India. He is a Fulbright scholar, with 50 years of professional experience in India and abroad and authored 352 Research publications on Environment and Natural Resource Management. He led Indian Delegation to the Ramsar Convention in Japan, acted as a member of Indian Delegation to the Asian Wetlands Conference to Malaysia, Indo-Russia Meet on Forests to Russia, IUCN General Assembly to Argentina and other International Meets in Kenya, China and Mexico.

Debashish Debnath is Associate Professor at Indian Institute of Forest Management, Bhopal (an Autonomous Institute under Ministry of Environment and Forest since 1994). He is the author of two books, 60 research papers and 9 popular articles. He attended number of International and National Seminars. He organized number of training programmes at National and regional levels. He undertook number of consultancy Projects at the National and State level. His areas of Interest are Indigenous Knowledge system, Forest Governance, Corporate Social Responsibility, Climate Change and Sustainable livelihood, Tribal women empowerment, rural environment and Development Management.

K.N. Krishna Kumar is the Professor in Communication and Forestry Extension at Indian Institute of Forest Management, Bhopal. He did his Ph.D. in Agricultural Extension from Tamil Nadu Agricultural University and got first class in M.Sc. in Agricultural Extension from Benaras Hindu Vishvavidyalaya, Varanasi. He has published more than 50 research articles and chapters in edited books. He has completed several research projects and undertook consultancy projects at the national and international level.

P.K. Viswanathan, Associate Professor, Gujarat Institute of Development Research, Ahmedabad, was earlier with the Rubber Research Institute of India. He has also worked at the School of Environment Resources and Development, Asian Institute of Technology, Bangkok, been a Visiting Fellow at the Chinese University, Hong Kong, and a Wellcome Trust Visiting Fellow at Mahidol University, Thailand. His research interests include institutional and governance aspects of water resources development, collective action and sustainable livelihood outcomes in smallholder agriculture; agrarian transformation in Asia; ecological economics and community benefits of mangrove restoration; industrialisation and its impacts on natural resources and ecosystems. His Ph.D. is from ISEC, Bangalore.

Pradeep Kumar Mathur, Senior Scientist is a member of the Faculty of Wildlife Science at the Wildlife Institute of India, Dehra Dun. Dr. Mathur pursued M.Sc. 'Experimental Biology' and Ph.D. 'Ecology' with a focus on 'Grazing land and desert ecosystems'. Firstly, he had a short stint as Lecturer at the Regional College of Education, NCERT, Ajmer (Rajasthan). Subsequently, Dr. Mathur served for five years as a field practitioner — "Pasture Expert" and responsible for managing semi-arid grassland reserves. Since 1986, Dr. Mathur has been involved in capacity building programmes relevant to wildlife management and biodiversity conservation through professional training, research, and higher education at WII. His specific interests are in Rangeland ecology; protected area management and planning; and landscape approach to conservation. He has several publications to his credit.

Prodyot Bhattacharya is the Dean at School of Environmental Management in Guru Gobind Singh Indraprastha University, New Delhi. He has worked as faculty at Indian Institute of Forest Management, Bhopal. He did his Ph.D. in the field of Ethnobotany

& Forest Ecology and got first class M.Sc. in Botany with specilization in in Forest Ecology from Saugar University. He has published more than 80 research articles in reputed journals, chapters in books. He completed several research projects and undertook consultancy projects at the national and international level. His areas of specialization are Community Forestry, Non-Wood Forest Products & Agroforestry.

Samit Ghosal is currently employed as Anthropologist (Cultural) in the Anthropological Survey of India. He has obtained Ph.D. in Social Anthropology from the North Bengal University. His areas of interests include Cultural Ecology, Ethnicity, Tribal Studies, Forest and Natural Resource Management with special reference to Biosphere Reserve situation, Maritime Anthropology and Anthropology of Tourism. He has conducted intensive field investigation among the tribal population in Sikkim, Andaman, Madhya Pradesh, Orissa and Maharashtra. He has published a number of articles in national and international journals and edited a book on 'ethnicity and ethnic situation in Central India tribes'. He has participated in various conferences in India and abroad.

Subhabrata Palit is a senior forestry consultant who advises on community forestry strategies throughout the Asia and Africa region. He retired from the Indian Forest Service in 1997 as Chief Conservator of Forests, West Bengal, where he took primary responsibility for conceptualizing and developing Joint Forest Management (JFM) in India. He has published widely on participatory forest management and forest agency reform. His specialities include the training and orientation of key personnel involved in Community Forest Management (CFM) programs in India, including foresters and non-governmental organizations. His books include *Structural Changes in Forest Departments* (1999), published by the World-wide Fund for Nature, New Delhi and *Comparative Analysis of Institutional and Policy Dimensions of Community Forestry in India and Nepal,* by International Centre for Integrated Mountain Development, Kathmandu, Nepal.

Umesh Kumar is Human Ecologist at the Anthropological Survey of India. He was awarded Doctoral degree in 2009 from North-Eastern Hill University. He is also on the editorial board of the journal, 'Practising Geographer'. During his initial posting at Andaman & Nicobar Islands he has completed a number of projects; important among them are studies of tribes of Andaman and Nicobar Islands particularly the Jarawa, the Onges, and the Nicobarese and impact assessment of tsunami at Little Andaman. He is presently engaged in Biosphere Reserves studies. His current research interests include study of livelihood practices of communities residing in the biosphere reserves of India, anthropogenic pressure and conservation prospects. He has published more than two dozen papers in different journals and books.

V.K. Melkani is an Indian Forest Service since 1982 and worked as Field Director, Kalakad Mundanthurai Tiger Reserve and coordinated implementation of a World Bank Project on "Improving Park Management and Eliciting Local People's Support for Biodiversity Conservation through Eco-development". He has about 30 research papers published in national and international journals, proceedings of workshops/seminars. His special areas of interest include inclusive conservation with local communities and other stakeholders on board, capacity building of stakeholders, resolving conflicts on natural resource ownership and use and landscape/seascape conservation issues. Presently, he has been working as Professor & Head, Landscape Level Planning and Management Department in Wildlife Institute of India since December 2008.

Part I

INTRODUCTION

1

Biodiversity Conservation
Current Approaches and Future Options

Bidhan Kanti Das and *Ajit Banerjee*

Introduction

It is widely agreed that increasing population and the accelerated economic growth in a number of developing countries are the main drivers of environmental degradation. One of its forms is biodiversity loss, meaning the depletion of genetic resources, species variety, and natural ecosystems coverage. Global biodiversity in terms of species is likely to be substantially undermined by the year 2100. Some authors believe that about 18 per cent of the species available in the global 'hotspots' within which about 30-50 per cent of all species may exist (Myers *et al.*, 2000) will be lost by 2050, even if all of those areas are fully protected.

The growth of human population has been increasing alarmingly, particularly in developing countries. The world's human population has increased near fourfold in the past 100 years (UN Population Division, 2007). An overwhelming majority of this population is found within the economically poor but biologically rich countries of the developing world (Brechin et al 2003). The rate of population growth, however, is still relatively high in Central America, and highest in Central and parts of Western Africa. In relative numbers, Africa will experience the most rapid growth, over 70 per cent faster than in Asia (annual growth of 2.4 per cent *versus* 1.4 per cent in Asia, compared to the global average of 1.3 per cent and only 0.3 per cent in many industrialized countries) (UN Population Division, 2007). While the number of floral faunal species has decreased alarmingly, the number of protected areas, IUCN categories I-V, designed to protect them, has increased tremendously from about seven thousand in 1991 to more than twenty-eight thousand in 2000, protecting around 6.4 per cent of the world's land mass, up from 4.8 per cent in 1991 excluding hundreds of marine protected areas, biosphere reserves, world heritage sites, or wetlands of international importance (*ibid.*). These events have been compounded by a myriad of commercial and economic development related activities which create greater demand on scarce natural resources and ecological systems. As a result, access to natural resources is being contested by stakeholders at many levels. So the competition over access to resources is bound to rise in future.

Biodiversity as a Concept

Ecologists have found 'biological divesrsity' as a concept difficult to define and measure. In fact, Knopf (1992) asserted that the definitions of biodiversity are "as diverse as the biological resource." Some consider it to be synonymous with species richness (Heywood 1998), others see it as species diversity (Bond and Chase, 2002) whereas others consider it 'full variety in life on Earth' (Takacs, 1996). It is a broad unifying concept, encompassing all forms, levels and combinations of natural variation, at all levels of biological organization (Gaston and Spicer, 2004). After studying 85 definitions of biodiversity, Delong (1996) suggested that 'biodiversity is a state or attribute of a site or area that specifically refers to the variety within and among living organisms, assemblages of living organisms, biotic communities, and biotic processes whether naturally occurring or modified by humans.' That means, biodiversity is the variety of living organisms on earth, the range of species, the genetic variability within each species, and the varied characteristics of ecosystems (O'Riordan, 2002).

Recently various International Organisations or Conventions have attempted to define biological diversity. The International Convention on Biological Diversity (2003) defined it as the variation at the levels of genes, species and ecosystems. According to International Convention on Biological Diversity (CBD), 'Biological diversity' means the variability among living organisms from all sources including *inter alia*, terrestrial, marine and other aquatic ecosystems and the ecological complexes of which they are part; this includes diversity within species, between species and of ecosystems. The same Convention stressed on those biological resources which are relevant for *human use*. That means 'biological resources' includes genetic resources, organisms or parts thereof, populations, or any other biotic component of ecosystems with actual or potential use of value for humanity. On the other hand, 'Ecosystem' means a dynamic complex of plant, animal and micro organism communities and their non-living environment interacting as functioning unit' (Convention on Biological Diversity, June 1992, Article 2, "Use of Terms"). This definition has been further refined by the World Resources Institute (WRI) as comprising genetic diversity, the variations between individuals and populations within a species, and species and ecosystem diversity; to which some also add functional diversity (WRI, 1994). In the Millennium Ecosystem Assessment (MEA), the definition of biodiversity is further extended. Biodiversity is defined as "the variability among living organisms from all sources including, *inter alia*, terrestrial, marine and other aquatic ecosystems and the ecological complexes of which they are part; this includes diversity within species, between species and of ecosystems."(2005). It explicitly recognizes that every biota can be characterized by its taxonomic, ecological, and genetic diversity and that the way these dimensions of diversity vary over space and time is a key feature of biodiversity. This variety can usefully be thought of in terms of three hierarchical sets of elements, which capture different facets: *genetic diversity* which refers to the diversity of genes within a single species as well as between species; *organismal diversity* which recognises the variety of roles that different organisms — including the separate life stages of individual species — play in the ecosystem; and *ecological diversity* that recognises the different taxa contained within an ecosystem (Harper and Hawkesworth, 1995).

All these definitions have actually given importance on species richness. They speak equally of the biodiversity of some given area or volume (be it large or small) of the land or sea, of the biodiversity of a continent or an ocean basin, or of the biodiversity of the entire Earth.

Likewise, one can speak of biodiversity at present, at a given time or period in the past or in the future, or over the entire history of life on Earth. However, the tendency to define biodiversity in terms of species richness is, in fact, a poor political strategy in marine ecosystems, since global (as opposed to local) extinction is virtually unknown in marine populations, with the exception of mammals and birds. In order to achieve this we need to move away from the traditional definitions of biodiversity, often expressed in terms of obscure taxonomic distinctions, and identify socially meaningful effects of species and habitat loss. For example, agronomists have long promoted biodiversity by arguing that monocultures are prone to disease, and pharmaceutical companies have publicised the number of new drugs that they have discovered in obscure species (Gaston and Spicer, 2004).

Biodiversity can be measured in terms of genetic diversity and the identity and number of different types of species, assemblages of species, biotic communities and biotic processes, and the amount (e.g. abundance, biomass, cover, rate) and structure of each (Delong, 1996). It can be observed and measured at any spatial scale ranging from microsites and habitats to the entire biosphere. Considering species diversity as biological diversity, some models and indices have been developed (Hamilton, 2005). However, some matrices have also been developed to include broader concept of biodiversity. For example, Parkes and his colleagues developed 'habitat hectares index' that combines vegetation area with its quality (2003). Quality parameters include canopy cover, the number of large trees, number of logs, patch size and proximity to a stand of vegetation. The extended version of the habitat hectares index is known as Biodiversity Benefit Index (Oliver and Parkes, 2003). But these indices have been criticised due to absence of strict ecological meanings, assigning subjective weights for various components. Moreover they are not representative of actual ecological processes and the statistical distributions associated to each component are not considered (Hamilton, 2005).

Importance of Biodiversity

Biodiversity, in terms of species and functioning of ecosystems, provides global and local benefits. These include food, water, genomes, regulation of floods and climate, waste treatment, recreation and aesthetic enjoyment, soil formation, nutrient cycling, breeding grounds of prey, and plant pollination (MEA, 2005). It is the key to ecosystem health, as it serves as an absorptive barrier, providing protection from environmental shocks and stresses (Stolton *et al.,* 2008).

The Millennium Ecosystem Assessment Report (2005) provides a comprehensive account of the usefulness of bio-resources to maintain life. For example, biodiversity is used by many rural communities directly as insurance and coping mechanism to increase flexibility and spread or reduce risk in the face of increasing uncertainty, shocks, and disasters. The availability of this biological "safety net" has increased the security and resilience of some local communities to external economic and ecological perturbations, shocks, or surprises (MEA, 2005). Coping mechanisms based on indigenous plants are particularly important for the most vulnerable people, who have little access to formal employment, land, or market opportunities.

Secondly, agricultural biodiversity can improve food security. It is important for agicultural production. Wild strains of domestic crops provide genetic variability that can be crucial for overcoming outbreaks of pests and pathogens and new environmental stresses. Many agricultural communities consider increased local diversity a critical factor for the long-term productivity and viability of their agricultural systems. Incidences of natural disasters have been increasing over the past few decades, creating an increase in human suffering and economic losses. Mangrove forests and coral reefs—a rich source of biodiversity—are excellent natural buffers against floods and storms. Their loss or reduction in coverage has increased the severity of flooding on coastal communities.

Thirdly, it is estimated that about 7,000 plant species and several hundred species of animals have been used for human food consumption at one time or another. Some indigenous and traditional communities currently consume 200 or more species. Wild sources of food remain particularly important for the poor and landless to provide a somewhat balanced diet. Wild meat, fish and insects provide much of their protein, while forest fruits and vegetables are a source of vitamins (Scoones *et al.,* 1992). A conservative estimate suggests that wild plants and animal provide at least 20-30 per cent of rural people's income in developing countries (Vedeld *et al.,* 2004). Fuel wood provides more than half the energy used in developing countries. In rural areas, 95 per cent is consumed in the form of firewood, while in urban areas 85 per cent is used in the form of charcoal. Shortage of wood fuel occurs in areas with high population density without access to alternative and affordable energy sources. Women and children in rural poor communities are the ones most affected by wood fuel scarcity. They must walk long distances searching for fire-wood and therefore, have less time for tending crops and school. According to World Health Organisation (2002), about two billion people who lack adequate access to Western medicine largely depend on wild and semi-wild plants and animals for much of their treatment. Wild resources are considered as the most important resource for families facing individual or social hardships like poverty, sickness, drought, economic crisis (World Resource Institute, 2005).

Fourthly, many cultures attach spiritual and religious values to ecosystems or their components such as a tree, hill, river, or grove. Thus, loss or damage to these components can harm social relations—for example, by impeding religious and social ceremonies that normally bind people. Damage to ecosystems, highly valued for their aesthetic, recreational, or spiritual values can damage social relations, both by reducing the bonding value of shared experience as well as by causing resentment towards groups that profit from their damage.

Fifthly, biodiversity offers directly the various goods—often plants, animals, and fungi—that individuals need in order to earn an income and secure sustainable livelihoods. In addition, it also contributes to livelihoods through the support it provides for ecosystem services. Nature-based tourism, "ecotourism" — one of the fastest-growing segments of tourism worldwide—is a particularly important economic sector in a number of countries and a potential income source for many rural communities. Biodiversity also contributes to a range of other industries, including pharmaceuticals, cosmetics, and horticulture.

Conservation as a Concept

The idea of conserving the nature or 'wild' species evolved from America with the early wilderness philosopher like Henry Thoreau and George Catlin (Nash, 1973). The basic idea was to preserve the pristine landscape, the wildlife and the Native American Indian as a specimen for the world to see. Several acts were passed to curtail rights of American Indians and for forced eviction In 1891, an amendment of the existing land laws had taken place which categorically pointed that state had the authority to create 'forest reserves' by withdrawing lands from the public domain. By this, fifteen 'forest reserves' totalling about 52,60,913 hactares of land were created (Nash, 1973). Since then parks and nature reserves became the most dominant approach of conserving wildlife areas throughout the globe. These areas have been seen as 'pristine environments similar to those that existed before human interference, delicately balanced ecosystems that need to be preserved for our enjoyment and use and that of future generations' (Gompez-Pompa and Kaus, 1992). It does not recognise the importance of local management and land use practices in sustaining and protecting biodiversity. The basic philosophy is that conservation can only be possible without human interference.

In common usage, the term refers to the activity of systematically protecting natural resources such as forests, including biological diversity. Carl F. Jordan defines the term 'biological conservation' as being a philosophy of managing the environment in a manner that does not despoil, exhaust or extinguish (1995). It is the preservation and protection of living nature: species, habitats and ecosystems (Adams, 2009). Conservation measures could have different forms, which are usually divided in two categories: statutory, administrative or contractual measures and management plans.

Loss of Biodiversity

At the first Earth Summit, the vast majority of the world's nations approved that human actions were dismantling the Earth's ecosystems, eliminating genes, species and biological traits at an alarming rate (Cardinale *et al.*, 2012). It is argued that a wide range of human interventions actually leads to gradual degeneration of ecosystem structure and function with its associated loss of species. The increasing rate of species extinction is a clear indication of biodiversity loss. Data on the IUCN Red list of Threatened Species in 1996 suggests that some one thousand species are lost each year. IUCN's recent assessment shows that the number of critically endangered species has increased —

mammals from 169 to 180 and birds from 168 to 182 (2000). The number of of critically endangered primates has increased from 13 to 19 and fresh water turtle species in the same category rose from 10 to 24 (*ibid.*). In fact, habitat loss and degradation are believed to be the most important threats to species. The 2000 IUCN Red List reports that changes in habitat affected 89 per cent of all threatened birds, 83 per cent of mammals, and 91 per cent of threatened plants that were assessed (IUCN, 2000). Conversion and reduced quality of forested lands has been the most important cause of habitat loss all over the world. One-fifth of all tropical forest cover was lost between 1960 and 1990. In respect of forest quality, timber cutting and atmospheric pollution continue to affect forest cover, species composition, and age stratification (Abramovitz, 1998). The Pilot Analysis of Global Ecosystems (PAGE) of the World Resources Institute provided a comprehensive account of weakening of the capability of natural ecosystems to maintain life (2000). For example, half of the world's wetlands have been lost in the past century. Logging and conversion of forest ecosystems have reduced world's forests by as much as half, another quarter is being fragmented by roads, farms and settlements. About one in ten of all tree species is at risk of extinction. Most freshwater and coastal ecosystems no longer have the capacity to maintain healthy water quality. Over extraction for cultivation exceeds natural replinishment by over 160 million cubic metres annually. Introduced species, transmission of pathogens and incurable damage to natural immune protection are leading to a chaotic reduction in species numbers and densities (2000). An estimated 4160 to 10,000 medicinal plants are under threat of extinction by habitat loss or over exploitation (Hamilton, 2004). In several parts of the world, overexploitation of fish and game along with forest destruction and water pollution have reduced the availability of fish and wild meat, and local people have lost a rich source of nutrition. In effect, the poor are most affected. Environmental degradation impacts heavily on the poor causing greater poverty (MEA, 2005). This often leads to migration from rural to urban settings, forest areas or marginal lands. Uncertainty forces people to adopt unsustainable short-term survival tactics — leading to further environmental destruction and a cycle of decline (MEA, 2005; WRI, 2005).

The loss of biodiversity will diminish the capacity of ecosystems to provide society with a stable and sustainable supply of essential goods and services (Tilman, 2000). Loss of biodiversity disturbs essential ecosystem functions such as pollination, the maintenance of soil health, water cleanliness, the assimilation of wastes, especially toxic wastes, and the cycling of carbon, nitrogen and sulphur (O'Riordan, 2002). Wood and his colleagues tried to identify the root causes of biodiversity losses. They pointed out that interconnectedness of major drivers like economy, social selections, civil rights, property rights and political power is the key to biodiversity loss. But they vary in the most diverse and unexpected ways at any point on the ground. It is the global to local and local to global interconnectedness that shapes biodiversity loss. The proximate determinants range from climate change, overharvesting, habitat loss and pathogenic incursion to socio-economic drivers like demographic change, inequality and poverty, public policies and markets, social changes and development (2000).

Current Biodiversity Conservation Approaches

For conservationists, species extinction is the clear indication of biodiversity loss. It is beyond doubt that there is a rapid decline in biological diversity and extinction rates are currently estimated to be 100 to 1000 times normal (Lovejoy, 2002). It is also argued that the rapid loss of species is due to human actions (Hails et al 2006; Cardinale *et al.,* 2012). Three-quarters of the habitable area of the Earth has been disturbed by human intervention (Hannah *et al.,* 1994). About 40 per cent of terrestrial net primary production was used directly by human activities; co opted or lost as a result of those activities. These activities are things used for consumption like crops, timber or fish; grazing livestock or other activities like fires or human induced soil erosion (Vitousek *et al.,* 1986).

Though impact on biodiversity has been recognised in recent past, the concern for nature has long history. Though Europeans deliberately exploited non-human nature in Europe, the understanding and importance of nature changed with the extention of global trade in Asia. As a part of colonial control, European rulers intensified their control on the environment, opening up newly discovered diverse nature and cultures to exploitation (Adams, 2003). Since then, colonial rulers felt that forests could be managed rationally to increase production and sustain human benefit.

In twentieth or twenty-first centuries, conservation became a dominant movement. Wildlife or nature conservation organizations had started their activities for preservation of particular species by the end of nineteeth century. For example, Yellowstone National Park was established in 1872 in the USA. The strategies of those conservation organizations were to create reserve places for nature, and to separate humans and other species (Adams, 2003, 2004). The idea of this conservation model of game or hunting reserves was drawn from US idea of national parks as 'pristine' or wilderness areas and the British notion of smaller or more managed nature reserves (Adams, 2009). Since then park and reserve creation across the globe continued even after the Second World War. Basic philosophy was that the public good was best served through the protection of forests and water resources, even if this meant the displacement of local communities (McCracken, 1987). This strategy and philosophy was transferred to all colonies of United Kingdom. At present, all national parks in Latin America, Asia, Africa and the rest of the developing world have been created based on Yellowstone model.

The area protected globally more or less doubled over the 1970s. It doubled again within 2004. By 2005, over 1,00,000 protected areas (PAs) covered more than 2 million square kms, or 12 per cent of the Earth's land surface (Chape, 2005). The expansion of protected area networks and fruitful governance system became problematic as the social and political reality and institutional structure varies from one region to other regions of the globe. Recognising diverse socio-political reality and institutional settings from one region to another region, the World Commission on Protected Areas developed six different management categories with two sub-categories : (a) areas managed primarily for biodiversity conservation (categories I and II) and (b) areas managed mainly for sustainable use of resources (categories III-VI). IUCN modified the original definition of protected area for wider applicability in different settings. The IUCN defined protected area 'an area of land and/or sea especially dedicated to the protection and maintenance of biological diversity, and of natural associated cultural resources, and managed through legal or other effective means' (IUCN, 2003). Most of the world's protected areas (84.5% of those with assigned IUCN categories) are open to some form of human use (Nauton-Treves *et al.,* 2005). Individual surveys show that settlement rates of 56-72 per cent is for national parks and sanctuaries in India

Table 1.1: The six categories of protected areas recognized by the World Conservation Union (IUCN)

Category	*Description*
I(a and b)	Strict nature reserve, wilderness protection area, or wilderness area managed mainly for science or wilderness protection.
II	National park, managed mainly for ecosystem protection and recreation.
III	National monument, managed mainly for conservation of specific natural features.
IV	Habitat / species management area, managed mainly for conservation through management intervention.
V	Protected landscape/seascape, managed mainly for landscape/ seascape conservation or recreation.
VI	Managed resource protected area, managed mainly for sustainable use for natural resources.

Source: Nauton-Treaves et al 2005

(Kothari *et al.*, 1989) ; 85 per cent for national parks in South America (Amend and Amend, 1995); 70 per cent for PAs in well populated tropical areas (Bruner *et al.*, 2001); and 70-100 per cent for PAs in Myanmar, Mongolia and East Kalimantan (Bedunah & Schmidt 2004; Jespon *et al.*, 2002; Rao *et al.*, 2002). Within each state the actual management of a type of protected area may vary from the description offered by IUCN (Borrini- Feyerabend, 1996)

Conservationists argue that extensive human use is incompatible with the preservation of a full complement of species in habitats (Oates, 1995). It is believed that biodiversity can only be preserved by creating areas that are strictly protected from all human interference (Wilshusen *et al.*, 2002; Hutton *et al.*, 2005). But studies have shown that many protected areas, particularly in biodiversity rich developing countries, are managed ineffectively and thus provide little or no real protection of biodiversity (Brandon *et al.*, 1998; Bruner *et al.*, 2001). Conservation practitioners identified lack of governance and corruption as the major reasons for ineffectiveness of protected area management and argued for more stricter regulation (Terborgh, 1999). However, there are also advocates for incentive-based conservation in addition to or in place of protected areas (Hutton and Leader Williams, 2003). Incentives like direct payments, giving money to communities, undertake specific conservation actions that maintain wildlife populations (Feraro and Kiss 2002) may be the possible options.

Though the protected areas are successful to a certain extent in reducing deforestation rate, preventing species extinction and in conserving land and water bodies, it creates huge social costs. The greatest social costs of PAs are the forced removal of people from their homes and/or curtailment of access. So socio-economic impacts can be of three different kinds : complete physical displacement, economic displacement through restrictions on resource use (e.g. on collection of firewood and other NTFPs, grazing, water use) and cultural displacement through restricted access to locations of cultural and symbolic value (Lele *et al.,* 2010). Critics of protectionist approach have identified several problems. Firstly, decline in deforestation rate is somewhat mixed. PAs are more successful in arresting deforestation rate in less accessible areas but not in others. Secondly, it is not clear whether complete exclusion of human activities is necessary for conservation effectiveness, and whether wilderness or pristineness is a meaningful goal, in the context of historical modifications of landscapes. In some place, mega fauna inside the PAs have disappeared even after stricter protection (e.g. Sariska Tiger Reserve in India). In a few places, excluding resource use has actually been deleterious to the key biodiversity value of the PA. Thirdly, alienation of local communities by curtailing access rights or forced removal has turned potential conservation allies into adversaries. Fourthly, an exclusionary approach inevitably produces ethical challenges, calling into question the legitimacy of such conservation programmes (Lele *et al.,* 2010).

In 1990s, a new paradigm has emerged in the conservation thinking that recognising the need to ensure the participation of local people (Adams and Hulme, 2001). It is argued that conservation cannot be undertaken without the support and participation of local people. To make conservation viable, livelihood issues of local people should be at the centre of conservation strategy (Pimbert and Pretty, 1995; Barrett *et al.*, 2005). It is morally incorrect not to take account of the interests and needs of the local people. Some researcher's argue that a more pragmatic problem is that the imposition of conservation measures against the wishes of local people in a protectionist strategy is likely to be expensive, difficult and likely to fail (Brandon and Wells, 1992; Hulme and Murphree, 2001). However, it is a key element in the concept of the UNESCO Biosphere reserves, that specified a strictly protected core and a surrounding buffer zone (Adams, 2009). These participatory and people centred approaches are popularly known as Integrated Conservation and Development Projects (ICDPs) (McShane and Wells, 2004) or community based conservation or community based natural resource management (Brosius *et al.,* 2005). ICDPs were designed to reduce poverty and improve income levels, nutrition, health care and education as well as to conserve biodiversity (Christensen, 2004).

In practice, it is difficult to integrate conservation of biodiversity and development of local people. Various ICDPs tried to address many different aspects of household economies which are complex in nature and vulnerable to over-optimistic planning and the limited knowledge planners (Stocking and Perkin, 1992). This approach has been criticised for its effectiveness (Wilshusen *et al.,* 2002; McShane and Wells, 2003, Garnett *et al.,* 2007). A primary criticism has been that projects have failed to achieve either goal (Brown, 2003). Moreover, there has been little evidence that improving the living standards of local people will translate into positive impact on conservation (McShane and Wells, 2004). Critics also pointed that projects were generally paternalistic, externally imposed, representing the ideas and agendas of outside conservation organizations. Projects tended to give local people little actual control over natural resources (Chapin, 2004, Kaimowitz and Sheil, 2007).

On the other hand, some authors point out that PAs are usually too small to meet the requirements of either ecosystem or biodiversity conservation. Studies in island biogeography suggested that biodiversity could not be sustained on small preserved habitat islands (Shafer, 1990). While some PAs are vast, most are small. Reserves are increasingly isolated in a matrix of intensively managed land, or managed for industrial agriculture (DeFries *et a*l., 2005). There is a possibility of extinction of species in PAs, even if they are firmly protected (Shafer, 1990). So conservation strategy needs to extend beyond PAs. One approach would be conservation at landscape level (Sayer and Campbell, 2004). Other approach is creation of biosphere reserves (BRs), which will be discussed later. Landscapes are considered as mosaics of land cover types that provide environmental services and development opportunities for the multiple needs of diverse stakeholders. A landscape approach seeks to understand landscape dynamics and the desired changes from different viewpoints, the aim being to identify interventions and policies that will achieve the stated goals of stakeholders. Constituting a forum for stakeholder negotiations is a fundamental first step in considering a landscape approach (Sayer and Maginnis, 2005).

Recognising the presence of human settlements, the dominant protectionist paradigm has extended its conventional approach of protection to improve man and environment relationship which is known as biosphere reserve approach. In fact, the UNESCO, under its 'Man and its Biosphere programme' in early 1970s has developed an ecological programme aimed for improvement of the relationship between man and the environment and thereby to increase man's ability to manage efficiently the natural resources of the biosphere. The approach emphasizes the importance of the structure and functioning of ecological systems and their mode of reaction when exposed to human intervention including the impact of man on the environment and *vice-versa*. Biosphere reserves have three very different, but equal, aims: *conservation* of genetic resources, species, and ecosystems; scientific *research and monitoring*; and promoting *sustainable development* in communities of the surrounding region. Biosphere reserves primarily serve three roles: a conservation role; a logistic role that includes the international network for research and monitoring, which had been a salient feature of biosphere reserves from the earliest days, and a development role, which was an attempt to associate environment with development (Batisse, 1986). The UNESCO defined biosphere reserves (BRs) as an area of terrestrial and coastal ecosystems promoting solutions to reconcile the conservation of biodiversity with its sustainable use. That means, "Biosphere reserves, by definition and intent have economic and social benefits for local people, but also have value in demonstrating sustainable development tied to conservation in the wider biogeographical region" (UNESCO, 1984).

The biosphere reserve as a concept and a tool of UNESCO has its origin in the protected areas domain but has now evolved into an international designation that allows context-specific conservation and development relationships to be developed in land and seascapes where more than 80 per cent of the designated area lies outside of legally protected core zones. As such, each biosphere reserve could be a context-specific experiment in sustainable development at varying scales (Iswaran *et al.*, 2008). It deals with one of the most important questions of reconciling the conservation of biodiversity, the quest for economic and social development and maintenance of associated cultural values. BRs are thus special environments for both people and the nature and are living examples of how human beings and nature can co-exist while respecting each others' needs (GOI, 2007). It may be noted that the BR is not intended to replace existing protected areas but it widens the scope of conventional approaches of protection and further strengthens the Protected Area Network. Existing legally protected areas (National Parks, Wildlife Sanctuaries, Tiger Reserves and reserve/protected forests) may become part of the BR without any change in their legal status. On the other hand, inclusion of such areas in a BR will enhance their national value. However, these reserves differ from protected areas due to their emphasis on :

(i) Conservation of overall biodiversity and landscape, rather than some specific flagship species, to allow natural and evolutionary processes to continue without any hindrance.

(ii) Different components of BRs like landscapes, habitats, species and land races.

(iii) Developmental activities, and resolution/mitigation of conflicts between development and conservation.

(iv) Increase in broad-basing of stakeholders, especially local people's participation and their training, compared to the features of scheme on Wildlife Sanctuaries and National Parks.

(v) Research and Monitoring to understand the structure and functioning of ecological systems and their mode of reaction when exposed to human beings.

About the Text

As the editors of the present compilation, it would be pertinent to say some words about the essays that feature in this volume. The present volume is primarily based on the proceedings of the two-day national conference on 'Potential of Diverse Biodiversity conservation Approaches and Livelihood Concerns in India' held between 11th and 12th March 2011 at the Institute of Development Studies, Kolkata (IDSK). The conference was successful to bring academics from national level research institutions, scholars from NGOs, Forest Administrators, decision makers and PA inhabitants to the intense debate so as to enrich the collective understanding on how to conserve forest resources and promote livelihood, to identify areas and measures to advocate policies and programmatic action as well as to guide future research.

The first four essays try to focus on current management strategies in protected areas and their effectiveness in conserving dwindling bio-diversity resources and argue for changes in current management strategies. The Union Government of India, since inception of Department of Environment and Forest on November 1, 1980 has published the forest policy and strategy paper on Environment and Development, in June 1992. Since then the Government has conceived conservation of forest resources as an exclusive domain and provided policies, laws, and Acts for conservation of forest resources. In the opening essay 'Re-examining Conservation and Development Strategy in India', A.K. Ghosh tries to examine those Acts, Policies and Programmes and attempts to analyse the current situation to evaluate the status of promises, rhetoric and action and attempts to suggest some remedial measures. Bidhan Kanti Das's article 'Critiquing 'Fortress Conservation Approach': Is 'people centred conservation approach' a viable option in Indian context?', tries to analyse the arguments in favour of 'Fines and Fences Approach' or 'Fortress Conservation Approach' particularly in the context of social, economic and political realities in developing countries like India. He argues that 'people centred conservation' approach is the only viable option in the context of high dependence on forest resources, continuous conflicts and resistance, and failed relocation processes leading to further marginalisation of local people especially tribal/indigenous communities in Indian situation. On the other hand, Ajit Banerjee's essay on 'Problems of Present Practices of Protection Area (PA) and Management in India: Need of Change' identified current constraints in management practices in Protected Areas in India. He argued that unlike non-interference of local people in protected area management, people's participation in protection is extremely important. Co-existence of animal and man should be a major plank as it has happened in the past millennium. The dependence of the people on the forest will continue but with innovation and to a certain degree that will not upset biodiversity. A landscape approach may be the best alternative in the present context. The new management may include production and even animal culling to avoid man-animal conflict if necessary. This is possible if the planning is done in a rational manner by the core people themselves in consultation with forest technicians. The paper stresses for initiating such approach at least in a limited scale. Similarly, P.K. Mathur advocated for landscape approach for conservation of wildlife in his article 'Landscape Approach to Conservation in Context of Gir Forests—Challenges and Prospects' by highlighting a successful case study in the context of Gir forests and conservation of the Asiatic lion and emphasizes on the management interventions in the "Greater Gir" adopted by the PA management and emerging challenges in dealing with such a large landscape. It amply illustrates that small PAs neither conserve the entire array of representative biodiversity nor they provide adequate habitat to wide ranging faunal species. He argued that better use and focus on concepts of landscape ecology and conservation biology within boundaries of PAs and managed forests, and outside to community, revenue, and other lands are of paramount significance to help ensure protection and restoration of forests and other natural areas in India for future generations. This article presents the relevance, challenges and opportunities of this approach to conservation in the context of the country's wide array of natural resources, land use, growing demands and developmental needs. It specifically stresses on the need of ecological restoration in different regions on a war footing for health, integrity and sustainability of diverse ecosystems. Subhabrata Palit in his essay 'Conserving Wildlife and Biodiversity through People's Participation' opined that conservation areas need to be seen as a part of wider human influenced landscapes and ecosystems, where goods and services they provide are better and more widely understood. For this, protected area management strategies should be evolved from a species-based conservation approach to a livelihood-based landscape approach. It is argued that biodiversity must be recognized and managed to support local livelihoods as well as for global public good. P.B.Gongopadhyay and H.S. Pabla in their article 'Relocation from Protected Areas – Need for a balanced approach' argue that 'exclusion' theory of forest management for only small percentage of villages which are in crucial habitat should be implemented for survival of endangered wild life. However, sincere efforts should be given for inclusive management of villages which are not in the crucial habitat of endangered species. According to them, this seems to be a balanced and pragmatic approach to secure at least some 'inviolate' habitat for survival of endangered wild life.

With the acceptance of UNESCO's Man and Biosphere (MAB) programme in 1972 and the concept of Joint Forest Management in 1988, the role of and people's rights, however, restricted, become acknowledged. The Biological Diversity Act, 2002 is perhaps the only law empowering local communities to determine the extent of bio-resource that could be used for commercial purposes and put provisions for access and transfer of such resources on a principle of benefit sharing. Biosphere Reserve in India is unique with the presence of human habitation inside the core zone. This creates a man animal and man nature conflict for utilisation of natural resources and subsistence livelihood. Moreover local population living inside encounter with various contradictory and conflicting forest policies and acts from time to time. As a result, tribals and other forest dwellers are continuously facing threats of displacement, annexation of cultivable land to the forest and restriction on the use of natural resources. Samit Ghosal in his essay 'Biodiversity Conservation and Utilisation of Natural Resources in the Biosphere Reserve Situation in India : Some observation' has shown that how local people have evolved and adapted to unique sustainable livelihood strategies which are suitable to the local ecology against the backdrop of these exogenous factors by synergized traditional and modern economic practices. He argued that by optimal utilisation of limited natural resources at their disposal they produce ecologically appropriate agricultural crops at par land and soil types and availability of water and follow crop rotation to maintain the production level based on observation in terrestrial (Pachmarhi BR and Similipal BR) and marine (Gulf of Mannar BR) ecosystem. He advocated for Biosphere Reserve management strategy that would integrate the management of natures' domain (Ecology) and humans' domain (socio-economics) and prescribed a model for human kind in the conservation and sustainable management of nature. Debashish Debnath and others in their article 'Biosphere Reserve Management in Similipal of Orissa: some emerging issues' draw attention about socio-economic status of local inhabitants and identify challenges in Biosphere Reserve governance and discuss the programmes under Management Action plan and suggest for future perspectives based on micro level field data in Similipal Biosphere Reserve of Orissa. Living in the areas rich in natural resources, traditional societies fulfil many of their livelihood requirements from the rich biodiversity around them. The ecosystems such as forests not only meet a variety of livelihood needs of the forest dwelling societies through products such as timber and non-timber forest products, but also sustain traditional shifting cultivation and agricultural practices contributing to the food security of the people within Biosphere Reserves. But human population living within the Biosphere Reserves has always been a matter of conflicting interests and debate. So Biosphere reserve concept needs to be seen from the view point of both biodiversity and cultural diversity. The Biosphere Reserve management, therefore, necessitates understanding of not only ecological issues but also the socio-economic and cultural issues linked with the former. Umesh Kumar in his article 'Livelihood Concerns and Conservation Prospects in Biosphere Reserves of India' stressed that proper understanding of the societal perceptions of natural resources as cultural resources and integrating them in the management strategy is crucial for the successful execution of conservation linked development strategy. The present paper endeavours to analyze the anthropogenic pressure and conservation prospect in Khangchendzonga Biosphere Reserve in India using people preference for resources and contingent valuation method.

Various forms of participatory forest management approaches have evolved in the context of forest resources in India since the early 1970s. These approaches are broadly based on the assumption that communities would have incentives to protect forests if they receive adequate returns from the resource. However, the precise nature of economic gains that communities make, and the ways in which these gains are distributed among groups within communities are inadequately studied. Anirban Ganguly and Adrian Lopes in their essay 'Participatory Forest Management in Himachal Pradesh – Benefit Flows and Equity' present an analysis of the tangible benefit flows from selected forested villages of Himachal Pradesh where the state-implemented (and donor-supported) Participatory Forest Management (PFM) is in operation. It shows changes in levels of forest dependence post-implementation of PFM, and makes an analysis of the equity impacts of the programme. Benefits from major forest products for PFM villages exceed those from non-PFM villages based on flow calculations. The study finally provides broad policy pointers based on the analysis, arguing that participatory approaches to management of forests start yielding economic benefits even in the short-run, especially in sites where the background level of forest dependence is relatively high. There are several evidences of positive role of the local resource dependent communities. They help in natural resource conservation planning and action but they are neither acknowledged, nor given a genuine consideration.

Various conventions reiterated the role of local communities and their involvement in such initiatives for sustainable forest management and biodiversity conservation. Various workable approaches such as Joint Forest Management (JFM) for participatory forest protection, regeneration and conservation efforts and Eco-development processes for participatory biodiversity and wildlife conservation were attempted. In this context, development researchers and international donors believed that development programmes failed due to lack of belongingness towards assets created and that could be countered through people's contribution. V.K. Melkani in his essay 'Sustaining Livelihoods under Eco-development Initiative in Kalakad Mundanthurai Tiger Reserve in Southern Tamil Nadu : Key Results and Future Challenges' tries to show the successful implementation of development programmes with active participation of local people under World Bank assisted project. It is argued that this approach contributed significantly in improving the situation and reducing the rising conflicts between the management and the communities. It provides a learning experience for refining the strategy and the protocols of these approaches to build in equity, both in participation and benefit sharing and securing long term sustainability of these efforts. Though V.K. Malkani presented successful implementation of eco-development programmes with active participation of local people, Bidhan Kanti Das presented an account of the different findings of eco-development programmes in another national park of North Bengal in his essay 'Cost sharing strategy to create belongingness: experiences from an ecodevelopment project in a national park of India' based on micro level field based study. It intends to assess how far eco-development activities are successful after implementation in different protection committees. In addition, it tries to explore the nature of villagers contributions in eco-development investments as well as how poor, marginalized people respond to the strategy of sharing cost for investments. These findings may be important in the context of emerging assumption that specifies that most development programmes fail to achieve desired success due to lack of belongingness. To counter this problem, Donor Agency believed that any form of cost bearing by beneficiaries is essential to create belongingness towards assets created under development programmes.

Research on mangroves and the supporting ecosystems reveals the multiple functions of mangroves in the conservation of biodiversity, livelihood security in addition to coastal protection from Tsunami, tropical cyclones, reduction of intensity of sea waves and the stabilisation of coastlines. Studies argued for protection of the coastal ecosystems, livelihoods and marine biodiversity in Gujarat. This concern evolved from the development dilemma caused by the unbridled pace of industrialisation taking place along the coasts of Gujarat. P.K. Viswanathan in his essay 'Community Based Mangrove Restoration as Instruments of Conserving Marine Biodiversity and the Protected Areas: An Exploratory Analysis from Gujarat' analyses the potential role of Community Based Mangrove Restoration (CBMR) activities as effective instruments of sustainable biodiversity conservation and the protection of coastal ecosystems, including marine protected areas in the coastal state of Gujarat. The study called for a policy as well as institutional necessities for legitimising the community based mangrove restoration activities as critical instruments of sustainable biodiversity conservation in the coastal environments, including the marine protected areas (MPAs).

Ways Forward

About 90 per cent of the world's poor depend on forests for at least a portion of their income (USAID, 2006). In India, about 50 million people directly depend on forests for subsistence alone. About 600 million African people depend on forest resources for their livelihoods (Coad *et al.*, 2008). Ethnographic studies have shown that these people use hundreds of species for a wide range of purposes. The utility values of bioresources to maintain livelihood of local communities have already been discussed in detail. If different species become scarcer and disappear, these forest user groups who are already poor will become further marginalised. So, the conservation of bio-resources is closely linked to the sustainable development of local communities and to the conservation of their way of life. As a result, the problem concerning the conservation of resources has immense and direct implications on local communities and greatly affects their own development and living in conditions. To put it in another way, conservation of bio-resources is not only important in terms of aesthetics, ecology or leisure, but also includes the issues of equality and justice. At the same time, bio-resources are also depleting at faster rate. So conservation of bio-resources, the resources which have utility values, is absolutely essential. But what should be the possible approaches of conservation of depleting bio-resources, particularly in developing countries like India?

Distribution of the costs and benefits of conservation varies widely across conservation strategies. In developing countries, creation of PAs has often given rise to considerable conflict between governments, conservation agency and the local population, and led to expulsion or marginalisation of local inhabitants. In fact, many costs of PAs are borne locally, especially poor communities while benefits accrue globally. Local costs vary from forced eviction, restricted access to forest resources and aesthetic and religious purposes to conflict related human and wildlife interaction. This approach ignores the local knowledge and traditions of the rural population in the conservation of natural resources and biodiversity. Social impacts of such conservation have both ethical and practical implications. Curtailing rights to access to local resources and means of subsistence is ethically incorrect, socially unjust and contravention of legal human rights. In practical sense, a continuous flow of positive benefits to local people from forest resources can enable and provide incentives for sustainable management in future. On the other hand, negative social impacts can erode local support, making conservation more difficult and less sustainable.

In developing countries like India, communities coexist with the environment, with production and reproduction systems that depend on biodiversity of forest ecosystems. They have intricate relationships with forests in every sphere of life. Distribution of forests and 'indigenous', tribal people is correlated in different parts of the World. Areas of high biodiversity overlap with places where traditional communities maintain and control over resource management. This is particularly true in African, Asian and South Asian countries including India. Keeping in mind the huge social and ecological costs of protected areas and overlapping nature of high biodiversity zones and presence of traditional forest dependent communities, inclusion of local people in conservation initiatives seems to be most viable option. Introduction of some development measures among the local communities can reduce pressure on forest resources and thereby provide positive conservation outcomes. These development activities range from alternative economic opportunities to revenue sharing from parks, services etc. The level of management operations might be zonation of areas like core and buffer zones or at the landscape level depending on the biogeography of local areas, i.e. context specific.

Above all, the attitude of forest managers about the local people has to change. They have to recognise that local people are co-partners in management of natural resources. The idea that local people are the destroyers of forests or 'economically irrational' or 'ignorant', 'underdeveloped' has to be changed. Such negative attitudes clearly undermine the mutual trust essential for effective partnership and joint management of resources between conservation authorities and the local communities. Forest managers have to be trained more on social concerns that dominate now-a-days than timber extraction and revenue generation.

REFERENCES

Abramovitz, J, 'Sustaining the World's Forests', in L.R. Brown, C. Flavin and H. French, eds., *State of the World 1998*, New York : Norton, 1998.

Adams,W.M., *Against Extinction: the story of conservation.* London : Earthscan, 2004.

Adams, W.M. and D Hulme, 'If community conservation is the answer in Africa, What is the Question ?' *Oryx*, vol.35(3):193-200, 2001.

Adams, W.M. ed., *Conservation*, London : Earthscan, 2009.

Adams, W.M., 'Nature and the colonial mind',. In, W.M. Adams and M. Mulligan, eds., *Decolonizing nature : Strategies for conservation in a post colonial era,* London : Earthscan, 2003.

Amend, S. and T. Amend, National parks without people? The South American experience. Gland, Switzerland: IUCN. 1995.

Batisse, M. 'Developing and focusing the biosphere reserve concept', *Nature and Resources*, Vol. 22, No. 3, pp.1–12. 1986.

Barrett, C.B., D.R. Lee and J.G. McPeak, 'Institutional arrangements for rural poverty reductions and resource conservation', *World Development* vol.33(2): 193-197, 2005.

Bond, E.M., Chase, J.M., Biodiversity and ecosystem functioning at local and regional spatial scales. *Ecology Letters* 5, 467–470. 2002.

Brandon, K. K.H. Redford and S.E. Sanderson, *Parks in peril: People, politics and protected areas*. Washington.: Island Press, for the Nature Conservancy, 1998.

Brandon, K.E. and M, 'Wells Planning for people and parks: Design dilemmas', *World Development,* vol. 20:557-567, 1992.

Brechin, S.R., P.R. Wilshusen, C.L. Fortwangler and P.C. West, 'Beyond the square wheel : toward a more comprehensive understanding of biodiversity conservation as social and political process', *Society and natural resources,* vol.15: 41-64, 2002.

Brosius, J.P. A.L. Tsing and C. Zerner, *Communities and Conservation : Histories and politics of community based natural resource management,* Altamira Press : Walnut Creek, CA. 2005.

Brown, K., 'Three challenges for a real people centred conservation', *Global ecology and Bio geography,* 12:89-92, 2003.

Bruner, A.G., R.E. Gullison, R.E. Rice and G. A. B. da Fonseca, 'Effectiveness of parks in protecting the tropical biodiversity', *Science,* 291(5501) : 125-128, 2001.

Budenah, D.J, S.M. Schmidt, Pastoralism and protected area management in Mongolia's Gobi Gurvansaikhan Mational Park. *Development and Change,* vol: 35 (1), pp. 167-91. 2004.

Cardinale, B.J. *et al.* Biodiversity loss and its impact on humanity. *Nature*. Vol. 486, pp. 59-67, 7 June 2012.

Chapin, M, 'A challenge to conservations', World Watch Institute, Nov. Dec. : 17-31. 2004.

Christensen, J. 'Win win illusions (www document)', *Conservation in practice* 5(1): 12-19. URL: www. Conbio.org/CUIP/articles51wwi.cfm., 2004

Coad, L., A Cambell, L. Miles and K. Murphrees, 'The costs and Benefits of Protected areas for local livelihoods: a review of the current literature', Working paper. UNEP WCMC, Cambridge, IK, 2008.

DeFries, R., R., Hansen, A.C. Newton and M.C. Hansen, 'Increasing isolation of protected areas in tropical forests over the past twenty years', *Ecological Applications,* vol:15: 19-26. 2005

DeLong Jr., D.C., Defining biodiversity. *Wildlife Society Bulletin* 24, 738–749. 1996.

Ferraro, P.J. and A. Kiss, 'Direct payments to conserve biodiversity', *Science,* vol. 298: 1718, 2002.

Garnett, S.T., J. Sayer, and J. du Toit., 'Improving the effectiveness of interventions to balance conservation and development: a conceptual framework', *Ecology and Society,* vol. 12(1): 2. [online] URL: *http://www.ecologyandsociety.org/vol12/iss1/art2/.*, 2007.

Gaston, K. J. and J.I. Spicer., *Biodiversity: an introduction,* 2nd edition, Oxford: Blackwell Publishing, 2004.

GOI, *Protection, Development,Maintenance and Research in Biosphere Reserves in India : Guideline and Proformance,* Ministry of Environment and Forests, 2007.

Gunderson, L.H. and C.S. Holling (eds). *Panarchy: Understanding transformations in human and natural systems.* Island Press, Washington, DC. 2002.

Hails, C., J., Loh and S., Goldfinger, eds., *Living Planet Report 2006,* WWF International, Zoological Society of London and Global Footprint Network, Gland, 2006.

Hamilton, A.C. 'Medicinal plants, conservation and livelihoods', *Biodiversity conservation,* vol: 13. pp: 1477-1517. 2004.

Hamilton, A.J. 'Species diversity or biodiversity?' *Journal of Environmental Management,* vol. 75, pp. 89-92. 2005.

Hannah, L., D, Lohse, C., Hutchinson, J., L. Carr and A., Lankerni, 'A premininary inventory of human disturbance of world ecosystems', *Ambio,* 23: 246-250, 1994.

Heywood. V. H. 'The species concept as a social cultural phenomenon : a source of the scientific dilemma.' *Theory in Biosciences,* vol: 117, pp. 203-212.

Hulme, D. and M., Murphree, eds., *African Wildlife and Livelihoods: The promise and performance of community conservation,* Oxford : James Curry. 2001.

Hutton, J., W.A. Adams and J.C. Murombedzi, 'Back to the barriers ? Changing narratives in biodiversity conservation', *Forum for Development Studies,* vol. 32:341-370, 2005.

Hutton, J.M. and N. Leader Williams, 'Sustainable use and incentive-driven conservation : realigning human and conservation interests', *Oryx,* 37:215-226, 2003.

Iswaran, N., A. Persic and N.H. Tri., 'Concept and practice: the case of UNESCO biosphere', *International Journal of Environment and Sustainable Development,* Vol. 7, No.2 pp. 118-131, 2008.

Jespon, P. F. Momberg, H. van Noord, A review of the efficiency of the protected area system of East Kalimantan Province, Indonesia, *Natural areas Journal,* vol: 22(1), pp. 28-42. 2002.

Jordan, Carl, *Replacing Quantity with Quality As a Goal for Global Management.* Wiley 1995.

Kaimowitz, D. and D., Sheil, 'Conserving what and for whom? Why conservation should help to meet basic human needs in the tropics,' *Biotropica,* 39 (5) : 567-574, 2007.

Knoff. F. L. Focussing conservation of a diverse wildlife resource. Cited in *Delong, Jr* (1996). 1992.

Kothari, A., P. Pandey, S. Singh and D. Variava, *Management of National Parks and Sanctuaries in India : a status report.* New Delhi: Indian Institute of Public Administration. 1989.

Lele, S., P. Wilshusen, D. Brockington, R. Seidler and K. Bawa, 'Beyond exclusion: alternative approaches to biodiversity conservation in the developing tropics', *Current opinion in environmental Sustainability,* 2:1-7, 2010.

Lovejoy, T.E., 'Biodiversity: threats and challenges', In: Tim O'Riordan and S. Stoll Klemann, eds., *Biodiversity, sustainability and Human communities.* Cambridge: Cambridge University Press, 2002.

McCracken, J. 'Conservation priorities and local communities', In: D. Anderson and R. F. Grove, eds., *Conservation in Africa: People, politics and practice,* Cambridge : Cambridge University Press, 1987.

McShane, T. and M. Wells, eds. *Getting Biodiversity Projects to work: towards more effective conservation and development,* New York, USA: Columbia University Press. 2004.

Millennium Economic Assessment, *Ecosystems and Human wellbeing: Biodiversity synthesis.* Washington, USA : Island Press, 2005.

Myers, N., R.A. Mittermier, K.G. Mittermier, G.A.B. da Fonseca and J. Kent, 'Biodiversity hotspots for conservation priorities', *Nature,* vol: 403: 853-858, 2000.

Myers, N., 'Biodiversity and bio-depletion: the need for a paradigm shift', In: Tim O'Riordan and S. Stoll Klemann, eds., *Biodiversity, sustainability and Human communities.* Cambridge: Cambridge University Press, 2002.

Nauton-Treves, L., M.B. Holland and K. Brandon, 'The role of Protected Areas in conserving Biodiversity and sustaining local Livelihoods', *Annu. Rev. Environ. Resour.* Vol: 30: 219-52, 2005.

O'Riordan, T. 'Protecting beyond the protected', in, T. O'Riordan and S. Stoll-Kleeman (eds) *Biodiversity, Sustainability and Human Communities,* Cambridge : Cambridge University Press, 2002.

Oates, J.F., 'The dangers of conservation by rural development: A case study from the forests of Nigeria', *Oryx,* 29: 115-122, 1995.

Oliver, I. and Parkes, D., A prototype toolkit for scoring the biodiversity benefits of land use change. Department of Sustainable Natural Resources, NSW, Australia. 2003.

Parkes, D., Newell, G., and Cheal, D., Assessing the quality of native vegetation: the habitat hectares approach. *Ecological Management and Restoration* 4, 29–38. 2003.

Rao, M., A. Rabinowitz, S.T. Khaing, Status review of the protected area system in Myanmar, with recommendations for conservation planning. *Conservation Biology,* vol: 16 (2). pp. 360-68. 2002.

Sayer, J.A., and S. Maginnis, eds. *Forests in landscapes. Ecosystem approaches to sustainability,* London, UK : Earthscan, 2005.

Sayer, J., and B. Campbell, *The science of sustainable development: local livelihoods and the global environment,* Cambridge, UK: Cambridge University Press, 2004.

Schafer, C.L., *Island Theory and Conservation Practice,* Smithsonian Institution Press, Washington DC. 1990.

Scoones, I. M. Melnyk, and J. Pretty. The hidden harvest: wild foods and agricultural systems, a literature review and annotated bibliography. International Institute for Environment and Development, London, UK.1998.

Stocking, M. and S., Perkin, 'Conservation with development : an application of the concept in the Usambara Mountains, Tanzania', *Transactions of the Institute of British Geographers NS,* 17:337-349. 1992.

Stolton, S., N. Dudley and J. Randall, *Natural security : Protected areas and hazard mitigation,* Gland: WWF International, 2008.

Takacs, D., 1996. *The Idea of Biodiversity: Philosophies of Paradise.* The Johns Hopkins University Press, Baltimore, MD, pp. 393.

The International Convention on Biological Diversity, 2003. Convention on Biological Diversity: Article 2: Use of Terms. http://www.biodiv.org/convention/

Terborgh, J. *Requiem for nature,* Washington DC : Island Press, 1999.

Tilman, D., 'Causes, consequences and ethics of biodiversity', *Nature,* vol. 403:208-211, 2000.

UN Population Division, In: Trends in population, developed and developing countries, 1750-2050 (estimates and projections), 2007.

UNESCO; 'Action plan for biosphere reserves', *Nature and Resources,* Vol. 20, No. 4, pp.1–12. 1984.

USAID, 'Issues in poverty reduction and natural resource management', Washington DC : United States Agency for International Development, 2006.

Vitousek, P.M. P.R. Ehrlich, A.H. Ehrlich and P.A. Matson, 'Human appropriation of the products of photosynthesis', *BioScience,* 36: 368-373, 1986.

Wilshusen, P.R., S.R. Brechin, C.L. Fortwangler and P.C. West, 'Reinventing a square Wheel : Critique of a resurgent 'Protectionist paradigm' in International Biodiversity Conservation', *Society and natural resources,* vol: 15(1):17-40, 2002.

Wood, A., P., Stedman-Edwards and and J. Mang, eds., *The root causes of biodiversity loss,* London : Earthscan, 2000.

World Resources Institute, 'World Resources 1994-1995', Washington DC: WRI, 1994.

Vedeld P., A. Angelsen, E. Sjasstad and G.K. Berg. Counting on the environment, forest incomes and the rural poor. *Enviroment Economics series paper 98.* World Bank: Washington DC. 2004.

World Health Organisation, Annual Report 2002, WHO: Geneva. http.://whqlibdoc.who.int/hq/2003/test.pdf. 2003.

World Resource Institute. World Resources 2005: The wealth of the poor-managing ecosystems to fight poverty. World Resource Institute: Washington DC. 2005.

PART II

POLICY AND MANAGEMENT

2

Re-examining Conservation and Development Strategy in India

A.K. Ghosh

Introduction

India in 1947, when it became independent, continued with many colonial traditions, one such being the issue of governance of natural resources. It is acknowledged that a paradigm shift was made during colonial period to convert Common Pool Resource (CPR) into State owned resource. Guha and Gadgil (1993) pointed out that 'while state management had not been unknown in the pre-colonial period, it was...oriented towards highly specific end, e.g. the reservation of elephant forests in the Maurya Period or...later a state monopoly over commercial species like teak and sandal wood'. One has to remember that India had a significant geographical area under forests and colonial rulers identified forests as a potential area for exploitation, for revenue earnings. By a single legislation, viz. Indian Forest Act, 1878, British Government took over all the customary rights of the local community from the forest land. The objective of such an act was not to conserve forest ecosystem with better management but to meet the need of the Imperial Government (e.g. large timber for the railways) and introduce a system of commercial production of timber.

Conservation of species diversity, it is well known, can best be done in mixed forest but the new Act and guidelines changed such prime forest into monocultural stands, one such notable change being "pure coniferous stand" of the Himalayas from eastern broad leaved forests. Such drastic changes could also be noted in the changing law over hunting (notwithstanding the laws since 1887); while traditional hunting communities were denied rights, mass-scale hunting of Indian Wildlife was patronized by the system of colonial governance- such incidences include killing of 400 elephants in the Nilgiris by one person in nineteenth century (Beneet, 1984) or 700 tigers by another person in twentieth century (Eliott, 1973). With Independence the concept of conservation emerged, albeit slowly, perhaps due to myriads of other problems the country was facing during that period.

Conservation Strategy : Approach

The post-independence period witnessed the forest conservation approach in the enactment of Indian Wildlife (Protection) Act in 1972. It must be noted that even in 1887, a Wild Birds Protection Act (No. X of 1887) was passed which only prohibited sale or possession but not killing of any specified wild birds, during breeding season (Panjawan, 1994). The 1887 Act was followed by Wild Birds and Animal Protection Act (Act VIII of 1912) which prohibited capturing or killing of wild animals, violation of which called for penal action; the Act was amended in 1935 where Provincial Government was given the power of declaring any area as "Sanctuary" for protection of wild animals and birds. So this was the beginning of "Protected Area" (PA) system in India, but with Second World War "wildlife protection" was relegated to low-priority. After Independence, the Indian Parliament passed Wildlife Protection Act in 1972 (Act 53 of 1972). This is considered to be the most comprehensive Act driven by concern for fast depleting wildlife in the country but still it allowed hunting with a permit for some specific categories, viz. special game, big game, small game and also allowed wildlife trapping. The Wildlife (Protection) Act, 1972, however, showed concern for only selected species of fauna, which represent much less than even one per cent of the total faunal diversity. However, while conservation of country's rich faunal resources received a positive legal protection in selected protected area (PA) and outside, the conservation of flora only received little legal support, restricted to six species through amendment of the Act with effect from October 1991; a Schedule VI was added to the Act and title changed into "An Act to provide protection of wild animals, birds and plants...". One has to remember that Botanical Survey of India (1983) had already prepared materials for a catalogue of threatened plants of India, enlisting 519 species from Peninsular India, 62 species from Gujarat and Rajasthan, 162 species from Western Himalayas and 112 species from North East India, totalling 855 species (BSI, 1983). Protecting only six species, therefore, looked rather meaningless or symbolic! This becomes more critical when one looks at the current trend of conversion of forest land for non-forestry purposes in some of the richest virgin forest areas in India, viz. Jharkhand, Odisha, Chhatisgarh, Madhya Pradesh etc. If one considers only the floral species enlisted under Indian Wildlife (Protection) Act and not the Red Listed plants of Botanical Survey of India, the impacts of such conversion can easily be understandable.

The Wildlife Conservation Act, 1972 also empowered to declare its intention to constitute any area, other than reserve forest or territorial water as a sanctuary for the purpose of "protecting, propagating or developing wildlife or its environment". This power has been under Section 18 of the Act but logically, resident population, if any, in such areas had rights: Before they were evicted from the declared sanctuary, certain procedures are to be followed but in many cases they were ignored leading to litigation. Customary Rights of traditional forest dwellers have often been taken away with the purpose of conservation, leading to conflicts which may not be conductive for 'conservation' purpose. So the very purpose of conservation for future generation becomes questionable as it tended to exclude people.

The concept of "Man and Biosphere" (MAB) a programme launched by UNESCO, Paris in 1972 was accepted by the Government of India. It was admitted for the first time that conservation cannot be without peoples' participation and the approach can best be made keeping interest of the local community in view. The efforts of the Government in setting up Biosphere Reserve can be viewed as more pro-people; it may be noted that due to opposition from within the Government, declaration of Biosphere Reserve was delayed inordinately; it took 14 years for India to declare Biosphere Reserves. The total number of Biosphere Reserve set up between 1986 to 2009 now stands at 16 (MoEF, 2010).

Forest Conservation

An attempt can be made to analyse the approach and strategy adopted by the National Government towards one of the most important areas for Ecosystem Services — the forests. Till 1980, the word 'Conservation' was not a part of vocabulary for the foresters in India.

Forest (Conservation) Act, 1980, may be marked as the first significant step towards appropriate conservation strategy. Forests are regarded as the site for highest level of productivity and people dependent on forests considered as the primary stake-holders, and yet have so far been excluded from the conservation strategy. As such, the new Act providing restriction on de-reservation of forests or controlling use of forest land for non-forest purposes, were welcome steps. The Act for the first time made an attempt to regulate rampant process of de-reservation. Nevertheless, it remained silent on the rights of forest dwellers or the roles they can play towards making conservation efforts more fruitful. Till 1980, the rampant conversion of forest land has never been questioned but with the Forest (Conservation) Act, 1980, there was significant decline in use of forest land in the country. According to Khushoo (1986), it came down to 14600 ha per year from 1,50,000 ha per year. Forests occupy nearly 77 mha of land area being variably distributed over 31 states and seven Union Territories. Only Eight States of India could be listed as in possession of good land resources (67%), viz. Chhattisgarh, Madhya Pradesh, Andhra Pradesh, Arunachal Pradesh, Odisha, Maharashtra, Uttarakhand, Uttar Pradesh. Maximum conversion of forest land has been seen for Multipurpose River Valley Project, Mining Projects, besides for other industrial projects, viz. Iron and Steel, Thermal Power, Fertilizer and infrastructure development project especially for expansion of Railways and Roadways. In all such cases forest land acquisition was an easy process before 1980 but with the Environment Protection Act, 1986 and Environmental Impact Assessment, 1994, amended in 2006, the process of forest land clearance became more regulated. Some development projects like Railways continued to be exempted from such laws.

But the current events of much concern are connected with sudden spurt of forest conversion for development project in recent years. An analysis of the forest area which has been permitted to be converted

Table 2.1: Diversion of Forest Area

Period/Year	*Forest Area Diverted* (in ha)*
1981-92	1,98,421.19
Eighth FYP (1992-97)	84,587.07
Ninth FYP (1997-2002)	1,47,397.57
Tenth FYP (2002-07)	1,96,262.32
Eleventh FYP (2007-12)	2,04,425.06
Total	8,30,244.00

* For all projects excluding regularization of encroachments.

Source: "Forest Clearance", Centre for Science and Environment, viewed on July 17th 2012. *http:/www.cseindia.org/userfiles/Forest%20clearance.pdf%20*

from 1981 i.e. the year after the Forest (Conservation) Act, 1980 to 2012 can elucidate the point (Table 2.1). Currently, a separate permission is being needed from the Forest Advisory Committee (FAC). However, the mode of functioning of FAC has been repeatedly questioned by the non-official members. Diversion of forest land after Forest (Conservation Act), 1980 till 2012 has been calculated at 8,30,244 ha and with every Five Year Plan an upward trend of diversion can be noted (Table 2.1). In a recent issue of *Economic and Political Weekly*, a correspondent commented on the way of functioning of FAC as follows:

> "*Past and present non-official members of the FAC concur that performing their role on the committee is an uphill task. The FAC meets once a month for a day and may have to appraise as many as 40 project proposals at a time. Since it is impossible to scrutinize all the documents that make up a proposal, the committee confines itself to evaluating the "fact sheet" prepared by ministry officials which sketches the main forest-related features of the project area such as flora and fauna, tree density, proximity to protected areas such as national parks and sanctuaries, extent of human displacement, land identified for compensatory afforestation, and the recommendations of the district forest officer and the conservator of forests. In addition, the fact sheet may include comments from the site inspection report*

(mandatory for projects requiring more than 100 ha of forest land), information on compliance with state government conditions (such as preparing a wildlife management plan), and so on. In order to make a more persuasive case before the FAC, many private and public sector user agencies send their representatives to Delhi to present proposals in person. On the basis of the limited information contained in the fact sheet, sometimes fortified by the hearty assurances offered by the project proponent, the FAC decides whether to allow forests to be diverted or not." (Anon. 2011)

The forest land diverted has been used for several purposes and at least 30.7 per cent comes under the process of "regularization of encroachment" but irrigation, mining, power and industrial projects together account for more than 50 per cent of the total land converted during last 30 years (Table 2.2).

Table 2.2 : Forestland diverted in post Forest Conservation Act (1981-2011)

Purpose/sector Forest land diverted	*Area (in ha)*	*Percentage (%)*
Defense	46570	3.9
Regularization of encroachment	368432	30.7
Social services	65089	5.4
Transport (Road, Railways)	63292	5.3
Power projects (Hydel, Thermal, Wind and Transmission lines)	164128	13.7
Mining	148860	12.4
Irrigation	167237	14.0
Others (including industries)	175067	14.6
Total forest land diverted	1198676	100

Source: CSE, 2011, *http:/www.cseindia.org/userfiles/Forest%20clearance.pdf%20*

Figure. 2.1 down below clearly shows sudden spurt of conversion since 1999-2000 with a dip in 2003 and then a upward curve with highest conversion in 2010. One can relate it with the era of globalization and the urge of the government for faster economic growth without any concern for natural resource accounting.

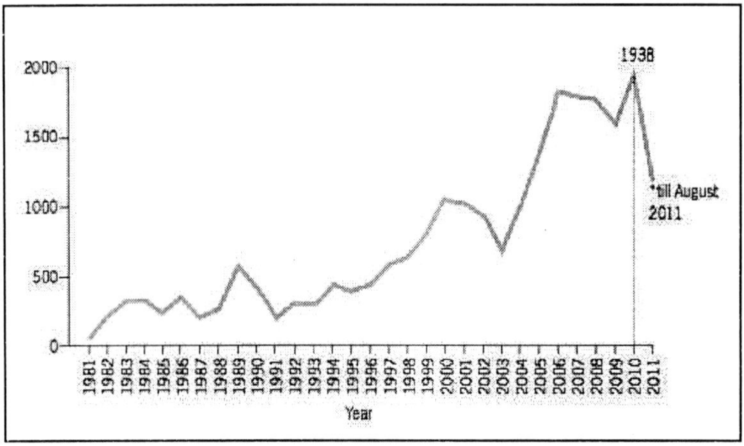

Source: CSE, 2011, *http:/www.cseindia.org/userfiles/Forest%20clearance.pdf%20*

Fig. 2.1 : Forest clearances granted (number of projects)

However, the next major step after promulgation of Forest (Conservation) Act, 1980, by the Government of India may be seen in the "National Forest Policy" of 1988. The Resolution (MoEF, 1988) admitted that 'forests in the country have suffered serious depletion'. It further stated as one of the basic objectives, is 'meeting the requirement of fuel wood, fodder, minor forest produce and small timber of the rural and tribal population'. It further stated 'a primary task... should be to associate the tribal people closely in protection, regeneration and development of forests as well as to provide gainful employment to the people living in and around the forest.' This is perhaps the first admission of the authority on the importance of making people partner in forest conservation. The entire concept of Joint Forest Management (JFM) leading to the formation of thousands of Forest Protection Committees (FPCs) across India thus had its origin in the new National Forest Policy, 1988.

By the year 2000 A.D., "JFM arrangements for production and regeneration of degraded forest" is stated to cover 70,000 sq. km, out of a total of 6,33,400 sq. km (Khare *et al.*, 2000). It is alleged that "Conservationist favour expansion of protected areas for biodiversity conservation but are less concerned about forest dependent people (Khare, *op.cit.*). But conservationists are rather a part of the "growing policy community" comprising government foresters, forest industrialists, social activists, larger farmers and locally powerful political elites and international agencies. The concern for people living in and around forest remained yet to be fully visible in the government policy and actions.

After a period of prolonged struggle by the forest dwellers and civil society organizations, the Government of India enacted 'Forest Rights Act in 2006'. The Act provides rights over the forest land for those tribal families and other traditional forest dwellers who could prove continuously inhabiting forest for three generations or for 75 years; a family can claim up to four acres of forest land subject to authentication of such claim under FRA 2006. One has to remember that Panchayati Raj Extension to the Scheduled Areas (PESA) provided the first entitlement of the forest dwellers to certain benefits but due to turning process of implementation the real benefit did not reach the people. While implementing FRA, it is observed that the State Forest Departments often put obstacle to grant titles to the forest dweller families and invariably rejects community rights granted under the law. The State Forest Departments are more eager to use the provisions of the law to shift the forest dwellers family from the declared protected areas. Such a tendency obviously comes from a psyche of disbelief that forest dwellers can be one of the most important communities to ensure conservation as evidenced from the history of last 5000 years. Apparently this trend of mistrust contradicts the very doctrine of participatory management enshrined under the Principles of Joint Forest Management.

Impacts of Development

One of the major impacts of development in the post-independent India can be seen in the loss of agriculture and forest land for more than 30 sectors and developmental projects. Such impacts include not only the loss of yet to be documented biodiversity both in the field of agriculture and in the forest land, but also social impact on the human population due to the loss of agricultural and homestead land acquired by the Government for the purpose of developmental projects. For instance, India is considered as 3rd largest Dam builders in the World for constructing 100s of multipurpose river valley projects during 1st to 11th

Five Year Plan and the process continued in the 12th Plan period. Obviously such projects always affect the rural populations and worst affected are the backward communities of tribal. An analysis of the tribal population displaced due to river valley projects would be revealing (Table 2.3). It will show that in 10 of the 28 states in India the percentage of the tribal population amongst the displaced people is above 50 per cent in 80 per cent of these States, sometime the percentage of tribal population displaced reaching up to 100. In absence of a proper Rehabilitation & Resettlement Policy, resentments amongst the displaced people soared over the years and have taken the shape of violent political movements often damaging natural resources, thereby defeating the purpose of conservation. The Land Acquisition and Rehabilitation and Resettlement Bill, 2012 has taken 5years to come to the present shape and is still awaiting to be placed before the House of Parliament till July 2012. Most of the violent movements have now spread in 8 densely forested States of India challenging the very concept of conservation goals. Still efforts to convert more forest land and biodiversity rich area continue unabated.

Table 2.3: Displacement of Tribal Population due to River Valley Projects

Project	*State*	*Displaced Population*	*Tribal Percentage*
Karjan	Gujarat	11,600	100
Sardar Sarovar	Gujarat	2,00,000	57.60
Maheshwar	Madhya Pradesh	20,000	60.00
Bodhghat	Madhya Pradesh	12,700	73.91
Icha	Bihar	30,800	80.00
Chandil	Bihar	37,600	87.92
Koel Karo	Bihar	66,000	88.00
Mahi Bajaj Sajar	Rajasthan	38,400	76.28
Upper Indravati	Orissa	18,500	89.20
Ichampalli	Andhra Pradesh	38,100	76.28
Tultuti	Maharashtra	13,600	51.61
Daman Ganga	Gujarat	8,700	48.70
Bhakra	Himachal Pradesh	36,000	34.76
Masan Reservoir	Bihar	3,700	31.00
Ukai Reservoir	Gujarat	52,000	18.92
Upper Indravati	Odisha	18,500	89.20
Pong	Himachal Pradesh	80,000	56.25

The number of Indian citizens displaced for River Valley Projects alone has been variably calculated by different analysis, ranging from

21 million to 40 million (Singh, 2003). Such massive displacements obviously had serious impacts directly on conservation issues and indirectly, antagonizing people without ensuring social justice, against the very concept of development benefiting an "exclusive society".

National Conservation Strategy and Policy on Environment and Development

So far the discussion veered around the forests of India from conservation perspectives. The first National Conservation Strategy and Policy Statement on Environment and Development was published by the Government of India in June 1992, coinciding with the UN Conference on Environment and Development (UNCED), held at Rio de Janeiro, Brazil.

In the Preamble, it stated that "The survival and well-being of a Nation depend on sustainable development. It is a process of social and economic betterment..." The policy document listed besides others, the Water Act of 1974, Air Act of 1981 and Environment Protection Act of 1986 but failed to mention any earlier policies that are supportive to the National Conservation Strategy. Under Priorities and Strategies for action, 'Population Control' tops the list followed by 'Conservation of Natural Resources' which included land and water, atmosphere, biodiversity and biomass. It may be added that in subsequent years, National Water Policy (2000), Biological Diversity Act (2002) and Rules (2004) lent support to the objectives.

The conservation strategy emphasized on the needs for integrating environment concern in every major sectors dealing with development under "Development Policy from Environmental Perspectives". Towards the end it also calls for a policy on 'Rehabilitation of Project affected People' which is yet come up in full form, even after 18 years of the Policy Statement.

It will be worthwhile to recall that with 73rd and 74th Constitutional amendment, decentralization of governance became a part of the system. Panchayati Raj, however, benefits the revenue villages keeping forest village outside the purview, till the 'Panchayat Raj Extension to Scheduled Areas' was enacted in 1996. The period between 1980-1996, therefore, can be marked as an era of changing perception, apparently more in favour of community participation. The democratic process of governance in India still believed in the colonial process of ruling for more then three decades after independence.

The dawn of twenty-first century was expected to lead to a more effective system of conservation. However, in between 1991-2011, the process of globalization and market economy had its palpable impacts on National Policies, as evidenced by newly drafted or changes made of as many as 15 National Policies, advocating role of private sector in the name of corporate efficiency during the period (Ghosh, 2005).

But one has to admit that at least two of the bills passed by the Indian Parliament are unique Biological Diversity Act, 2002 (BD Act) and Forests Rights Act (FRA) in 2006. The BD Act declared for the first time sovereign rights of the nation over its biological resources and put in place a decentralized plan of governance with provision of benefit sharing between the conservers and providers of biological resource and traditional knowledge, i.e. the Local Community and the Stakeholders. The second Act, viz. Forests Rights Act, 2006 corrected a historic injustice, so far meted out to the traditional forest dwellers.

Biodiversity Act, 2002 stated that "Every local body constitutes a Biodiversity Management Committee within its area for the purpose of promoting conservation, sustainable and documentation….." [Section 41(i)]. Similarly FRA stated under Chapter III, Section 5, to "ensure that the decisions taken in the Gram Sabha to regulate access to community forest resources and stops any activity which adversely affects the wild animals, forest and biodiversity...". While our analysis has tried to follow a historical path of genesis of acts and policies supporting conservation and development strategy in India within a limited space, necessary to have research with supporting data to confirm our contention.

Way Ahead

The concept that conservation and development may be synergistic rather than antagonistic has been evident since the publication in 1988 of Brundt land Commission Report "Our Common Future". The issue of sustainability is intrinsically connected with conservation and appropriate use of finite natural resources. Earlier, The Report of Club of Rome (Meadows & Meadows, 1972), on the Predicament of Mankind in twenty-first century, alarmed the world and put enough caution to limits to growth. Nearly 50 years have passed since its publication but apparently global powers and emerging economies are yet to implement the strategies that guarantee sustainability. Economic growth leads to development; obviously such belief can be the driving force to scale up GDP following classical economic model. In India, for instance in last 10 years, coal production has tripled, iron ore production has jumped by 286 per cent, and bauxite by 350 times. Union Government has decided that 450 coal blocks covering 3,80,000 ha of forest land will be open to mining in coal sector (Sethi, 2010).

The fallacy is that while Forest Rights Act, 2006 provided "Gram Sabha" to decide on the fate of the forest they live, i.e. conversion for economic development or otherwise, their views are often not sought. Biological Diversity Act, 2002 mandated formation of Biodiversity Management Committees at local level to ensure regulation of access and derive benefit, but implementation remains pathetic. State Governments vying with each other continue to put "development" at any cost, relegating "conservation" to the last priority. The time to act has been delayed. The question remains how long the civil society and informed public will act as viewers?

REFERENCES

Anon. Projects and Forests: Flawed Clearances and Complicit Foresters. *Economic & Political Weekly*, Vol 46 (41): 15-17. 2011.

Beneet, Scott 'Shikar and the Raj'. South Asia N.S. 7:72-88. 1984.

BSI. Materials for a Catalogue of Threatened Plants. Botanical Survey of India, Department of Environment, Government. of India, 1-69. 1983.

Elliot, J.G., Field Sports In India. (1800-1947). London. 1973.

Ghosh, A.K., Civil Society and Environmental Governance. *Ishan*, 22:31-35. School of Fundamental Research, Kolkata. 2005.

GOI National Conservation Strategy and Policy Statement on Environment and Development. Ministry of Environment and Forests, Government of India, New Delhi. 1992.

Guha, Ramchandra and Gadgil, Madhav, State Forestry and Social Conflict in British India. 104-124. In, Indian Forestry: A Perspective, ed Ajay S. Rawat. Indus Publishing Company, New Delhi. 1993.

Khushoo, T.N. Environmental Priorities in India and Sustainable Development. Presidential Address: 73rd Session. Indian Science Congress Association, New Delhi. 1986.

Khare, Arvind, Sarin, M.I., Saxena, N.C., Palit, S., Bathla, S., Vama, F., and Satyanarayana, M. *et. al.* (2000): Joint Forest Management: Policy, Practice and Prospect. World Wide Fund for Nature. India, New Delhi and International Institute for Environment and Development.

Meadows, Donella H., Meadows Dennis, L., Randers, J., Behrem, W.W.,1972. The Limits to Growth: A Report for Club of Rome's Project on the Predicament of Mankind. Universe Books.

MoEF National Forest Policy: Resolution No 3-1/86- F. Dated 7th December, 1988. Ministry of Environment and Forests, New Delhi.

MoEF (2010): Annual Report 2009-2010. Ministry of Environment and Forests, New Delhi. 1988.

Ray, Panjawani. Evolution of Wildlife Laws. The Wildlife (Protection) Act, 1972 (as amended up to 1991). Notary Publishers, Dehra Dun. 1994.

Sethi, Nitin, Plundering India: India undermined, *Times of India,* Crest Edition, October 30, 2010. 2010.

Singh, Sekhar, Social and Environmental Impacts of Large Dams in India. *Ecologist Asia,*11(1); 61-70. 2003.

3

Critiquing 'Fortress Conservation Approach'

Is 'People Centred Conservation Approach' a Viable Option in the Indian Context?

Bidhan Kanti Das

Introduction

Conservation of biodiverse resources of the Earth is one of the major agendas for international conventions, international environmental NGOs, national and state agencies as well as conservation biologists for the last two decades. There is rapid decline in biological diversity, though large parts of ecosystems have not yet been explored (Heywood, 1995). It is argued that since early period of human history, people have overexploited the diverse resources, which is manifested recently in the negative effects of tropical logging (Bawa and Seidler, 1998) and marine fisheries exploitation (Pauley *et al.,* 1998). About 40 per cent of the Earth's terrestrial primary productivity was appropriated by human action (Vitousek *et al.,* 1986). Chapin *et al.,* (2000) calculated that about 10 per cent of all known bird species, 20 per cent of known mammal species, 5 per cent of known fish species and 8 per cent of all recorded plant species are under the threat of extinction. The extinction rates are currently estimated to be 100 to 1000 times normal (Lovejoy, 2002), which is much greater than ever experienced in recorded history. Conservation Biologists argued that loss of biodiversity contributes to undermining the capability of life to survive and reproduce itself with vigour and reliability (O'Riordan, 2002).

To preserve the denuding biodiversity, various conservation efforts have been initiated. Some efforts are reactive in nature. Conservationists argued that biodiversity habitats are being depleted by the population increase and human consumptive use. Creation of parks is the most effective way to counter ever increasing human impacts (Myers, 2002).They see nature separate from humans. This protectionist approach to biodiversity conservation has become widely unpopular, particularly in developing and less developed countries for their socio-economic impacts (Adam and Hulme, 2001). Second approach is people centred conservation or community based conservation that emphasized the need not to exclude local people, but to ensure their participation in decision making process in conservation (Western and Wright 1994; Adams and Hulme, 2001). However, this approach has also been criticized by conservationists. In between these two extreme positions, there is another approach, neoliberal approach like 'payment for ecosystem services', 'ecotourism', 'bio prospecting' etc. advocated by economists. They argue that community based conservation approaches do not link local communities directly through markets and payments are not performance based (Ferraro and Kiss, 2002).

In developing countries, most biodiversity rich zones or biodiversity 'hotspots' are also social and political 'hotbeds' (Wilshusen *et al.*, 2003). These areas are characterized by high levels of poverty, insecure land tenure and landlessness, unstable political systems, and state sponsored repression (*ibid.*). For example, more than 75 per cent of the total population of Tri National de la Sangha area of Cameroon, Congo, and the Central African Republic live below the poverty line of US $ 1 per day (Sayer *et al.*, 2007). Against this backdrop, the present paper tries to examine the current conservation strategies in the context of socio-economic realities of developing countries like India. Further I would argue which strategies might be the best possible options for sustainable development of bio-resources in developing countries like India.

The paper is structured as follows: The first section deals with philosophical background and arguments in favour of 'protectionist' paradigm of conservation and its impact on local inhabitants. The second section discusses the conservation and development approach and its impact. Critical assessment of neoliberal approach to conservation will be discussed in the third section. Section four presents some facts on socio-economic realities of local forest dependent communities. Finally, I argue that integrated conservation and development approach might be the best possible options for conserving biodiversity resources in future.

Protectionist Paradigm of Conservation

Historically, conservation strategies have been dominated by attempts to reserve places for nature, and to separate humans and other species. This model is called as the 'fortress conservation' or the 'fines and fences approach'. Conservationists historically focused on wilderness, wild species and natural ecosystems and have been concerned with conservation of the structure and elements of biodiversity. This philosophical approach is termed as 'compositionalism' (Callicot *et al.*, 2000). People fall outside this sphere of interest. The management philosophy stressed that 'the public good was best served through the protection of forests and water resources, even if this meant the displacement of local communities' (McCracken, 1987). Local communities overstocked, overgrazed or otherwise overused the natural environment and were thus barriers to effective natural resource management (Chatty and Colchester, 2008). So the general expectation was that human use of resources would invariably affect biodiversity in a negative way. Deriving from this philosophy, much conservation practice has had the goal of the preservation and restoration of biological diversity and integrity. The establishment of parks and protected areas (PAs) historically has been the primary approach to conserving biodiversity. It involves the exclusion of people as residents, the prevention of consumptive use and minimisation of other forms of human impact (Brockington and Schmidt-Soltau, 2004). This has led to forced displacement from the Reserve, creating a new group of impoverished and marginalised people who are often called 'Conservation refugees' (Dowie, 2005). But why do conservation scientists believe in protectionist paradigm of conservation strategy? What are the elements of protectionist arguments? Wilshusen and his colleagues have identified four core elements of 'protectionist' argument (2002) which are as follows:

(i) Protected Areas Require Strict Protection

It holds that in all existing PAs, restricting human occupation and use (IUCN categories I-IV accounts 64.8 per cent of all PAs) must be enforced. Proponents of this strategy argue that PAs have been and continue to be essential elements of global biodiversity conservation strategies. Conservation programmes should dedicate significant time and energy to PA management (Terborgh and van Schaik, 1997). In particular, many species—especially large mammals—need extensive, undisturbed tracts of habitat to ensure their survival. It is beyond doubt that some sort of management strategy has to be enforced to preserve denuding bio-resources including large mammals in biodiversity 'hotspots'. Similarly, life and livelihoods of rural communities revolve round the forest resources for generations particularly in developing countries. An IUCN study reveals that about 86 per cent of national parks had permanent resident populations (Amend and Amend, 1992), who were historically dependent on resources of PAs for their livelihood. In India, the same phenomenon also exists in over 65 per cent of the PAs (Kothari *et al.* 1989). Considering the above facts, the issue is not whether PAs should be enforced but how. Advocates of protectionist paradigm emphasize only on maintenance of ecological structure and function. That means, they are undermining or ignoring the 'politicized' nature of PAs. It is important to recognize 'politicized' nature of PAs for awareness generation and attempts at consultation or 'cosmetic participation' most likely, will not change many rural people's suspicions and resistance. This approach has to address broader social and political factors to gain people's confidence. The political trajectories of PAs to a large extent shape how they are perceived by local people and other actors (Wilshusen *et al,* 2002). Moreover, it depends on the degree of legitimacy that management restrictions carry. This approach involves significant curltailment of people's access to forest resources that leads to diverse socio economic impacts. In most cases, these people become impoverished and marginalised. PA managers deal with these political realities on a daily basis and yet the broader policy implications have been explored only superficially (Wilshushen *et al.,* 2002). As a result, conflict and resistance often develop in response to parks and their management. For example, local populations destroy important components of wildlife resources, even negotiate with professional poachers and ivory traders by helping them kill rhinos and elephants as a form of protest against loss of traditional rights in Nagarhole in Karnataka, Kanha in Madhya Pradesh and Keoladeo National Park in Rajasthan, India (Chatterjee 2009).

Traditional management strategy focuses on zonations (core, buffer, multiple uses). But the Western scientific and managerial explanations *mask* other political understandings of the roles that PAs play in the context of wider social and cultural spheres. For outsiders like resource dependent agrarian communities, PAs are not necessarily understood as a means of providing ecological and economic services but rather as territorial control strategies (Wilshusen *et al.,* 2002). In many cases, members of rural communities have not been told that they live near or adjacent to PA and even if they do know, they may not be familiar with the strategies employed for the protected area. As a result, local reactions are not positive, and are rather violent.

When viewed from historical perspective, many outsiders including local communities view such conservation efforts as yet another expression of external control. This strategy, in some contexts, reflects earlier eras of imperial domination (Chan *et al.*, 2007). Many PAs in former colonies were established by Europeans and essentially for Europeans, whereas others were established in post-independence period with the explicit objective of luring wealthy international tourists (*ibid*). PAs also serve foreign 'elite' interests in developing countries like East Africa and India with the creation of royal game reserves for trophy hunters (Neumann, 1998).

(ii) Biodiversity Conservation is a moral Imperative

Proponents of 'protectionists' paradigm often cited a combination of pragmatic and moral arguments for protection of biological diversity. Pragmatic arguments are based on explaining the utilitarian importance of preserving biodiversity in terms of economic use and non-use values (Wilshushen *et al,* 2002). This basically emphasizes on real and potential use values of plant and animal species as sources of new pharmaceuticals, genetic banks for key agricultural crops, and environmental services like flood control, as well as non-use values like 'wilderness' areas for recreation and aesthetic value.

The moral argument is based on two basic rights : (i) the intrinsic right of nature to exist (i.e. humans do not have the right to eradicate other species) and (ii) the right of global, regional and local communities to enjoy the aesthetic qualities of nature (Terborgh, 2004). Underlying belief is that the international communities can and should act on behalf of nature in different parts of the earth as 'global citizens'. This typically justifies foreign involvement in the management of a country's biodiversity (van Schaik and Kramer, 1997).

Though the arguments are fine, it fails to account in two crucial points : firstly, the arguments do not acknowledge that there are different ways of understanding and appreciating nature (Wilshushen *et al.*, 2002). Conservation professionals educated and trained in positivist traditions in the West, would only accept priority to scientific explanations and strategies for protecting biodiversity. This assumes the existence of only one reality. In fact, they consistently ignore the intricate intertwined relationship between indigenous people and immediate nature that shapes their beliefs and practices (Folke, 2004). But by failing to understand the world and how it changes from pluralistic way, conservationists are not interested to dialogue with other groups, including a wide variety of local communities. Moreover, it ignores the complex social and cultural histories that shape different people's understanding of and relationship to the natural world (Wilshushen *et al.,* 2002). The idea of looking to ecosystem of plants and animals as a function of unique past has progressively changes to see ecosystem as *dynamic*, and continuously changing and thereby, acknowledges the importance of people in functioning of ecosystem (Chatty and Colchester, 2008). Various regional and local ecological studies show that not allhuman use is detrimental to wildlife conservation. All over the world, quality of forest and biodiversity patterns are reflections of past land use activities (Ramakrishnan, 1992; Western, 1989; Saberwal, 1996). Comprehensive scientific study reveals that there are many differences among flora population of grazed and ungrazed lands. In fact, the grazed areas had greater number of plants as well as variety though vegetation cover is more in ungrazed lands. They concluded that light to moderate grazing in the Great Basin certainly has no ill effects on the ecosystem (Courtois *et al.* 2004). In southeast Asia, the intermittent clearance of tracts of land in the forest of the Pwo Karen never caused forest degradation, but rather encouraged the larger wild herbivores to enter by creating sporadic open access in the forest (Ewers,

1998). Moreover, a study revealed that resource management to protect and control the elephants caused severe deterioration of the land within the park while inhabited area outside the park remained forested (Botkin 1990).

Secondly, protectionists advocate that local concerns should not automatically supersede regional, national, and global concerns. It is beyond doubt that nature protection serves the common good which both justifies local restrictions and impacts as well as the stakeholder's status and the international community (Wilshushen *et al.*, 2002). At the same time, the argument assumes that both types of interests (local and nonlocal) are of the same order and carry the same weight. This is important because it affects the legitimacy of claims. Forest people often question about the opportunity cost to be borne by themselves for common good. How should we respond to the common 'local' argument that imposed conservation restrictions produce not only economic hardships but also irreversible cultural impacts? People residing in and near PAs perceive their interest as tangible and immediate and the 'common' interest as unclear and intangible. This view only reflects the issue of distributive justice, including the widely accepted belief that the common good refers to elite special interests imposed on rural poor (*ibid.*). This argument suggests that dialogue on conservation would need to clarify this balance of interests in specific context. It should address the perception that local people carry a disproportionate burden in terms of negative social, cultural and economic impacts.

This moral approach tends to create a false moral dilemma in which the rights of humans are pitted against the rights of nature. This type of binary understanding often creates a vacuum for dialogue where nature 'loses out' by default when humans 'win'. Win-lose scenarios imply that there is no space for dialogue or negotiation. Since the issue of nature protection is framed as a moral, win lose proposition, debate along these lines produces opposing camps that might be described as 'pro-nature' *versus* 'pro-people'. This confrontational dichotomy forces a separation between humans and nature as a means of protecting 'wildlands' (Jhonson, 2000).

(iii) Harmonious, Ecologically Friendly Local Communities are Myths

Proponents of protectionist paradigm believe that community based natural resource management (CBNRM) or community based conservation (CBC) by indigenous and other traditional people cannot guarantee species protection. It is argued that local communities who historically live in harmony with nature, are losing traditional qualities due to rapid social change (Terborgh, 1999). Further, it is a myth that a community member is living in perfect harmony with other community members (Oates, 1999). John Oates argued that there is little evidence that traditional African societies have been natural conservationists. Rather they exploit nature for immediate gains without regard to sustainability. He continued that such exploitation has usually led to marked resource depletion or species extinction.

But available evidences from all over the world show that communities are protecting forest for generations. Globally 11 per cent of the world's total forest land is under community ownership or administration. In South America, one-fifth of the Amazon is under indigenous protected area control which is 5 times more than the area of formal protected areas integrated under official PA system like the 68,000 hectares Alto Fragua-Indiwasi National Park of Colombia. Australia has a network of over 20 indigenous PAs, comprising about 20 per cent of the country's terrestrial PAs. In India, there are over 10,000 community managed forests, ranging from a few hectares to several hundred thousand hectares. They are protecting resident and wintering waterfowl, antelope and deer species, nesting Olive Ridley sea turtles, freshwater fish poplations, and threatened pheasant species (Pathak *et al* 2006). Many community forestry activities in Nepal not only protect the habitat and species but communities also sustainably harvest forest resources and benefit from ecological functions such as availability of water. In Brazil, indigenous and extractive reserves (forest reserve managed by rubber tappers and other folk communities) protect much larger areas of native forest than do uninhabited protected areas. They have been far more effective in halting deforestation and in expanding the frontier regions where the pressure for deforestation is high (Nepstad *et al.*, 2006). In Mayan zone Quintana Roo, Mexico, where community forestry has been implemented, deforestation rate between 1984 and 2000 was almost 'imperceptible' and was comparable with or lower than those of areas under PAs (Bray *et al.*, 2004).

However, homogenous nature of community has been criticized by some social scientists and they have cautioned against overlooking the heterogeneity and extant power hierarchies that exist in rural communities that can marginalise less powerful sections of the society (Agarwal and Gibson, 1999; Nygren, 2005). Identity politics—class, gender, age, caste — within local communities act in such a way that empower some members and marginalise others. For example, women in many developing countries are not legally right holders though they are locally recognised as community members through kinship networks, residence and other social factors (Charnley and Poe, 2007). That doesn't mean that one should ignore the evidence that in many instances such communities have demonstrated their capacity to manage natural resources effectively over time (Hutton *et al.*, 2005). Critics create false impression that all resource dependent people act only to maximise short term gains without considering wider political and economic factors that might encourage them to do so. In the words of Redford *et al.*, 'it is clearly not that communities are bad but rather that they must not be stereotyped. Some will actively work to conserve some components of biodiversity, others will not, and have not' (1998). By arguing such simplistic way about community functions, protagonists are oversimplifying rural communities motivations and cultural practices. Sceptics also overlook how decision making organization, and governance institutions — both customary and modern — that structure the resource use within and among rural communities (Wilshusen *et al.,* 2002). It is wrong to assume that local institutions cannot adapt to social change. Traditional groups might be able to adapt patterns of use to a more sustainable way, especially with outside support.

(iv) Conservation linked to Development does not Protect Biodiversity

The main argument revolves around the perceived failure of conservation and development in protecting species in parks. Conservationists believe that integrated conservation and development projects (ICDPs) have not effectively safeguarded PA core zones. They argued that conservation programmes have become diluted with social goals like poverty reduction and social justice. ICDPs and participatory strategies have emphasized development much more than nature protection (Brandon, 1997). John Terborgh asserted that ICDPs actually increase rather than reduce human use pressures on PAs (1999). For conservationists, community based approaches do not provide enough protection for endangered species and environments and fail to achieve conservation goals.

However, studies available have shown that outcome of ICDPs is positive in nature. A review of 28 conservation and development projects found that greater levels of community input into decision making were associated with better conservation outcomes (Brooks *et al.,* 2006). Other studies also document positive ecological effects from community forestry, for example, Poffenberger (2006) for southeast Asia, Wily (1999) for Tanzania, and Nittler & Tschinkel (2005) for Guatemala. Some social scientists criticized ICDPs function similar to conventional development projects and results are highly inequitable outcomes that severely limit the local people's rights (Schmidt, Soltau, 2004) as well as potentially becoming poverty traps for local communities (Dove, 1993). Social scientists raised questions in the inherent assumption within ICDPs which focus local people as the agents of environmental destruction while disregarding larger scale extraction of resources by loggers and miners (Dove, 1993 ; Christensen, 2004). Only focusing local people as threat which is a minor one, contributed to their lack of success and further alienates local support for conservation activities (Christensen, 2004).

Some evidences, however, show that ICDPs appear not to offer biodiversity conservation at a sufficient scale or degree to guarantee species survival as in Indonesia, Nepal and Kenya. But it would be a mistake to assume that if ICDPs do not sufficiently address biodiversity conservation then we have nothing to learn from the approach and should be discarded as a policy tool. Whatever perceived lack of effectiveness *may be real* but success mainly depends on how the programme is implemented rather than concept. On the ground, ICDPs were generally paternalistic, lacking expertise and one sided, driven by agenda of conservation with little indigenous input (Chapin, 2004). Conservationists and foresters adopt development activities as secondary strategy to achieve their primary objective. According to Songwora (1999) 'outsiders/initiators are more interested in wildlife than the local communities and that the outsiders intend to put as much of the community's land as possible under protected area management'. 'Most ICDPs have treated local people as passive beneficiaries of project activities and have failed to involve people in decision making related to the process of change and their own development (Wells and Brandon, 1993)'.

Secondly, protagonists believe that sustainable use depletes biodiversity (Redford and Richter, 1999). Regarding sustainable use, Brandon *et al.*, in *Parks in Peril* (1998) state,

> *'Not all things can be preserved through use. Not all places should be open to use. Without understanding of broader ecosystem dynamics at specific sites, strategies promoting sustainable use will lead to substantial losses of biodiversity'.*

That means authors critique sustainable use as means of achieving species protection in and around parks. A recent evidence regarding sustainable use in Amazonia contradicts the assumption made by proponents of protectionist paradigm (Redford and Sanderson 2000 ; Schwartzman *et al.*, 2000). Even if we accept the view that sustainable use will not maintain species diversity, most critics undermine the important role that it plays as one component of a broader landscape strategy. John Robinson of Wildlife Conservation Society (1993) also criticized the issue of sustainable use debate entirely in ecological terms and opined that exclusive reliance on this approach actually lowers biological diversity. Actually sustainable use strategies have played central role in reversing large scale land use conversion of tropical dry forests in Quitanaa Roo, Mexico without any government intervention (Wilshushen *et al.*, 2002).

Moreover, in most cases, parks overlap with or adjoining areas with pre-existing land use rights. In some cases, landless migrants may come from other regions in search of resources (Wilshusen *et al.*, 2002) like forced displacees. These political realities can be managed with the intervention of local developmental programme with involvement of local communities in buffer zones to reduce pressure from core protected zones. If this strategy has not been effective, as critic's claims, it would appear to be more a problem of implementation rather than concept (*ibid.*). They further argued that exclusive reliance on 'fortress conservation' paradigm will not protect species. More likely, it would prove politically suicidal for foresters and produce violent resistance by resource dependent populations, as we observed in several protected areas in developing countries including India (Mukherjee, 2009 ; Torry, 2011).

Neoliberal Approach to Conservation

Proponents of neoliberal paradigm, dominating the late twentieth century, argue that uncontrolled, open markets give individuals the greatest freedom in selection what to produce and consume and that patterns of natural resource use (including conservation) are best determined by market processes (Hulme and Murphee, 1999). That means, privatization of resources that can be traded in markets without intervention of government give freedom to local authorities and non state actors like NGOs (Castree, 2008). From conservation perspective, it is argued that if species or habitats are to be conserved they must not be protected from market forces. If it is under the control of an inefficient state, they will allow them to be destrroyed as 'rent seeking' public officials take bribes from poachers and timber companies. Instead, it is better that they must be fully exposed to a market (free from distortions that create perverse incentives) where their uniqueness and scarcity will lead to high economic values being placed on them. So the possibility of conservation is greatly improved (Hulme and Murphee, 1999). Consumers (tourists, trophy hunters, and local people who intrinsically value a species or habitat) will bid prices up so that alternative uses that would degrade the environment, particularly agriculture, will no longer be attractive to producers (i.e. proprietors and managers of the resources). It emphassizes on economic efficiency, commodification of biodiversity, marginalisation of certain groups, transformation of property rights and accountability of governance networks.

These arguments have been presented most publicly over the issue of elephant trophy hunting and ivory sales. They claim that where elephants are conserved but not utilized then local resource users view them as a pest (a very big pest) destroying livelihoods through crop raiding and threatening human life (Hulme and Murphee, 1999). By contrast, where elephants are fully utilized (tourism, trophy hunting, ivory, skin, meat sales) in ways that provide economic incentives to local resource users then people will protect and manage elephants and give a high priority on the maintenance of elephant habitat.

This neoliberal paradigm is varied in nature in conservation practice. It is evident in terms of increasing prominence and power of big international environmental NGOs like Conservation International and The Nature Conservancy and partnership with multinational financial institutions like the World Bank, IMF (Chapin, 2004). Other forms are : the promotion of economic activities (like eco tourism, bio prospecting, and payment for environmental services) to commodify natural resources and create market for trading (West, 2006) ; the spurt of private owned 'nature reserves' (Langholtz, 2003) ; the decentralisation of resource control to NGOs and community members (Brockington 2002; Igoe, 2004). One consequence of the growing importance of neo-liberal approaches to conservation is the increasing involvement of the private sector in the tenure and management of PAs, raising complex issues of rights, ownership, governance and legitimacy. The concept of private parks, or parks managed by corporate non state actors, is of increasing importance in conservation (Langholtz and Kruz, 2004). The increasing private sector engagement in conservation landholding has been driven partly by growing dissatisfaction with the issue of effectiveness of tropical PAs (Krammer *et al.*, 2002).It is argued that most biodiversity exist outside formally protected land, much of it private (Langholtz and Kruz, 2004). In fact, policies to promote the conservation value of private land have been widely developed in the game ranching and safari industries.

However, researchers critiqued the assumption that economic efficiency is the only answer for conservation of biodiversity. There is a lack of scientific evidences that market forces always favour conservation (Chan *et al.*, 2007). In fact, it is very difficult to predict market behaviour. It depends on various externalities. So, it cannot be a dependable option for conservation which seeks a continuation in protection of biodiversity. They argued that native bees at one point of time are important because they provide pollination services to coffee cultivators; they become less important when coffee prices go down and coffee cultivators become pineapple cultivators. So internalization of externalities and harnessing market forces may be good for biodiversity for some time, but such management option will not work continuously. This approach may be problematic in Indian context where marginalised tribals mostly inhabiting the most biodiverse region (TTF, 2005) are incapable of handling market forces. This may lead to further marginalisation. Secondly, neoliberalization of conservation constitutes an institutional and cultural shift towards privatization of property rights and marketization of exchanges. For example, a shift to neoliberal policies in Mexico in 1990s brought an end to agrarian reform, allowing dissolution of collective property rights (*ejidos*) among other changes (Lele *et al.*, 2010).Thirdly, neo-liberalization may allow international NGOs and corporations to increase their influence over local resource use through the decentralised governance in which community members participate rather than truly transferring control to community members, (Levine, 2002). Fourthly, local values and meanings may change with commodification of resources that may affect social cultural dynamics within communities (Sullivan 2006; West, 2006); Fifthly, commodification of resources may actually accelerate rather than reduce resource degradation if revenues are used to buy extractive equipment (like tractors)(West, 2006). Sixthly, forced displacement may be increased due to market based conservation initiative (Adams and Hutton, 2007).

Community based Conservation Approach

This approach gets impetus with the publication of the Brundtland Commission report where meeting development needs of local people have been explicitly recognised. It explicitly links conservation and human livelihood and moves beyond the development philosophy of the Brighten Wood Institutions (World Bank, IMF) (Robinson, 2006). A new community conservation narrative has emerged that stresses non exclusion of local people, either physically from PAs or politically from conservative policy process, but to ensure their participation (Western *et al.*, 1994; Adams and Hulme, 2001). This approach sees local communities as integral part of the ecosystems — a 'functional' perspective-based on human rights perspective mainly advocated by anthropologists/social scientists (Shah, 2007). This paradigm recognised both the moral implication of costs of conservation borne by local people and the pragmatic problem of the hostility of displaced or disadvantaged local people to conservation organizations practicing a 'fortress conservation policy' (Adams and Hulme, 2001).This functionalist approach is, in fact, less concerned with static structure and elements of biodiversity, more on maintaining dynamic ecological processes. The basic assumption is that human influence is pervasive. Wilderness is no more than a matter of degree and humans are a natural part of nature (Callicot *et al.*, 2000). Implication of community based conservation (CBC) theory is that there can be no universal meta truths about conservation that can be separated from, or implemented in isolation from, the context within which people interact with the species/ ecosystem for which conservation strategies are being designed. The knowledge of communities with the environment, including access to, and control over use of natural resources, is basic to the explanations and visions of conservation as well as the choice of appropriate conservation strategies (Campbell and Vainio Mattila, 2003). So, conservation is impossible without support and participation of local communities and also without improving livelihoods (Pimbert & Pretty, 1995; McShane, 2003; Barret *et al.,* 2005). It leads to emergence of management strategy of protected areas *linking local communities* towards *participatory and people centred* approach with the objective of conserving biodiversity as well as of ensuring livelihood security of local traditional communities like ICDPs, eco-development etc., (Pimbert & Pretty, 1995). Moreover, inhabitants are more likely to take responsibility for forest health if they feel a sense of ownership and control over them (Glasmeier and Farrigan, 2005). In other way, conservation can best be achieved by raising the standards of livelihood of rural people that may play incentive for survival of species (Hutton and Leader Williams 2003). In India, National Forest Policy (1988) advocated this inclusive approach.

This approach has gained wide acceptance within international policies due to following perspectives : Firstly, it evolved from rediscovery of 'community' as idealistic unit and bottom up approach against top down approach as an alternative that serves as a means of achieving positive social change (Adams and Hutton, 2001). Secondly, there is a need for pragmatic approach associated with protecting resources in developing countries, where exclusionary protection has failed to incorporate 'the human dimension of ecological issues' (Meyer and Helfman, 1993), increasingly seen as key to the success of conservation undertakings (Ghimire and Pimbert, 1997). This failure can undermine biological goals of conservation because of encroachment and illegal harvesting activities by local people and efforts to enforce exclusion can consume disproportionate amount of conservation funds. Thirdly, a critique of the philosophical basis of parks and protected areas embedded in North American romanticism and European utilitarianism (McCormick, 1989) and put emphasis on the separateness of human from nature. When the idea was imported by developing countries, this idea had at times conflicted with local ideas of human environment relations (Ghimire and Pimbert, 1997) and can undermine local cultural and social norms and regulations, and traditional or indigenous knowledge system (Marks, 1984). Fourthly, interest in environmental justice and a critique of the way of traditional conservation activities impinge on rural livelihoods. The already marginalised local human populations bear a disproportionate share of the conservation costs, through lost access to land and resources (Hackel, 1999; Wainwright and Werhmeyer 1998) and through reduced variety of economic activities (Turton, 1987). That means, parks can exacerbate existing inequities between the rural poor living next to them and those who gain through visiting as tourists or receiving wider environmental benefits of protection.

Some Harsh Realities

In developing countries, rural communities have always been dependent on natural resources for their sustenance and it is true even today for millions of forest dwellers (Gibson *et al.*, 2001). Studies have shown that the distribution of forests and indigenous population is correlated particularly in developing countries including India and it was noted that areas of high biodiversity overlap with areas where traditional communities maintain control over resource management (Maffi, 2005). More than half of PAs of the world are inhabited by local population whereas, in India, it is about two-third of total PAs (Kothari, 1997). Analysing the relationships between the extent of PAs and national wealth in Africa, Geisler and deSouza concluded that those countries with highest indices of poverty also have the greatest extent of PAs (2001). Similar situation is also available in India. It is also observed that poorer African countries established many more PAs than richer African countries (Geisler, 2003).

In India, the 150 poorest districts, constitutionally designated Schedule V areas, are primarily inhabited by tribals and are also the prime 'tiger districts' (TTF, 2005). Similarly, other communities who are also equally impoverished—live in and around those areas. Equally forests in these areas are in fact under greater pressure. Forced exclusion led local people to struggle for their lands and rights over lands (Adams *et al.*, 2004). This has led to violent protests, rallies and acts of sabotage against national parks and sanctuaries themselves. In India, national parks and sanctuaries have witnessed more than a hundred clashes in the early 1980s. Local inhabitants had set fire to large areas of the Kanha and Nagarhole national parks in the early 1990s due to denial of access to the park for forest resources. Insurgent forces have taken advantage of local resentment to drive out forest guards in the Manas Tiger Reserve in Assam, and to invade the Kutur Tiger and Buffalo Reserve in Madhya Pradesh (Roy and Jackson, 1993).

There is no proper assessment of the total number settlements in core and buffer areas of the PAs. People living in and around PAs are about 4.5 million in India (Kothari, 1996). The TTF estimated that the core and buffer zones of PAs alone contain around 65,000 families or 3,25,000 people (2005). Only 80 villages and 2904 families (and 46341 livestock) relocated from different TRs (as per TTF 2005; Kabra 2009). If we calculate costs of relocation, about 665 crores would be required to relocate all families from PAs as per current rate of compensation (i.e. 1 lakh per family). If we enhance money to 10 lakh per family one can imagine how much money is required. Moreover, rehabilitation programmes are largely ineffective except in Bhadra sanctuary, Melghat Tiger Reserve (Kabra, 2003). There are very few systematic studies or long-term studies to show changes to take due to relocation of people except some anecdotal evidences. That may actually be due to long standing human interactions with resources (Lasgorceix and Kothari, 2009). Conversely, the environmental impact is the destruction or degradation of natural ecosystems due to clearance for cultivation, housing sites, roads etc. Those who are forcefully relocated, people primarily *Adivasis* become more impoverished and marginalised in most cases (Lasgorceix and Kothari, 2009). They face hardship in getting resources like fuel, fodder, medicinal plants, wild foods etc. at relocation site.

The current strategy of conservation is expensive. Much of the budget for PAs has to be spent on aircrafts, radios, weapons, vehicles, salaries of armed guards, night goggles and other anti poaching instruments (Duffy 2000). In India, under 'Project Tiger', a flagship programme for conservation of Tigers, crores of rupees have been spent in 28 odd reserves in the country and the central funds are increasing with time but without any fruitful results. Notably the reserves where most funds have been invested are not necessarily best protected areas in the country (TTF, 2005). For example, Sariska and Ranthombore, both in Rajasthan, where the tiger is under threat, have received very high investments for infrastructure development. That means, high investments in these reserves have not yielded meaningful results. The report further pointed that providing staffs for patrolling reserves with varying size and shape is almost impossible.

Moreover, there are evidences that much of the biodiversity loss observed in PAs results from the curtailment of activities by local people. For example, the wildlife rich savannah ecosystems of East Africa have emerged as a result of the connectedness and co-evolution of pastoralists, their cattle and local wildlife. Without one, the others suffer. In Kenya, exclusion of Masai from their lands, scrubs and woodland increased that inhibited grazing opportunity for antelopes (Adams and MacShane, 1992). Evidences from various parts of the earth suggest that local people do value, utilize and efficiently manage their environments as they have done for millennia (Novellino, 1998; Abin, 1998; Sabewal, 1996). That means, when local people are excluded then degradation is more likely to occur (Chatty and Colchester, 2008). Forced relocation cuts the very intricate and intertwined relationship of man with immediate forest ecosystem and destroys the very essence of life. As a result, they engaged in destructive behaviour and malicious killings of the very wildlife they valued earlier (Mukherjee, 2009). Some others negotiate with professional poachers and ivory traders by helping them to kill rhinos and elephants.

Best Possible Alternatives: People-centred Conservation

The 'island model' or 'fortress model' of protection in India as well as in other developing countries have been frequently criticized for their adverse socio-economic impacts. The issues are: costs may outweigh benefits; cost may be borne by local communities especially the poor, marginalised who are not compensated, and imposition of certain projects planned by outside agencies without consultation of local communities (Adams and Hulme, 2001/9). The creation of PA causes curtailment of future land use options with potentially significant economic opportunity costs. The forced eviction of settlers or right holders in land or resources cause exacerbation of poverty (Brockington, 2002) and contravention of legal or human rights (Geisler and de Souza, 2001). Further, it is ethically unfair that displacing some groups without their consent is undemocratic, and displacing already disadvantaged group is doubly so (Brechin *et al.*, 2002).

Moreover, there is lack of consensus among researchers about effectiveness of PA strategy to conserve biodiversity though PA creation has halted deforestation rate to some extent, prevented species extinction and conserved land and water resources in some parts of the world. In fact, effectiveness in conservation is more mixed (Lele *et al.*, 2010). Significant forest decline has continued in other areas (Curran *et al.*, 2004). Many PAs are currently parks in paper in the tropics. One-third of such areas in the tropics are already subject to encroachment by landless and impoverished peasants (Myers, 2002). A survey of ninety three national parks of 5000 ha or more in size in 22 tropical countries has shown the importance of this measure in preserving biodiversity (Bruner, *et al.*, 2001). What is worthwhile to note that 70 per cent of all the studied parks are inhabited by local people. Local residents are contesting with Government about ownership rights in half of the studied parks. Still more than 80 per cent of the parks had much vegetation since establishment of parks. Parks affected less degradation compared to undesignated surrounding areas. However, Jules Pretty argued that success depends on clearly marked boundaries and close relations between authorities and local communities, including machining payments to local people (2002).

Other estimate suggests that 40 per cent of tropical parks are in no better condition than the land outside them (Bruner *et al.*, 2001). PAs are selected in less accessible areas so that they are less subject to degradation pressure. In some places, large mammals inside PAs have disappeared even after exclusion like in case of Sariska Tiger Reserve in India. It is not clear whether complete exclusion of human activities is really necessary for conservation effectiveness, in the context of historical modifications of forest landscapes. Evidences suggest that in some places, excluding resource use has actually been deleterious to the key biodiversity value to the PA like the case of Bharatpur Bird Sanctuary (Lewis, 2003). Alienation of local communities turned potential conservation allies into adversaries (Kothari, 2008). Human impacts continue relatively unabated despite protection measures (Robbins *et al.*, 2006).

A lot of empirical evidence indicates that the imitating 'protectionist' paradigm of conservation approaches in developing countries has led to food insecurity and declining status of livelihoods of people residing in and around the reserve (Wells and Brandon, 1992; Kothari *et al.*, 1989). Access to forest resources for food gathering, grazing, fishing, collection of wood etc. has been curtailed with the creation of PA. In some cases, local communities have been excluded from their habitat without provision of alternative means of livelihood and income (Pimbert and Pretty, 1995). The net effect is people in and around PAs get further impoverished and marginalised. Though this approach helped to improve biodiversity and growth of wild population, but it is clearly unreasonable to expect the rural poor to incur the opportunity costs, restrictions and potential harm that are often imposed by global conservation programmes (Arjunan *et al.*, 2006). An emerging consensus was that traditional and indigenous people should have incontrovertible rights to their land and one should support their struggle as morally responsible human being (Redford and Sanderson, 2000: 1362).

Considering the above facts, it is realized that management of PAs should aim at providing livelihood to the local community, which will in turn assure the protection of the PAs and its effective management. This is widely known as community based conservation (CBC) or community based natural resource management (CBNRM) or people centred conservation. It looks to a direct cooperative relationship between the integrity of ecosystems and the sustainable livelihoods of local people (Salafsky and Wollenberg, 2000). It is assumed that greater local control over forest management will result in more ecologically sustainable management of biodiversity as local people have greatest vested interest in them, and therefore, most incentive to do so (Wily and Mabya, 2001). Further, if they have sense of ownership and control, they are more likely to protect forest resources. In effect, management policy has been shifted to more 'participatory' approaches emphasizing equitable and sustainable use of natural resources by local communities (McNeely and Miller, 1984). Keeping the policy objective into consideration, stress has been given in searching new employment opportunities from biological resources which do not lead to further losses of biodiversity conservation. For this, participation and active support of local residents has become a major strategy in PAs (McNeely *et al.*,1990). The Integrated Conservation and Development Project (ICDP) is one such example. The ICDPs were implemented to reduce poverty and increase income levels, nutrition, health care and education as well as to conserve biodiversity (Christensen, 2004). Basic assumption is that if the income level of people gets enhanced as a result of development project, they will not engage themselves in illegal exploitation of nearby forests even in the absence of negative incentive provided by more effective penalties (Wells and Brandon, 1992). This approach has become the standard approach in linking the conservation of biodiversity with community development in PAs (Wells *et al.*, 2004). However, the approach of entrusting local communities in the management of forest areas has been criticized by protagonists of protection paradigm. They have raised doubt about the issues like the supposed closed relationship of local people with nature ; static view of local people's future; and the assumption that local institutions have the 'natural' capacity to manage a protected area for the sake of biodiversity conservation (Eghenter, 2002).

Though there are some limitations in ICDP approach that does not mean that ICDPs do not sufficiently address biodiversity conservation and so it should be discarded as a policy tool. It has tremendous policy relevance particularly in the context of overlapping status of poverty and biodiversity 'hotspots' in developing countries. In fact, there are instances of success in ICDPs approach (Schwartzman *et al.*, 2000; Hughes and Flintan, 2001; Brooks *et al.*, 2006). Whatever perceived failures have been observed are due to improper implementation of the programme rather than concept. The projects remained essentially protectionist in nature that seeks to save natural resources from local people. The projects were 'top down approach', designed and imposed by outsiders to meet predefined goals, with little local control (Kaimowitz and Sheil, 2007). It is true that conservationists advocate participation by local people, but at very low levels, often equating local people's participation with being educated regarding the necessity for conservation. Local people have been treated as passive beneficiaries of project activities and foresters have failed to involve people in decision-making related to the process of change and their own development (Wells and Brandon, 1993). The reasons for the perceived lack of effectiveness of community based projects range from the poor quality of project design and unqualified nature of many of those attempting implementation, to major policy failure in the devolution of power and authority (Gibson and Marks, 1995: Murphree, 2001) to real participation (Murombedzi, 2001).

So, how the people centred approach can be modified to conserve biodiversity as well as to improve livelihoods of local people? Keeping in mind the different approaches of biodiversity conservation, particularly in the context of developing countries, it will be legitimate and morally just to include resource dependent local people as active partners to achieve long term nature protection (Brechin *et al.*, 2001). If the biodiversity conservation is seen as social and political process (Brechin *et al.*, 2002) then consideration of economic, social, political as well as ecological impacts of different courses of action is inevitable. So conservation decisions depend on diverse stakeholders as well as societal interests (Song and M'Gonigle, 2001 ; Brechin *et al.*, 2002). To achieve success in 'people centred conservation' approach in meeting both conservation and development objectives, there is a need for pluralistic understanding of different knowledge, values and worldviews of different actors; for the adoption of deliberate inclusionary processes to decide and implement conservation, and for the need to transform conservation institutions to support a more dynamic, adaptive and integrated approach to conservation and development (Brown, 2003). To operationalize conservation, a framework linking conservation and development of local people for implementation of project activities on the ground may be useful which is schematised as follows:

To make conservation effective, participation of local people is absolutely necessary. Many forms of participation practiced are still passive and sometimes even coercive. For real inclusion we need to move beyond participation as practiced normally in ICDPs (Brown, 2003). Participation should occur at all stages of project implementation: information gathering, consultation, decision making, initiating actions and evaluation (Wells and Brandon, 1993). We need to apply methods and tools for 'deliberate inclusionary processes' that radically transform decision making and management processes and open up co-management frameworks. For this, a range of procedural techniques, mechanisms and methods like focus groups discussion, PRA exercise, workshops and working groups can be initiated. These methods put emphasis on working with small groups of people, focusing on the future

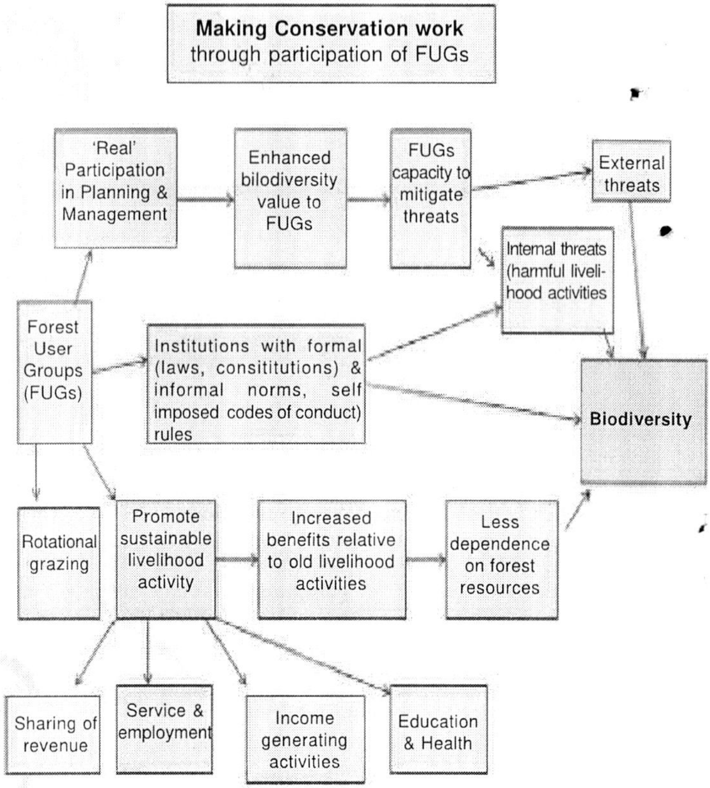

and on common ground; urging full attendance and participation; incorporating the widest possible range of interests and seeking public commitments to action (Brown, 2003). This may lead to fairer processes and better decisions and to the empowerment of marginalized actors like women. These empowered forest user groups can fight the external threats (like poachers) as well as internal threats (like illegal cutting of trees, destructive forest activities etc.).

Secondly, there should be institutional and legal frameworks 'to support the decisions made through such deliberate and inclusionary processes, otherwise processes and the stakeholders become undermined and disempowered' (Tompkins *et al.*, 2002). New institutions should be flexible and adaptable and able to manage complex ecosystems and accommodate diverse stakeholders' interests. Institutions in the broadest sense mean the formal and informal rules that govern human behaviour. They are made of formal constraints (rules, laws, constitutions) and informal constraints (norms of behaviour, self imposed codes of conduct) and enforcement characteristics (Brown, 2003).

Thirdly, strategies have to be evolved that promote sustainable livelihood activities. Various programmes have to be adopted like service provisions to neighbouring villages, employment of local people as guards as well as for other purposes and participation in park planning processes, income generating activities like sharing of revenues from wildlife tourism in PAs; investment in education and health sectors, or provision of locally acceptable alternatives to lost resources (Murombedzi, 1999).

Fourthly, the policy and legislative reforms have not resulted in sufficient community control over natural resources. In fact, there has been no real devolution of power and authority over resources, including land from the state to local people (Murombedzi, 2001). What is required is a process that gives communities control over their resources through tenure reform. It is based on the assumption that local communities have greater interest in sustainable resource use than Governments or corporations (Brosius, 1998) and that communities will develop a sense of proprietorship over wildlife (Hackel, 1999) with devolution of power.

Above all, lack of dialogue between forest authorities and local communities is the most important obstacle to make conservation a success. Forest officers always see local communities as ignorant, 'under developed' and 'economically irrational'. Such negative attitude undermines mutual trust necessary for an effective partnership and joint management of bioresources between forest authorities and local communities (Torri, 2011). The changing paradigm of control and sanction to development programmes for local communities requires changes in attitudes of forest managers. In addition, skill enhancement among forest managers to work with local communities, inculcating attitude of cooperation and trust as well as respect to partners is urgently needed which promotes healthy understanding between forest managers and local forest dependent communities in managing bio-resources in developing countries like India.

REFERENCES

Abin, R., 'Plantations : Village Development threatens the survival of Indigenous Dayak communities in Sarawak'. *Indigenous Peoples,* 4:15-23, 1998.

Adams, J.S. and T.O. MacSahane, *The Myth of Wild Africa.* New York: WW Norton and Co., 1992.

Adams, W.M. and Hulme, D., 'If community conservation is the answer in Africa, What is the Question ?' *Oryx,* 35(3):193-200, 2001.

Adams, W.M, and J. Hutton, 'People, Parks and Poverty : Political ecology and biodiversity conservation', *Conservation and Society* 5(2) : 147-183, 2007.

Agarwal, A. and C.C. Gibson, 'Enchantment and disenchantment : The role of community in natural resource management', *World Development* 27 (4) : 629-649, 1999.

Amend, S. and T. Amend, *Espacios sin habitants? Parques nacionales de America del Sur,* Editorial, Nueva Socieded, Caracas, 1992..

Arjunan, M., C. Holmes, J.P. Puyaravaud and P. Davidar, 'Do development initiatives influence local attitudes toward conservation ? a case study from the Kalakad Mundanthurai Tiger Reserve, India', *Journal of Environmental Management* 79 : 188-197, 2006.

Barrett, C.B, D.R. Lee, J.G. McPeak, Institutional arrangements for rural poverty reductions and resource conservation, *World Development* 33(2): 193-197, 2005.

Bawa, K.S. and R, Seidler, 'Natural resource management and conservation of biodiversity in tropical forests', *Conservation Biology* 12;46-55, 1998.

Botkin, D., *Discordant Harmonies: a new ecology for the 21st century.* New York: Oxford University Press, 1990.

Brandon, K., 'Policy and practical considerations in land use strategies for biodiversity conservation', in, R.A. Kramer, C.P. van Schaik and J. Johnson, eds., *Last stand : Protected areas and the defense of tropical biodiversity,* New York : Oxford University Press,. 1997.

Bray, D.B., E. A. Ellis, N. Armijo-Canto, and C.T. Beck, 'The institutional drivers of sustainable landscapes : a case study of the 'Mayan' zone in Quintana Roo, Mexico', *Land Use Policy,* 21:333-46, 2004.

Bray, D.B, E.A. Ellis; N. Armijo-Canto, and C.T. Beck, 'The institutional drivers of sustainable landscapes : a case study of the ' Mayan Zone" in Quintana Roo, Mexico'. *Land Use Policy* 21: 333-46, 2004.

Brechin, S.R., P.R. Wilshusen, C.L. Fortwangler and P.C. West, 'Beyond the square wheel : toward a more comprehensive understanding of biodiversity conservation as social and political process', *Society and Natural Resources,* 15: 41-64, 2002.

Brockington, D. and K. Schmidt-soltau, 'The social and environmental impacts of wilderness and development', *Oryx,* 38: 140-142, 2004.

Brokington, D,. *Fortress Conservation: The Preservation of the Mkomazi Game Reserve, Tanzania,* Oxford : Currey, 2002.

Brooks, J.S, M.A.Franzen, C.M. Holmes, M.N. Grote, M. Borgerhoff Mulder,' Testing hypotheses for the success of different conservation strategies', in *Conservation Biology.* 20 (5): 1528-38.2006

Brosius, J.P., A.L.Tsing and C. Zerner, 'Representing communities : histories and politics of community based natural resource management', *Society and Natural Resources* 11: 157-68, 1998.

Brown, K. 'Three challenges for a real people centred conservation', *Global ecology and Bio-geography,* 12:89-92, 2003.

Brunner, A.G., R.E. Gullison, R.E. Rice and G.A.B. da Fonseca, 'Effectiveness of parks in protecting the tropical biodiversity', *Science,* 291(5501) : 125-128, 2001.

Callicott, J.B., L.B. Crowder and K. Mumford, ' Current normative concepts in conservation biology', *Conservation Biology* 13:22-35, 2000.

Campbell, L..M. and A, Vainio Mattila, 'Participatory Development and Community based conservation opportunities missed for lessons learned ?' *Human Ecology,* 31(3):417-437, 2003.

Castree, N. 'Neoliberalising nature : The logics of deregulation and reregulation', *Environment and Planning A vol:* 40: 131-152, 2008.

Chan, K.M.A., R. M. Pringle., J.Ranganathan., C. L. Boggs, Y. L. Chan, P. R. Ehrlich, P. K. Haff, N.E. Heller, K.A. Khafaji, and D. Macnowski, 'When Agendas collide : Human Welfare and Biological Conservation', *Conservation Biology,* 21(1) : 59-68, 2007.

Chapin, M. *A challenge to conservations,* World Watch Institute, Nov. Dec. : 17-31, 2004.

Charnley, S. and M.R. Poe, ' Community Forestry in Theory and Practice : Where are we now ?', *Annual Review of Anthropology* 36:301-36, 2007.

Chatterjee, A. 'Conflict and Coexistence in a National Park.' *Economic and Political Weekly,* vol: XLIV, No. 23, pp. 52-59. June 6, 2009.

Chatty, D. and M. Colchester, 'Conservation and mobile Indigenous peoples', in D. Chatty and M. Colchester, eds. *Conservation and mobile Indigenous peoples,* Studies in Forced Migration, Vol. 10, UK :. Berghahn Press, 2008.

Christensen, J. 'Win win illusions' (www document) in *Conservation in Practice* 5(1) : 12-19. URL : www. Conbio.org/CUIP/articles51wwi.cfm., 2004.

Cincotta, R.P., J. Wisnewski and R, Engelman, 'Human population in the biodiversity hotspots', *Nature* 404 : 990-2, 2000.

Courtois, D.R., B.L. Perryman, and H.S. Hussein. 'Vegetation change after 65 years of Grazing and Grazing exclusion.' *Rangeland Ecology and Management,* 57 : 574-582, 2004.

Curran, L., S. Trigg., A. McDonald, D. Astiani, Y. Hardiono *et al.*, 'Lowland forest loss in protected areas of Indonesian Borneo', *Science,* 303: 1000, 2004.

Defo, S., N. Marikil, N. Doggart, and N. Burgess, 'Assessing environment and development outcomes in conservation landscapes', *Biodiversity. Conservation.* 16: 2677–94, 2007.

Dove, M.R. 'A revisionist view of tropical deforestation and development', *Environmental Conservation* 20(1) : 17-25, 1993.

Dowie, M. 'Conservation refugee', *Orion* Nov. Dec. : 16-27, 2005.

Duffy, R. *Killing for conservation : Wildlife policy in Zimbabwe,* Oxford : James Curry, 2000.

Eghenter, C. 'Planning for Community-based Management of Conservation Areas', in D. Chatty and M. Colchester, eds. *Conservation and Mobile Indigenous Peoples*', Studies in Forced Migration, Vol : 10, UK :. Berghahn Press, 2008.

Ewers, K. 'The politics of conservation: Pwo Karen forest people of Thailand', *Indigenous Affairs,* 4:32-5, 1998.

Ferraro, P.J. and A. Kiss, 'Direct payments to conserve biodiversity', *Science* 298: 1718. 2002.

Folke, C. Traditional knowledge in Social-ecological systems. *Ecology and Society,* vol. 9, No. 3, pp. 7, 2004.

Geisler, C., 'A new kind of trouble : Eviction in Eden', *International Social Science Journal.* 55: 69-78, 2003.

Geisler, C. and R, de Souza, 'From refuge to refugee ;The African case', *Public Administration and Development,* 21: 159-170, 2001.

Ghimire, K.B. and M.P. Pimbert, eds., *Social Change and Conservation,* Earthscan: London, 1997.

Gibson, C.C. and S.A. Marks, 'Transforming rural hunters into conservationists: An assessment of Community based wildlife management programmes in Africa', *World Development,* 23: 941-957, 1995.

Gibson, C.C., M.A. McKean and E. Ostrom, *People and forests : Communities, institutions, and governance,* Cambridge : MIT Press, 2000.

Gibson, C. 'Forest resources: Institutions for local governance in Guatemala', in J. Burger, E. Ostrom, R.B. Norgaard, D. Policansky, and B.D. Goldstein, eds., *Protecting the commons: A framework for resource management in the Americas*(pp. 71–89). Washington, DC: Island Press, 2001.

Glasmeier, A.K. and T. Farrigan, 'Understanding community forestry : a qualitative meta study of the concept, the process, and its potential for poverty alleviation in the United States case', *Geographical Journal,* 171(1): 56-69, 2005.

Hackel, J.D. 'Community conservation and the future of Africa's wildlife', *Conservation Biology* 13(4) : 726-734, 1999.

Heywood, V.H. *Global Biodiversity Assessment,* Cambridge : Cambridge University Press, 1995.

Hughes, R. and F. Flintan, *Integrating conservation and development experience : a review and bibliography of the ICDP literature,* International Institute of Environment and Development, London: UK, 2001.

Hulme, D. and M. Murphree, 'Communities, wildlife and 'new conservation in Africa', *Journal of International Development* 1:1 : 277-85, 1999.

Hutton, J., W.A. Adams and J.C. Murombedzi, Back to the barriers ? Changing narratives in biodiversity conservation', *Forum for Development Studies* 32:341-370, 2005.

Hutton, J.M. and N. Leader Williams, 'Sustainable use and incentive-driven conservation : realigning human and conservation interests', *Oryx,* 37:215-226, 2003.

Igoe, J., 'History, culture and conservation : in search of more informed guesses about whether 'community based conservation' has a chance to work', *Policy matters* 13. 2004.

Jhonson, L.M., ' A place that's good: Gitksan landscape perception and ethnoecology', *Hum Ecol.* 28(2) : 301-325, 2000.

Kabra, A., 'Displacement and Rehalitation of an Adivasi settlement : case of Kuno sanctuary, Madhya Pradesh', *Economic and Political Weekly,* 38(29) : 3073-87, 2003.

Kabra, A., 'Conservation-induced Displacement: A Comparative Study of two Indian Protected Areas', *Conservation and Society* 7(4): 249-267, 2009.

Kaimowitz, D. and D. Sheil., 'Conserving what and for whom ? Why conservation should help to meet basic human needs in the tropics', *Biotropica,* 39 (5): 567-574, 2007.

Kothari, A., ' Is joint management of protected area desirable and possible?', in, A. Kothari, N. Singh, and S. Suri, eds., *People and Protected Areas : Towards a participatory conservation in India,* New Delhi : Sage Publications, 1996.

Kothari, A., *Building bridges for conservation: Towards joint management of protected areas in India,* New Delhi: Indian Institute of Public Administration Publications, 1997.

Kothari, A., *Living in Wilderness.* Thelka(www.tehelka.com). 2008.

Kothari, A., P. Pandey, S. Singh., and D. Variava., *Management of National Parks and Sanctuaries in India: A status report,* New Delhi: Indian Institute of Public Administration, 1989.

Langholtz, J., 'Privatizing conservation', in, S.R. Brechin, P.R.Wilshusen, C.L. Fortwangler and P.C. West, eds., *Contested Nature : Promoting international biodiversity with social justice in the 21st century,* pp. 117-135, Albany : State University of New York Press, 2003.

Lasgoriceix, A. and A. Kothari, 'Displacement and relocation of protected areas : a synthesis and analysis of case studies', *Economic and Political Weekly,* XLV: 37-47+36, 2009.

Lele, S., P. Wilshusen, D. Brockington, R. Seidler and K. Bawa, 'Beyond exclusion : alternative approaches to biodiversity conservation in the developing tropics', *Current opinion in environmental Sustainability,* 2:1-7, 2010.

Levine, A. 'Convergence or convenience ? international conservation NGOs and development assistance in Tanzania', *World Development,* 30(6) : 1043-1055, 2002.

Lewis, M., 'Cattle and conservation in Bharatpur : a case study in science and advocacy', *Conservation and Society,* 1:1, 2003.

Lovejoy, T.E., 'Biodiversity: threats and challenges', in,Tim O'Riordan and S. Stoll Klemann, eds., *Biodiversity, sustainability and Human communities,* Cambridge: Cambridge University Press, 2002.

Maffi, L., 'Linguistic, cultural, and biological diversity', *Ann.Rev. Anthropol.* 29:599-617, 2005.

Marks, S., 'The imperial Lion : Human dimensions of Wildlife Management in Central Africa', UK. : Bowker Epping, 1984.

McCormick, J., *The Global Environmental movement : reclaiming paradise*, London: Belhaven, 1989.

McCracken, J., ' Conservation priorities and local communities', in, D. Anderson and R.F. Grove, eds., *Conservation in Africa: People, Politics and Practice*, Cambridge : Cambridge University Press, 1987.

McNeely, J..A. and K.R. Miller., eds., *National Park Conservation and Development: the Role of Protected area in sustaining society*, Washington DC: Smithsonian Institution Press, 1984.

McNeely, J.A., K.R. Miller., W.V. Reid., R.A. Mittermeir, and T.B. Werner, 'Conserving the World's biological Diversity, 'Gland, Switzerland: IUCN; WRI, CI, WWF-US and the World Bank, Washington D.C. 1990.

Meyer, J.L. and G.S. Helfman., 'The ecological basis of sustainability', *Ecological Applications* 3(4) : 569-571, 1993.

Mukherjee, A. 'Conflict and coexistence in a National Park', *Economic and Political Weekly*, vol: XLIV no. 23 pp. 52-59, 2009.

Murombedzi, J., 'Devolution and stewardship in Zimbabawe's CAMFIRE programme', *Journal of International Development*, 11:287-293,1999.

Murombedzi, J., ' Why wildlife conservation has not economically benefitted communities in Africa', in: Hulme and Murphree (eds) : 2001.

Murphree, M. 2001. A case study of ecotourism development from Mahenye, Zimbabwe, in, D. Hulme, and M. Murphree, 'Communities, wildlife and 'new conservationin Africa', *Journal of International Development* 11 : 277-85, 1999.

Myers, N., 'Biodiversity and bio-depletion: the need for a paradigm shift', in, Tim O'Riordan and S. Stoll Klemann, eds., *Biodiversity, sustainability and Human communities*. Cambridge: Cambridge University Press, 2002.

Nepstad, D., S. Schwartzman., B. Bamberger, M. Santilli., D. Ray *et al.* 'Inhibition of Amazon deforestation and fire by parks and indigenous lands', *Conservation Biology*. 20 (1): 65-73, 2006.

Neumann, P., P. 'Primitive Ideas : Protected area buffer zones and the politics of land in Africa', *Development and Change* 28: 559-582,1998.

Nittler, J., and H. Tschinkel, *Community Forest Management in the Maya Biosphere Reserve of Guetemala : Protection through profits*, Washington DC : US Agency Int. Dev., Sustain. Agric.Nat. resource. Manag. Collab. Res. Support Group/ Univ. of Georgia, 2005.

Novellino, D., 'Sacrificing peoples for the trees : The cultural; cost of forest conservation on Palawan Island', *Indigenous Affairs*, 4:4-14, 1998.

Nygren, A., 'Community based Forest Management within the context of institutional decentralization in Honduras', *World Development* 33(4):639-55, 2005.

O'Riordan, T., 'Protecting beyond protected', in, Tim O'Riordan and S. Stoll Klemann, eds., *Biodiversity, sustainability and Human communities*. Cambridge: Cambridge University Press, 2002.

Oates, J.F., *Myth and reality in the rain forest : How conservation strategies are failing in West Africa.* Berkeley : University of California Press, 1999.

Pathak N., T Balasinorwala, A Kothari, and B Bushley. People in Conservation:

Community Conserved Areas in India. Kalpavriksh, Delhi. 2006. www.iucn.org/themes/ceesp/Wkg_grp/TILCEPA/CCA% 20India%20brochure%20(2).pdf.

Pauley, D., V. Christensen, J. Dalsgaard., R. Froese and F. Torres, Jr., 'Fishing down marine food webs', *Science* 279: 860-863, 1998.

Poffenberger, M., *Communities and Forest Management in Southeast Asia : A regional profile of the working group on community involvement in forest management,* Gland, Switz.: World Conservation Union, 1999.

Poffenberger, M.. 'People in the forest : community forestry experiences from Southeast Asia', *Int. J Env. Sustan. Dev.* 5(1):57-69, 2006.

Pimbert, M.P. and J.N. Pretty. Parks, People and Professionals ; Putting participation into protected area management. IIED/WWF Discussion paper no.57. 1995.

Pretty, J., 'People, livelihood and collective action in biodiversity management', in, T. O'Riordan and S. Stoll-Kleeman, eds., *Biodiversity,, sustainability and Human communities : Protecting beyond protected,* pp. 61-86. Cambridge University Press, Cambridge, 2002.

Ramakrishnan, P.S. Shifting agriculture and sustainable development. Man and the Biospheres Series no. 10. Paris, UNESCO/Parthenon Publishing Group. 1992.

Redford, K.H. and B.D. Richter, 'Conservation of biodiversity in a world of use', *Conservation Biology* 13: 1246-1256, 1999.

Redford, K.H. and Sanderson, S.E., 'Extracting Humans from Nature', *Conservation Biology* 14(5) : 1362-4, 2000.

Redford, K.H., K. Brandon and S.E. Sanderson, 'Holding ground', in, K. Brandon, K.H. Redford and S.E. Sanderson, eds., Parks in Peril: People, politics, and protected areas, pp. 455-464, Washington DC : Island Press, 1998.

Robinson, J.G., 'Conservation Biology and Real World Conservation', *Conservation Biology,* 20(3): 658-669, 2006.

Robinson, J. G., 'The limits to caring : sustainable living and the loss of biodiversity', *Conservation Biology* 7 : 20-28, 1993.

Roy, S.D. and P. Jackson, 'Mayhem in Manas. The threats to India's wildlife reserves', in E. Kemf, ed., *Indigenous peoples and protected areas,* London : Earthscan, 1993.

Saberwal, V. Pastoral politics: Gaddi grazing, degradation and biodiversity conservation in Himachal Pradesh, India. *Conservation Biology* 10: 741-749. 1996.

Sayer, J., B. Cambell, L. Petharam, M. Aldrich, M.R. Perez, D. Endamana, Z.-L. N. Dongmo, L. Schimidt-soltau, "The costs of rainforest conservation: local responses towards integrated conservation and development projects in Cameroon, *Journal of Contemporary African Studies.* 22(1) : 93-117, 2004.

Schwartzman, S., A. Moreira, and D. Nepstad, 'Rethinking tropical forest conservation: Perils in parks', *Conservation Biology* 14:1351-1357, 2000.

Shah, A., 'Management of protected areas : exploring an alternative in Gir', *Economic and Political Weekly.* vol: XLII, Nos. 27 &28. pp. 2923-2930, 2007.

Song, S.J. and R.M.M'gonigle, 'Science, power and system dynamics : the political economy of conservation Biology' *Conservation Biology*, 15: 980-989. 2001.

Songorwa, A.N., ' Community based wildlife management in Tanzania : Are the communities interested?' *World Development* 27(12) : 2061-2079, 1999.

Sullivan, S., 'The elephant in the room problemitizing new (neoliberal) biodiversity conservation', *Forum for Development Studies* 33(1) 105-135, 2006.

Terborgh, J., *Requiem for nature.* Washington DC : Island Press, 2004.

Terborgh, J. and C.P. van Schaik, 'Minimising species loss : The imperative of protection', in, R.A.Kramer, C.P. van Schaik and J. Johnson, eds., *Last stand : Protected areas and the defense of tropical biodiversity*, New York : Oxford University Press, 1997.

Tiger Task Force, *Joining the Dots*, Report of the Project Tiger Task Force, 2005 *WWW.projectiger.nic.in.* accessed on 22.3.2011.

Tompkins, E., W.N. Adger and K. Brown, 'Institutional networks for inclusive coastal management in Trinidad and Tobago', *Environment and Planning* A, 34: 1095-1111, 2002.

Torri, M.C., 'Conservation, relocation and the social consequences of conservation policies in protected areas : Case study of the Sariska Tiger Reserve, India', *Conservation and Society* 9(1):54-64, 2011.

Turton, D., 'The Mursi and National Park development in the lower Omo valley', in, D.M. Anderson and R.H. Grove, eds., *Conservation in Africa : People, Policies and Practice*, pp. 169-186, : Cambridge : Cambridge University Press, 1987.

van Schaik and R.A. Kramer, 'Toward a new protection paradigm', in R.A. Kramer, C.P. van Schaik and J. Johnson, eds., *Last stand : Protected areas and the defense of tropical biodiversity*, New York : Oxford University Press, 1997.

Vitousek, P.K., P.R. Ehrlich, A.H. Ehrlich and P.A. MaTson, 'Human appropriation of the products of photosynthesis', *BioScience* 36:368-373, 1986.

Wainright, C. and W. Wehrmeyer, 'Success in integrating conservation and development ? a study from Zambia', *World Development* 26 : 933-44, 1998.

Wells, M.P., T.O. McShane, H.T. Dublin, S. O" Conner and K. Redford, 'The future of integrated conservation and development projects: building on what works', in, T. McShane and M. Wells, eds., *Getting Biodiversity Projects to work: towards more effective conservation and development*, pp. 397-422. New York, USA: Columbia University Press. 2004.

Wells, M., 'Biodiversty Conservation and Local People's Development Aspirations: New priorities for the 1990s', *Rural Dev. forestry Network paper* 18a : 1-24, 1994-95.

Wells, M. and K. Brandon, ' The principle and practice of buffer zones and local participation in biodiversity conservation', *Ambio* 22(2-3) : 57-162, 1993.

Wells, M. and K. Brandon, *People and parks : Linking protected area management with local communities,* Washington DC: World Bank, 1992.

West, P., 'Conservation is our government now : the politics of ecology in Papua New Guinea', Durham : Duke University Press. 2006.

Western, D. 1989. Conservation without Parks: wildlife in the rural landscape. In : Conservation for the twenty-first century (eds. D. Western and M.C.Pearl) Oxford University Press, New York.

Western, D., M. Wright and S. Strumm, eds., *Natural connections: Perspectives in community based conservation,* Washington DC : Island Press, 1994.

Wilshusen, P.R., S.R. Brechin, C.L. Fortwangler and P.C. West, 'Reinventing a square Wheel : Critique of a resurgent 'Protectionist paradigm in International Biodiversity Conservation', *Society and Natural Resources,* 15(1):17-40, 2002.

Wily, L. 'Moving forward in African community forestry : trading power, not use rights', *Society and Natural Resources* 19:49-61, 1999.

4

Problems of Present Practices of Protected Areas (PAs) and Management in India

Need of Change

Ajit Banerjee

Introduction

About 12 per cent of the global forest area is isolated from all forests for biodiversity conservation. In India, it is 29 per cent covering an area of about 19.8 million hectares. The management of these areas is carried out by the state forest departments.

In Protected Areas (PAs), management is different in certain respects from management of productive and other forests. The differences include emphasis on conservation and sustenance of quality and quantity of biodiversity specially wildlife and its habitat, strict protection from human intrusion, non-interfering scientific management of the existing and evolving natural parameters of the ecosystem in which the forest areas are located and sponsoring eco-tourism. Another important element in the PAs that needs attention is the role played by the forest dependent people in or on the forest fringe that have used the forest services for ages.

Problems

The major problems in management of PAs in India are:

1. *Conservation Failure*

Conservation has failed in respect of biodiversity at a global scale (Wilson, 1999).While some of the PAs in India have been managed well to desired objectives, many of them have in fact deteriorated. Animal census reports indicate failures in forest conservation with reduction in the overall population of keystone and other species such as tigers, elephants, crocodiles, *Gavialis* sp., pythons and also smaller animals like butterflies.

The number of endangered species in the country has increased and the extinction rate is also on the rise. Depredation of floral species especially of shrubs, herbs, epiphytes are common. Fragmentation of forest blocks, increase of soil erosion, loss of soil organic matter, incendiary fire damages, over-grazing leading to soil compaction and reduced water retention are some other features of the failures in the PAs.

Another feature often missed by us is that the major portion of the forest in the country not included in PAs, is neglected of biodiversity conservation. In India, it works out to 71 per cent of all forests.

2. *Size of PAs*

The size of the individual PAs in India, excepting a few, is comparatively small, predominantly below 100 sq.km to 250 sq.km.(Rodgero *et. al* 2002.) resulting in many families of animal species not having the required territory especially in the breeding time. Genetic diversity of the species concerned is reduced due to in-breeding (e,g. Gir lions). The smaller PA sizes and consequent loss of territory and food force some of the animals to stray out of the PAs causing damages to property and life of the local people.

3. *Deprivation of Forest Dependent People*

Isolation of areas and strict control of the use of PA resources deprive the local forest dependent people of their livelihood requirements. This produces a rift between the forest managers and the forest dependent people which ultimately causes forest degradation and animal loss. These people are also forced to earn money by collaborating with the smugglers and the *mafias* who damage biodiversity of the PAs. Participation of the people in PAs welfare schemes that are in place does not satisfy peoples' requirements and expectations.

4. *Paucity of Protection Staff and Infrastructure*

The State Forest Managers claim paucity of required protection staff and infrastructure to carry out satisfactory protection and conservation of PAs.

5. *Increase of Eco-tourism*

Increased ecotourism in PAs is considered to be a large detriment of its animal inhabitants.

Field Examples

As tiger is a major fauna and is also a keystone species, it attracts eco-tourism; Indian forestry attracts funds including foreign funds for its protection. We sometimes focus on these species and some other mega fauna such as elephants, rhinoceros, etc. in the protection implementation phase to the near-exclusion of others. We often neglect the whole concept of biodiversity.

In the context of what I have stated above it is obvious that the present PAs are focused more on trees and mega faunas; areas outside them whether it is forest or agriculture land, bio-diversity as constituted of all the living species including the smallest ones. Of them, some are really largest part of biodiversity, namely insects. It includes one of the most beautiful species, namely the butterflies. Because of this neglect, the data in respect of biodiversity species other than the important mega faunas are lacking in India. Biodiversity of the plant life is also focused on tree species and commercial shrubs and herbs to the exclusion of others. Worst is the situation in respect of biodiversity in subjects other than forests, e.g. the subjects of agriculture, fisheries etc.

It is well known now and realized by the entire world that the method of agriculture adopted throughout the world has literally curtailed the biodiversity of grasses, weeds and others. In most parts of the world these neglected species in agriculture have literally disappeared but little is said about them. But recent works in some of the developing countries such as India show that there is still scope of retrieving some of these species. One example, is that of MP (India) alone. It has been possible to collect seeds of many, now unused, varieties which can be again reintroduced. In the case of forests the number of endangered species has been listed. But these are really very few compared to what is really going on as there is hardly any specific data of the non-tree elements of the forests. This statement shows that if we are really serious about preservation of biodiversity, the method of isolating some percentage of forest alone for preservation is not a logical remedy.

At present some of the tiger reserves or Forest National Parks in India are portions of biodiversity reserves. These are recorded in paper alone as in most cases no care is taken of biodiversity outside the PAs. Loss of biodiversity over the years is rampant. One aspect for these non-forest areas forming a base of the PA, now being emphasized, is that the State Biodiversity Boards under the National Boards is the engagement besides other things in making out biodiversity registers. Local Gram Panchayats are involved in the survey and registers are published (Ref. West Bengal). The number registers that could be made is small compared to the huge requirement for India. Unfortunately the few done, is not followed up and no action is taken to introduce newly reported or old neglected elements of biodiversity nor is there any attempt to generate plans of action for doing so. Waste land or marsh land or habitation is completely neglected. The present concept, therefore, of having a PA of a portion of the forest of the country excluding all others has limited success even if the implementation is successful and needs change.

What I am suggesting is that isolation of PAs for more and more portions of the forest that has been conceived internationally is an escapist attitude based on the assumption that is impossible to look after the whole biodiversity as it is beset with so many problems. Most managing agencies and managers believe that protection is the 'stuff' of policing and not of the people who have a stake in the forest.

I will give another example in the context of developments that have taken place due to the ongoing implementation of Forest Rights Act of 2006. There is a provision, among others (Oxfam *et al.*, 2010), for the Act that the tribal people leaving inside in the margin of the forest can be relocated only on certain conditions from the core of the CTH (Core of the Habitat) areas of National Parks and sanctuaries. The relocation have to be voluntary on mutually agreed terms and conditions (Mutual means government and core inhabiting) people providing for livelihood for the affected individuals, communities etc. and adequate places of stay. In actual fact the data from four of the PAs where relocation is underway are unsatisfactory. Observations form the field are that the process of recognition and determination of acquisition of land or forest rights of Scheduled Tribes have not been completed, there are no studies to show that the people being relocated have been responsible for the irreversible damage for wild life and there are no evidences in the field that the co-existence of human being of these villages have led to any damage. There was also hardly any negotiation of mutual dialogue with the people to promote coexistence (Kalpavriksh. 2011).

I would, therefore, in brief say that the whole concept of impossibility of co-existence is more a celebral nature of well managing environmentalists, foresters or policy makers without attempting to see co-existence is a possibility.

Proposal

We argue that isolating forests for PA management in countries with large number of forest dependent population, is not an effective method of conservation. This isolation is possible in developed affluent countries as there are few people in those countries dependent on the forest for livelihood, except for its indirect services and ecotourism. In contrast PA management in India deprives forest dependent people of a portion of their livelihood.The people lose all stakes in forest conservation and become a party to its surreptitious use sometimes in collusion with mafias resulting in damage to biodiversity.

Smaller size PA with its associated problems earlier mentioned can be avoided if this concept of isolation of PA is rejected. Instead all the forests are considered as a part of the PA for conservation and productive use. It may be argued this will need a huge amount of funds due to increased staff infrastructure etc. for protection. Our counter agreement is that participation with people will be the major instrument for protection. Staff in fact will be reduced. This has been noticed in JFM and Community Management. Co-existence of animal and man should be a major plank as it has happened in the past millennium. The dependence of the people on the forest will continue but with innovation and to a degree that will not upset biodiversity. The new management may include production and even animal culling to avoid man-animal conflict if necessary. This is possible if the planning is done in a rational manner by the core people themselves in consultation with forest technicians.

Such a dramatic change from PA concept to what may be loosely termed as Landscape Management (Lindenmeyer *et al.*, 2002), will create a lot of other problems such as management of private areas, agriculture areas, introduction of now neglected species, possible change to organic farming, and other uses between the forest blocks and migration of animals at intervals and propensity of people to kill animals because of losses the farmers will be sustained from time to time, although the loss, I believe, will be less than what they suffer now. These are the issues on which our faith in the people, their goodwill and participation in working out the problems is required. In other words, there has to be a return to the reality, namely that the natural resources belong to all the people and not only to supposed-to-be well meaning few technical managers and NGOs. The 73 per cent of forests that are now not attended for biodiversity because of non-inclusion to PAs will then come under its fold besides the intervening non-forest areas that will make a significant contribution to overall biodiversity protection of the forests and the country-side.

We are not suggesting the change at one go. We propose that we start with a few PAs and monitor whether this change has the potential of replication. The next paper deals with Gir forests which may be relevant in this connection.

REFERENCES

Gadgil, Madhav. 'Grassroots Conservation Practices: Revitalizing the Traditions', in Asish Kothari *et al.*, eds., *'Communities and Conservation'*, London : Sage Publication, pp. 219-238, 1998.

Kalpavriksh, *'Legislation Brief; Recognition of Rights and Relocation in Relation to Critical Tiger Habitat (CTHs)'*, Pune, India, 2011.

Lindenmeyer, David B. and Jerry F Franklin, *Conserving Forest Biodiversity, Washington :* Island Press, 2002.

Oxfam, IIFM, SPWD, Workshop Report: Forest Rights Act, 2006—Status of Implementation and its Potential in Livelihoods Improvement of Forest Dwelling Communities, New Delhi : SPWD, 2010.

Rodgers, WA, HS, Panwar and VB Mathur Wildlife Protected Area Network in India : A review (executive summary), Wildlife Institute of India, Dehradun, 2002.

Wilson, Edward O., *The Diversity of Life,* London : Norton and Company; 1999.

5

Landscape Approach to Conservation in Context of Gir Forests

Challenges and Prospects

P.K. Mathur

The Rationale

Virtually all countries have seen the wisdom of protecting areas of outstanding values (natural, material, historical, spiritual and cultural) importance to society (McNeely, 1992; Miller, 1999). Over the years, these values have been redefined and new areas have been identified for evolving purposes. Presently, with the impetus of the 'Convention on Biological Diversity', the focus is on the protection, restoration and long-term *in situ* management of habitats, species and their genetic variations, and overall ecosystem functions and processes. The Wildlife Protected Areas (PAs) are widely held to be among the most effective means of conserving biological diversity.

The Protected Areas (National Parks and Wildlife Sanctuaries) in India have increased in number, and their extent during the past 3-4 decades (Rodgers *et al.*, 2000). A considerable amount of resources has been invested in their establishment, improved PA management, development of desired infrastructural support and capacity building by the State and Central Governments and various non-governmental agencies. In spite protected areas make significant contributions to modern society, they suffer from a number of problems. Unfortunately, there is a downside and some backlash against PAs in the past decade or so.

Today, most PAs are like 'islands' as their existing boundaries do not cover the complete range of biodiversity values they seek to protect. Further, most PAs are also faced with the situation of reconciling resource needs of various stakeholders and resolving their conflicts. Moreover, the non-compatible land use scenario around PAs also does not augur well for protected area management. In India and elsewhere in the world, PAs face seven significant obstacles that will limit their capacity to meet growing demands for their full array of benefits and values (Miller, 1999). Identified obstacles are: (a) the criteria adopted for the establishment of PAs, (b) small size, (c) irregular shape and long PA-people interface, (d) lack of desired organizational support, (e) inappropriate location, and (f) inadequate investments.

It is now increasingly being realized that storm-battered islands of biological diversity in a sea of human settlement as wild lands give way to farm, pasture and settlement require a new approach to PA management (Miller, 1996; Mathur and Sinha, 2008). There is little excuse for complacency about their future. Many are increasingly isolated and threatened by events both inside and outside their own borders. In order to mitigate various threats, conflicts and overcome above seven highlighted obstacles, there is an urgent need to look beyond the PA boundaries. Lessons learnt amply reflect that in future protected areas will have to be linked more effectively to sustainable development. A critical challenge is to ensure that well-managed PAs are regarded as integral parts of the landscape and seascape. Many conservationists are now stressing the importance of tackling conservation or PA issues on a wide scale. The precise scale and boundaries differ slightly. The concepts of Landscape, Integrated coastal management area, Bioregion, Ecoregion, etc. are being advocated, implemented and validated. Although the vocabulary may vary, the concepts are similar.

Integrated resource management calls for the process of planning, administration and management of the land resources in the light of social, economic and ecological considerations. Realizing this critical significance of including PAs in the landscape level or regional planning process, the Staff Appraisal Report of the World Bank (1996) stated that "PAs can be successful in realizing their long term conservation goals only to the extent that their priorities can become integrated into large-scale land use planning activities and regulations at the local and regional levels. The PAs – and the people responsive for PAs – will have to be more flexible, more responsive and more adaptable than has sometimes been the case in the past. Protected areas need to continue to expand both physically and philosophically, and to connect with each other, the wider landscape and more generally with society and the economy (Dudley *et al.*, 1999).

Landscape Management in the Context of Gir Conservation Area (GCA)

The Gir Forest

In the Kathiawar Peninsula in Saurashtra region of Gujarat State, Gir forests constitute the largest compact patch of natural dry deciduous teak *(Tectona grandis)* and thorn forests (Fig. 5.1). Its unique importance is the only home for the last surviving Asiatic Lion *(Panthera leo persica)*. The pastoralist community ('Maldharis') and their livestock constitute an integral part of the Gir ecosystem. Rugged and hilly terrain of Gir forms the catchment of seven principal perennial rivers flowing in the region. The four reservoirs located inside Gir protected area contributes to agricultural development in the PA surround (Fig. 5.2). The Gir landscape and the three temple complexes within PA attract tourists and pilgrims from far and wide. The Gir forests provide ecological security, environmental amelioration and opportunities for economic development in this otherwise drought prone region due to its various biological, ecological and cultural values.

Past Management

The present Gir forest (1,882.6 sq. km) has shrunk to almost half of its original area in 1880s (Singh and Kamboj, 1996; Singh, 2000). Once widely distributed in Asia, from Asia Minor and Arabia through Persia to India, the Asiatic Lion had become extinct from its range before the close of the ninteenth century, except in Gir. Even the population of

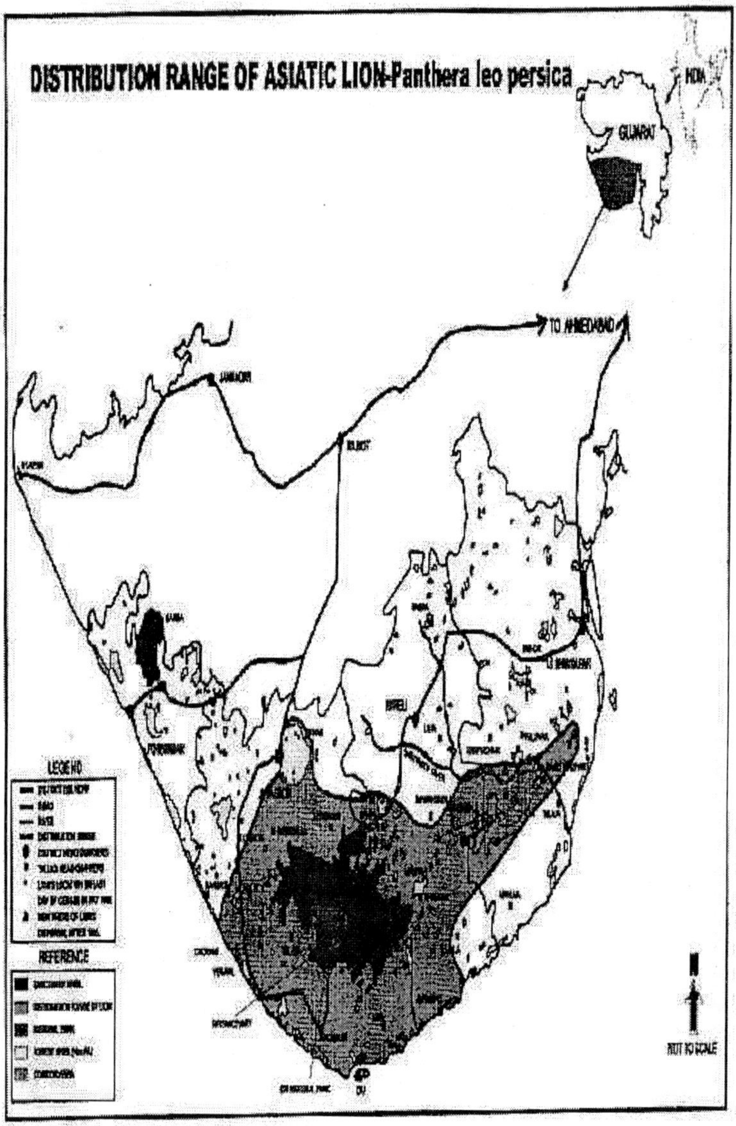

Fig. 5.1 : Gir Landscape showing Gir National Park, Gir Wildlife Sanctuary, Peripheral Forests/Grasslands and Agriculture Dominated Surrounding Matrix (*Source* : Gir PA Management).

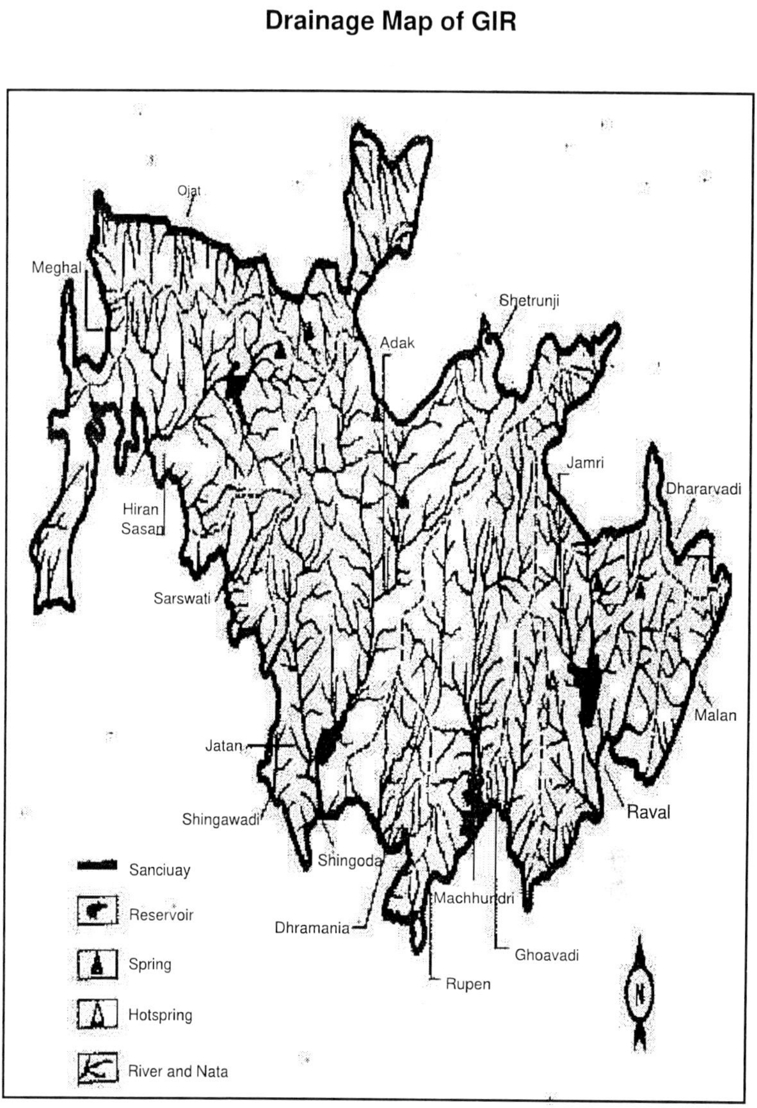

Fig. 5.2 : Drainage in Gir Protected Area and location of four reservoirs (*Source :* Management Plan by Singh and Kamboj, 1996).

lion in Gir forest has also dwindled to as low as just a dozen of animals during the beginning of twentieth century. Timely conservation efforts initiated by the then Nawab of Junagadh was able to save this endangered species from the brink of extinction. Maldharis have inhabited Gir forests since ages. They live in small temporary hutments ('Nesses') in the forested area. Historical records reveal that the lions in the Gir preyed mainly on domestic livestock (mainly cattle and buffalo) of Maldharis (Joslin, 1973; Berwick, 1974) which constituted almost 75 per cent of its diet.

The planned major conservation programme by the Gujarat Forest Department for the Asiatic lion commenced in September 1965 with declaring a large area of Gir forest as Gir Wildlife Sanctuary. The Gir Lion Sanctuary Project (1972-78) laid foundation for the restoration of forests from degradation. Subsequently, the Forest Department worked on the target to expand Gir Protected Area as and when opportunities occurred. Accordingly, the Government of Gujarat has declared an area of 1,412.1 sq. km as Protected Area (PA) which comprises Gir National Park (258.7 sq. km), and Gir Wildlife Sanctuary (1,153.4 sq. km), thus together forming 'core zone'. Besides this, 470.5 sq. km of peripheral forest and grassland ('vidi') areas constitute buffer zone including reserved forests (RFs), protected forests (PFs) and unclassed forests. Thus, a total area of 1,882.6 sq km (core and buffer zones) forms the present Gir forest or 'Gir Conservation Unit' (GCU). The area of GCU lies into two Districts, *viz.* Junagadh and Amreli.

The conservation values, past history, floral and faunal diversity, resource dependence of Maldharis and other local communities, management issues and strategies adopted for the management of endangered species (including Asiatic Lion), habitats, tourism, and PA-people conflicts are extensively dealt in the management plans or other relevant documents (Joshi, 1976; Singh and Kamboj, 1996; Singh, 2000; Singh and Pathak, 2000; Pathak, 2000; Singh and Patel, 2000). Mathur and Mathur (1998) have given an overview of research and monitoring activities in Gir and thus, provided a bibliography. Singh and Kamboj (1996) prepared a comprehensive management plan for the GCU and in principle they had conceded the concept of a Greater Gir Ecosystem. The main objective of this new concept was to integrate the management of adjoining areas having satellite populations of lion such as Girnar, Mitiyala and coastal forests in Junagadh and Amreli districts, and peripheral forests as part of Gir Protected Area Management. This concept or proposal of an enlarged Greater Gir Ecosystem during initial years of plan implementation largely remained on paper and half-hearted attempts were made not adequate enough to achieve the desired objectives.

Critical Conservation Issues

Human population of 72,000 within a 2 km radius of PA boundary in 97 revenue villages; 2,540 Maldharis in 54 settlements ('Nesses'); 4,500 residents including 239 'Siddis' (a Scheduled Tribe of African origin in 14 forest settlement villages); and 3 temple complexes occupied by 65 people within the PA itself exert direct pressure on the PA resources. Villages within and around the two PAs (Gir NP and WLS) maintain more than 100,000 cattle head. Thus, human settlement and the intense grazing pressure have direct impact on PA resources. Major continuing and growing concerns for PA management are impact of local demand for grazing and fuelwood; crop loss caused by wild animals; livestock predation; occasional human injuries and killing by lion; disturbance caused by four public roads traversing through PA; pilgrims and tourists. Key social issues are in Gir concern the processes of Maldhari relocation; the implications of tenure for forest villages and the relationship between PA authorities and local people. The above problems are further compounded by the fact that there is a mismatch between the administrative and ecological boundaries of the PA. In the changing scenario due to rapid changes in land use pattern, intensification of agriculture, industrialization, economic realities, excessive use of natural resources and desired support for the lion relocation programme, appropriate management interventions supported by a competent landscape/regional plan is a necessity of the hour for long term conservation of Gir ecosystem.

Landscape Level or Regional Planning

The integrated regional planning or bioregional management approach aims to find a balance between the resident community's needs for livelihood and the potential for natural resources in their bioregions (McNeely, 1992; Miller, 1996 and 1999; Craik, 1996; Olson and Dinerstein, 1999; Aberley, 1994; Dudley *et al.*, 1999; Badola *et al.*, 2000).

A large landscape or a bioregion is sufficiently large a land and water territory whose geographic limits are defined by human communities and ecological systems (Miller, 1996). Such areas must be capable to maintain ecological integrity (ecosystems, habitats and biological communities) in the region; support ecological processes (e.g. nutrient and waste cycling, migration and stream flow); meet the habitat requirements of keystone and indicator species; and to include the human communities involved in the management, use, and understanding of biological resources.

Major Achievements and Forerunning Activities – GCU

Drawing heavily from the concept and elements of bioregionalization, the Gir PA management has taken a lead to fulfil the requirements of this emerging approach of regional planning so as to strike a balance between the resident community's needs and the potential for natural resources. Some of the following forerunning activities/inputs by the Gir management are precursor to the current landscape management approach in the area:

(A) Establishment and Development of Gir PA

- The Gir sanctuary was declared in 1965. Realizing that the ecosystem was fast deteriorating, an extensive ecological research programme, the Gir Lion Project was initiated by the BNHS, Bombay in 1969 with the financial support of the Smithsonian Institute and Yale University of USA. Dr. Paul Joslin, the first research student was able to identify 10 major management problems highlighting habitat degradation and its probable causes.
- The research findings of the 'Gir Lion Project' were the main plank for launching 'Gir Development Scheme' (GDS) in 1971. Various measures undertaken led to the

increase in populations of carnivores (lion and leopard) and wild herbivores; drastic reduction in poaching, habitat recovery (vegetal cover, grass and browse availability), natural dispersal of lions to the adjoining areas (Girnar, Mitiyala, Coastal forests and peripheral grasslands), and ultimate establishment of satellitic lion population.

- Relocation of Maldharis (580 families out of 845 Maldhari families), their livestock and shifting of as many as 75 'Nesses' out of total 129 'Nesses' during 1972-86. This resulted into the establishment of Gir National Park (258.7 sq. km) devoid of Maldharis and their 'Nesses'. Consequent to Maldhari relocation, protection and habitat improvement programmes, the National Park area has shown a remarkable recovery of habitat-dense vegetation, permanent water and enhanced prey base. The Maldhari resettlement scheme included a 610 sq. m plot for house construction, 3.2 ha of agricultural land and cash compensation for house construction. By and large the resettlement scheme was quite successful in achieving its objectives. Now only 361 families inhabiting 54 'Nesses' and 14 forest settlement villages located in Sanctuary area exert direct pressure on Gir WLS and they remain to be resettled.
- Area demarcation and stone wall fencing all around the Gir NP and WLS undertaken as a part of the GDS have helped the Gir ecosystem in several ways.
- Mass awareness programmes and organizations of Nature Education Camps initiated by the Gir management in 1970s are two significant contributions and highly acclaimed programmes. About 125 Forest Youth Clubs and several NGOs are actively working in the Gir surrounds. Nearly 4,800 participants join 90 Nature Education Camps being organized every year for past. Such programmes have immensely benefited the PA management in building a positive rapport with masses.
- Over the years, the Gir PA management has developed several strategies to tackle man-wildlife conflict. The

management has developed a system wherein any lion or other carnivore encountered outside the PA. i.e. in surrounding areas are caught and released back in the forest interiors without loss of much time. The cash compensation is also being paid in the event of human injuries or killings as fast as possible.

(B) Ecodevelopment Initiatives in GCU

Eco-development is a strategy that attempts to conserve ecologically valuable areas, especially protected areas by reducing the adverse impact of local people on the PA as well as the impact of PA management on the local people (Panwar, 2001; Singh and Pathak, 2000). The practices of ecodevelopment activities are not new for Gir management. It was practised with different names and perspectives. The implementation of Maldhari resettlement scheme and other habitat protection and improvement programmes during the operation of above mentioned GDS were such pioneer efforts in this direction. Subsequently, at the behest of Government of India, a pilot project on Ecodevelopment was commenced in 1992-93 under the 'Eighth Five Year Plan'. The main objective was to minimize man-wildlife conflict and reducing the resource dependence of dependent communities. Activities, *viz.* provisioning of water harvesting structures, fodder development on the peripheral forest areas, installation of non-conventional energy system (Gobar Gas Plants) and immunization of cattle were undertaken. These ecodevelopment initiatives provided a good foundation for the actual launch of the Global Environmental Facility (GEF) supported India Ecodevelopment Project (Singh and Pathak, 2000).

(C) Comprehensive PA Management Plan

Subsequent to the first Management Plan for Gir NP and WLS by Joshi (1976), the comprehensive management plan prepared for the enlarged 'Gir Conservation Unit' (1,882.6 sq. km) by Singh and Kamboj (1996) was second significant forward step towards the process of landscape level planning. This plan was finalized in a workshop after obtaining inputs from various experts. This Plan (1996-2000) aimed to expand conservation efforts in new areas where lions have already established their home range or harboured satellite populations. The focus of this comprehensive plan was thus on: (i) the development of peripheral forests (400 sq. km) in ecodevelopment zone (97 villages) as multiple use area; (ii) development of satellite zones or extended Gir (i.e. Girnar – 180 sq. km; Mitiyala – 19 sq. km; coastal forests – 110 sq. km; and Barda – 192 sq. km to manage outside groups of lions already settled; (iii) corridor development/restoration; (iv) special programme for habitat improvement in 10 forest blocks where prey base and lions were in low densities; (v) manipulation of vegetation as experimental trials so as to improve lion habitat; and (vi) control of weed *Lantana camara*.

Regional Perspective and Landscape Management – GCA

As stated earlier, the concept of a Greater Gir Ecosystem (GGE) was conceded in principle in the management plan for GCU by Singh and Kamboj, 1996. The new initiative on the demonstration of landscape approach and several other management and ecodevelopment steps undertaken as a part of the ongoing India Ecodevelopment Project have set the desired stage for regional perspective and landscape management. The participatory exercise for revision of management plan for Gir has recently begun.

(A) Incorporation of Ecological Concerns

(i) Delineation of Bioregion

Singh (2000) and Pathak (2000) have provided more or less similar concept, details and extent of the proposed 'Greater Gir Ecosystem' (GGE) or 'Gir Landscape' from the perspective of regional planning. Accordingly, the present distribution of lion extends in three districts – Junagadh, Amreli and Bhavnagar, covering 18 talukas. Among these, 10 talukas of Junagadh (Una, Kodinar, Talala, Maliya, Mendarda, Junagadh, Visavadar and part areas of Keshod, Vanthali and Mangrol), five talukas of Amreli (Dhari, Khambha, Jafrabad, Rajula and Savarkundla) and part of three talukas in Bhavnagar (Mahuva, Palitana and Gariyadhar) are included where lions visit for food, water, shelter or have already established satellitic/meta populations. Pathak (2000) listed only 16 talukas in his paper. He omitted three talukas of Bhavnagar while included Veraval taluka in his list. Likewise, Singh omitted Veraval and Vanthali talukas. There was full agreement among the stakeholders and they endorsed for designating the Gir Landscape as proposed by Singh (2000) and Pathak (2000) except the minor omissions pointed out above.

The above-proposed 'Greater Gir Ecosystem' or 'Gir Landscape' includes:

(i) The Gir National Park (258.7 sq. km) and Gir Wildlife Sanctuary (1153.4 sq. km) forming the 'core' area,

(ii) Entire watershed and linkages (rivers, rivulets and streams) since water is the most important factor, both for conservation and sustainable development,

(iii) Adjoining and peripheral forests, grasslands and coastal vegetation serving as buffer,

(iv) Full range of corridors/connectivity/migratory routes for wider dispersal and movement of the flagship species – lion and other associated species, and

(v) Existing administrative units (talukas) in Junagadh and Amreli districts and parts of three talukas in Bhavnagar district.

Singh (2000) has recommended two sections in the proposed regional plan – first, dealing specifically with the management and conservation of Gir NP (258.7 sq. km), Gir WLS (1,153.4 sq. km) along with peripheral forests/grasslands occupying 470.5 sq. km area; and second section dealing with the entire area as described above for regional planning. The second section should focus on the identification, restoration and development of corridors and satellite areas; identification of encroached forests/grasslands and eviction, demarcation, and protection of such areas; development and maintenance of waterholes; establishment of adequate infrastructure for protection and addressing man-wildlife conflicts; and regulation of mining, industrial development and other anthropogenic activities detrimental to long term conservation goals and sustainable development.

(ii) *Management of Peripheral Forests and Corridors*

The peripheral reserved, protected and unclassified forests; reserved and non-reserved grasslands ('vidis'); and satellite areas (forests, grasslands and coastal plantations) constitute buffer area. Over the years, these areas have been under tremendous biotic pressure. Likewise, riparian areas outside Gir PA serving linkages/corridors/migratory routes need urgent management attention. Singh and Patel (2000) have assessed and mapped riparian areas serving as migratory routes/corridors for satellite populations of lion. Awareness and immediate efforts to conserve/restore such areas are critical components of any successful future conservation plan. The Government of Gujarat has recently initiated process to notify riparian areas and adjacent areas forming vital corridor links as "ecosensitive" zone (Fig. 5.3). Protection, regulated grazing, controls of fire and weeds, water management and other habitat improvement inputs are thus priority in all peripheral forests/grasslands.

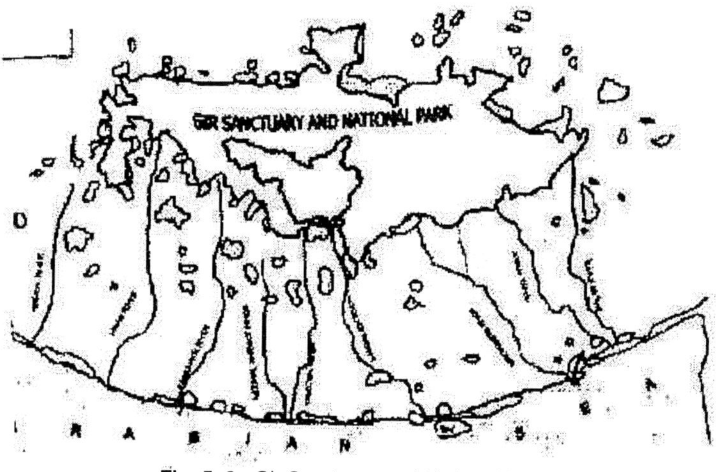

Fig. 5. 3 : Gir Sanctuary and National Park.

(iii) *Conservation of Water and Grass*

Water and grass are two important natural resources in the semi-arid tract of Gir. The Gir region experiences highly erratic rainfall. Highly variable number of rainy days (20 to 65) and total amount of rainfall (as low as 180 mm and as high as > 1800 mm with just 600 mm average annual rainfall) make entire area vulnerable to frequent droughts. On the contrary, much fold increase in ground water exploitation for multiple crops and industrial use in recent decades is a serious concern. Poor rainfall in a particular year leads to the shortage of grass and fodder; water scarcity; resultant poor agricultural production; inadequate employment opportunities; and overall impact on socio-economics and increase in man-wildlife conflict. The landscape plan thus needs to address water and grass management in the region on a priority basis.

(B) Broadening Participation

The landscape management calls for engaging local residents and other stakeholders, that is, those who depend upon, utilize, live within, or otherwise care about the place and its biological resources (Miller, 1996; Dudley *et al.,* 1999; Pandey, 2001). The Gir management has identified several primary and secondary stakeholders. An attempt to develop 'Gir Vision 21' has also been made by the Gir management through the participatory approach in a workshop (August 1997) of various stakeholders (Anon., 1997). As such, local people realize the significance of Gir forest, watershed and lion for the region. However, primary stakeholders (Maldharis and other local people living in 'Nesses' or villages in Gir and its periphery and their livestock) are wholly dependent on the resources of PAs and peripheral forests/grasslands. Requirements of these forest dependent communities have been assessed through micro planning process. Formation of Village Ecodevelopment Committees (VEDs) and intensive ecodevelopment inputs during the India Ecodevelopment Project have definitely broadened people participation. However, these activities require further augmentation and strengthening based on lessons learnt and keeping in view the expectations of local people. Activities those encourage cooperation with neighbours and partnerships among stakeholders and also support PA objectives need to be promoted. Initiatives of formal and informal dialogues and interactions with stakeholders need to be continued. These dialogues are always likely to be influenced by macro-economic policies, rural poverty, land tenure issues, inadequate funding, and lack of political commitment, PA-people conflict and often-inadequate management capacity. Thus, future landscape level programme should aim to plug the gaps in organizations and individuals capacities-building upon existing capacity wherever possible, while being able to respond to change in attitudes, the economy and the environment as necessary.

(i) *Linkages with Development Agencies and Inter-Agency Cooperation*

The people in Gujarat State are highly enterprising. This is evident in all round development (infrastructure, agriculture, industries, and coastal and marine resources) in the State as well as in the surrounds of Gir. The Constitution (73rd Amendment) Act, 1992 which came into force on April 24, 1993 provides constitutional status to the "Panchayati Raj" institutions. The Act provides a 3-tier system of Panchayati Raj for all States (having population more than 20 lakh); Panchayat elections every 5 years; reservation of seats for Scheduled Castes, Scheduled Tribes and Women (not less than 33%); adequate financial powers and to constitute a "District Planning Committee" to prepare draft development plan for the district as a whole. Panchayats have been given powers and authority to function as institutions of self-government. In the Panchayati Raj set up, the "Gram Sabha", the general assembly of villagers, has a key-role for effective functioning of Panchayats. The rural people, women and the marginalised people have been empowered to join in decision taking in 'Gram Sabha' on matters affecting their lives. Active functioning of the Gram Sabha is expected to ensure a participatory democracy with transparency, accountability and achievement.

The District Rural Development Agency (DRDA) is the nodal coordinating agency for implementation of various rural development programmes in each district and directly works under the District Development Officer and 'Zila (District) Panchayat'. Presently, the DRDA implements various developmental schemes, *viz.* the Watershed Development Programme, Integrated Wasteland Development Programme (IWDP), Employment Assurance Scheme (EAS), etc. Majority of these programmes aim to uplift rural people and are being implemented either by NGOs or Taluka Panchayats or various Government Departments. The District Forest official is a member of the Governing Body, Executive Committee as well as of the District Advisory Committee of DRDA. Though the Forest Department has come forward in implementation of select programmes (watershed development and wasteland development), the Gir management can take optimum benefit of various other programmes for implementation in rural areas of Gir.

Nearly a dozen development agencies (agriculture, irrigation, animal husbandry, tourism, fisheries, railways, PWD, industry, mining, health, education departments) along with other interested centers/groups, *viz.* temples and pilgrims are active in the Gir region. So far sectored approach and often counter productive activities are being undertaken by such agencies. They sometime adversely affect conservation goals. In recent past, several attempts have been made to bring together these sectored agencies so as to convince about the need of landscape approach. The response has been positive. However, their interest needs to be maintained and much more required to be done in this direction.

(ii) *Regional Steering Committee*

The inter-agency cooperation is vital for the effective planning and implementation of a landscape plan (Singh, 2001; Panwar, 2001). Promoting cooperation between organizations and institutions already working in the area is also critical. However, the experience elsewhere illustrates that the communities, institutions and developing agencies require space and time to adapt (Craik, 1996). Various stakeholder consultation processes recommended for the constitution of a high power Regional Steering Committee in the case of Gir. Accordingly, the Government. of Gujarat notified a high State Level Committee to steer the process of landscape level planning and to ensure conservation and sustainable development in the region.

Challenges to Regional Planning

The concept of landscape management is relatively new to Indian PAs, but several long running programmes in different parts of the world have amply illustrated that mainly three complex challenges await policy makers, managers and communities. These are (i) Building capacity, (ii) Stakeholder Involvement, and (iii) Institutional Cooperation. These challenges largely result due to deeply embedded values and practices of various development agencies, land use patterns, life styles and traditions of resource dependent people.

Conclusion

Notwithstanding the challenges and constraints, the landscape approach has the potential to foster a productive relationship between people and key biodiversity sites in the region. However, it urgently calls on all members of the protected areas community to *rethink* in a broader context; *re-orient* themselves to work for compatible management of surrounding areas; *respond* to local, regional, national and global concerns; and *reach out* to establish partnership and encourage cooperation with neighbours and other stakeholders. At the same time, governments (Local Panchayat, District, State and National) and private organizations need to complement efforts of the protected areas community through their skills, capabilities, authority, responsibility, and requisite funding support so as to realize their shared vision for the natural resources of the region.

REFERENCES

Aberley, D., *Future by Design: The Practice of Ecological Planning*. The New Catalyst Bioregional Series. New Society Publishers, Gabriola Islands, British Columbia and Philadelphia, PA. 1994.

Anon, "GIR VISION 21". Workshop on Integrated Management Planning for Gir National Park and Sanctuary under the India Ecodevelopment Project, Wildlife Circle, Gujarat Forest Department, Junagadh (Gujarat). 68pp, 1997.

Badola, R., A.K.Bhardwaj and S.K.Mukherjee, 'Integrating Conservation and Development in Protected Area Management – Can We Do It?', in *Indian Forester*, October, 2000:1054-1067, 2000.

Bhatnagar, Y., V.B. Mathur, T. McCarthy, 'A Regional Perspective for Snow Leopard Conservation in the Indian Trans-Himalaya', Paper presented in the GEF-India Ecodevelopment Project Initiative, National Workshop on Regional Planning for Wildlife Protected Areas, Background Literature, IHC, New Delhi: 118-141, 2001.

Bist, S.S., 'Regional Planning in the Context of Elephant Reserves', Paper Presented in the GEF-India Ecodevelopment Project Initiative, National Workshop on Regional Planning for Wildlife Protected Areas, Background Literature, IHC, New Delhi: 142-162, 2001.

Borrini-Feyeraband, G., ed., *Beyond Fences: Seeking Social Sustainability in Conservation*, IUCN, Gland, 1997.

Borrini–Feyerabend, G. 'Collaborative Management of Protected Areas', in, S. Stolton and N. Dudley, eds., *Partnership for Protection, New Strategies for Planning and Management of Protected Areas,* WWF and IUCN; Earthscan Publications Ltd., London: 224-234, 1999.

Choudhury, B.C. 'Integrated Regional Planning for Conservation of Marine Turtles in India', Paper presented in the GEF-India Ecodevelopment Project Initiative, National Workshop on Regional Planning for Wildlife Protected Areas, Background Literature, IHC, New Delhi:173-183, 2001.

Craik, W., 'The Great Barrier Reef Marine Park, Australia: A Model for Regional Management', *Natural Area Journal,* Vol. 16(4):344-352, 1996.

Crow, T.R., 'Landscape Ecology: The Big Picture', in *Approach to Resource Management*:55-65. 1999.

Dudley, N., B. Gujja, B. Jackson, J.P. Jeanrenaud, G.Oviedo, A. Phillips, P. Rosabel, S. Stolton and S.. Wells, 'Challenges for Protected Areas in the 21st Century', in, S. Stolton and N. Dudley, eds., *Partnership for Protection, New Strategies for Planning and Management of Protected Areas,* WWF and IUCN; Earthscan Publications Ltd., London: 3-12, 1999.

Forey, P.L., C.J. Humphires and R.I. Vane-Wright, eds., *Systematics and Conservation Evaluation,* Oxford : Clarendon Press, 1994.

Gopal, R. 'Regional Planning in the Context of Tiger Reserves'. Paper presented in the GEF-India Ecodevelopment Project Initiative, National Workshop on Regional Planning for Wildlife Protected Areas, Background Literature, IHC, New Delhi: 107-117, 2001.

Green, M.J.B. and J. Paine, 'State of the World's Protected Areas at the End of the 20th Century', in, S. Stolton and N. Dudley eds., *Partnership for Protection, New Strategies for Planning and Management of Protected Areas,* WWF and IUCN; Earthscan Publications Ltd., London: 18-28, 1999.

Haufler, J.B., C.A. Mehl., and G.J. Roloff., 'Conserving Biological Diversity Using a Coarse-Filter Approach with a Species Assessment', in, Baydack *et al.* eds., *Practical Approaches to the Conservation of Biological Diversity,* Washington, D.C., Covelo, California : Island Press, 107-125. 1999.

Hunter Jr, M.L., *Wildlife, Forests and Forestry, Principles of Managing Forests for Biological Diversity,* Englewood. Cliffs, New Jersey: Prentice Hall Career & Technology, 07632: pp. 370, 1990.

Hunter Jr, M.L. ed., *Maintaining Biodiversity in Forest Ecosystems,* Cambridge: Cambridge University Press, pp. 698, 1999.

Joshi, R.R. 'Working Plan for Gir Forests. Vol. I & II', Gujarat Forest Department: 152pp. 1976.

Mathur, V.B. and P.K. Mathur, 'Research Strategy for Protected Area Management for the India Ecodevelopment Project Sites. A Consultancy Report for the World Bank – India Ecodevelopment Project', Wildlife Institute of India, Dehra Dun, 153pp., 1998.

McNeely, J.A., ' Protected areas for the Twenty-First Century: Working to Provide Benefits to Society', in *Unasylva* 176, Vol. 45: 3-7, 1992.

McNeely, J.A.' Protected Areas Institutions', in, S. Stolton and N. Dudley, eds., *Partnership for Protection, New Strategies for Planning and Management of Protected Areas,* WWF and IUCN, London::Earthscan Publications Ltd., 195-204, 1999.

Miller, K.R., *Balancing The Scales: Guidelines for Increasing Biodiversity Chances Through Bioregional Management.* World Resource Institute. 73pp., 1996.

Miller, K.R., 'Bioregional Planning and Biodiversity Conservation', in. S. Stolton and N. Dudley, eds., *Partnership for Protection, New Strategies for Planning and Management of Protected Areas,* WWF and IUCN, London: Earthscan Publications Ltd., pp.41-49. 1999.

Olson, D.M. and E. Dinerstein., 'The Global 2000 Initiative: A Representation Approach to Conserving the Earth's Distinctive Ecoregions', in S. Stolton and N. Dudley, eds., *Partnership for Protection, New Strategies for Planning and Management of Protected Areas,* WWF and IUCN, London: Earthscan Publications Ltd., 59-68. 1999.

Pandey, S., 'Initiatives of Ecodevlopment and Regional Planning for Biodiversity Conservation at the Great Himalayan National Park Conservation Area', Paper Presented in the GEF-India Ecodevelopment Project Initiative, National Workshop on Regional Planning for Wildlife Protected Areas, Background Literature, IHC, New Delhi: 264-275. 2001.

Panwar, H.S., ' Ecodevelopment in Retrospect and Prospect', Paper Presented in the GEF-India Ecodevelopment Project Initiative, National Workshop on Regional Planning for Wildlife Protected Areas, Background Literature, IHC, New Delhi: 288-298, 2001.

Pathak, B.J.. 'Ecological Considerations for the Regional Planning for the Conservation and Development of the Gir Region', Paper Presented at the Workshop on Regional Planning for Conservation and Development, Jointly Organized by the Wildlife Institute of India and Gujarat Forest Department at the IIM, Ahmedabad:11pp. 2000.

Rahmani, A.R., 'Integrated Planning for the Conservation of Indian Bustards', Paper Presented in the GEF-India Ecodevelopment Project Initiative, National Workshop on Regional Planning for Wildlife Protected Areas, Background Literature, IHC, New Delhi: 231-240, 2001.

Rodgers, W.A., H.S. Panwar and V.B. Mathur, *Wildlife Protected Area Network in India: A Review, Executive Summary,* Dehra Dun: Wildlife Institute of India, 44pp., 2000.

Sawarkar, V.B., *A Manual for Preparation of Management Plans for Protected Areas and Managed Forests, IND-92/007,* Dehra Dun: Wildlife Institute of India, 1995.

Sawarkar, V.B. 'Conserving Biodiversity in Forested Landscapes', Paper Presented in the Workshop on Regional Planning for Conservation and Development, Gir Conservation Area, IIM, Ahmedabad: 28-46. 2000.

Scot, J,M., B. Csuti, R. Gerald Wright, P.J. Christ and M.D. Jennings., 'Regional Approaches to Managing and Conserving Biodiversity', in, Baydack *et al.* eds.,

Practical Approaches to the Conservation of Biological Diversity. Washington, D.C., Covelo, California: Island Press, pp. 55-70. 1999.

Singh, M. and B.J. Pathak, 'Ecodevelopment in Gir PA – Initiatives and Future Perspective', Paper contributed for India Ecodevelopment Project Workshop on Regional Planning for Conservation and Development, Gir Conservation Area, organizers: Wildlife Institute of India and Gujarat Forest Department; IIM, Ahmedabad, pp. 62-78. 2000.

Singh, H.S., 'Gir Lion – Present Scenario and Future Conservation Strategies', Paper contributed for India Ecodevelopment Project Workshop on Regional Planning for Conservation and Development, Gir Conservation Area, organizers: Wildlife Institute of India and Gujarat Forest Department; IIM, Ahmedabad, pp. 52-61, 2000.

Singh, H.S. and R.D. Kamboj, *Biodiversity Conservation Plan for Gir – A Management Plan for Gir Sanctuary and National Park*, Gujarat Forest Department, Vol. I & II, 1996.

Singh, M., ' Issues for Integrated Management Plan for Gir', Paper Presenteed in the India Ecodevelopment Project Workshop on Regional Planning for Conservation and Development, Gir Conservation Area, organizers: Wildlife Institute of India and Gujarat Forest Department; IIM, Ahmedabad, pp. 95-114, 2000.

Singh, M. and G.A. Patel, 'People – Park Issues', Paper presented in the India Ecodevelopment Project Workshop on Regional Planning for Conservation and Development, Gir Conservation Area, organisers: Wildlife Institute of India and Gujarat Forest Department; IIM, Ahmedabad, pp. 14-22,. 2000.

Singh, S., 'Sectoral Linkages and Inter-Agency Cooperation: Discussion Abstract', Paper Presented in the GEF-India Ecodevelopment Project Initiative, National Workshop on Regional Planning for Wildlife Protected Areas, Background Literature, IHC, New Delhi: 286-287, 2001.

Soule, M.E., 'Applications of Genetics and Population Biology: The What, Where and How of Nature Reserves' in *Conservation, Science and Society*, UNESCO-UNEP, Paris and Nairobi, 1983.

Stolton, S. and N.Dudley, *Partnerships for Protection, New Strategies for Planning and Management for Protected Areas,* London: Earthscan Publishers Ltd., 283pp., 1999.

Wilcox, B.A., '*In situ* Conservation of Genetic Resources: Determinants of Minimum Area Requirements' in National Parks', in, J.A. McNeely, and K.A. Miller, eds. *Conservation and Development: the Role of Protected Areas in Sustaining Society*, Washington D.C : Smithsonian Institution Press, 1984.

WII, 'WMF Project Report: Integrated Planning Framework', in, WII-USDA Forest Service Collaborative Project, Planning Workshop, Research Project Document, Dehra Dun : Wildlife Institute of India, India: 1-26, 1996.

WII, *Conserving Biodiversity in 21st Century through Integrated Conservation and Development Planning on a Regional scale*: Proceedings of the Workshop Organized at the Lal Bahadur Shashtri National Academy of administration,

Mussoorie in collaboration with Wildlife Institute of India, Dehra Dun: 146 pp. 2000.

World Bank. Staff Appraisal report, India Ecodevelopment Project, Report No. 14914-IN, South Asia Development II, Agriculture and Water division, the World Bank: 299pp. 1996.

6

Conserving Wildlife and Biodiversity through People's Participation

Subhabrata Palit

Introduction

Forest Departments in India have traditionally relied on custodial policing to safeguard protected areas (PAs). Where funds have been available, these have been used for fencing, gates, guards, and guns to protect parks and sanctuaries. However, these techniques have generally not proved effective in preventing exploitation of these areas by local communities, and they have often led to confrontation between wildlife authorities and villagers. As a result, there is a growing awareness in India, and in other countries as well, that another approach should be tried, one that secures willing cooperation of the people by providing alternatives to reliance on the natural resources of protected areas. There is also a recognition that conservation programmes must act to reduce any negative impacts that protected areas may have on nearby settlements, such as crop depredation by wild animals.

In recent years, protected area management has evolved from a species-based conservation approach to a livelihood-based landscape approach. The shift in the conservation paradigm has been gradual, and has included acceptance of communities as an integral part of national level conservation initiatives (Raman *et al.*, 2003), together with integration of many global conventions and directives. Scaling up conservation across larger landscapes, as facilitated by most global conventions, involves cooperation at various levels (Putz, 2001).

The strategic approach is based on addressing the landscape as a whole (Krishnaswamy and Hansoon, 1999). A landscape comprises the visible features of an area of land, including physical elements such as landforms, living elements of flora and fauna, abstract elements such as lighting and weather conditions, and human elements, for instance human activity or the built environment. Landscapes, are the places where people and nature meet, are shaped by the inter-relationships between humans and their environment. In turn, the natural setting has shaped how people live, their settlement patterns, livelihoods, cultural practices and beliefs – indeed their very way of life. Landscape approach is a strategy to overcome unsustainable and incompatible resource use practices by the dependent communities for their livelihood in and around PAs, through regulated ('sustainable' and compatible) use and alternatives ensuring collaborative efforts amongst different stakeholders.

Poverty and Conservation

Conservation has often been carried out at the expense of the poor-either through outright expropriation of land and resources or by imposing restrictions on the use of natural resources without adequate compensation.

In World Parks Congress in Durban September, 8-17, 2003 adoptions of the following principles in the conservation work have been recommended:

- The requirement of no net loss of biodiversity must be balanced with no negative impact on the livelihoods of the poor;
- Biodiversity must be recognized and managed to support

local livelihoods as well as a global public good;

- The global values of PAs must be harnessed in ways that create tangible benefits for the rural poor; and
- The PA category system must be made more responsive to local development needs.

It is, therefore, important to ensure that above principles are adopted for the existing PAs in the country, if necessary by amending the existing management plans and also while drawing up management plans for new PAs.

Biodiversity Conservation

Forests are one of the largest repositories of biodiversity in the world. By some estimates they contain 60-90 per cent of all terrestrial species found on the planet. Some of these could have widespread economic or medicinal uses that are still unknown to us. The conservation of these valuable genetic resources for future options that are yet undiscovered is a valuable service that forests provide to us and to future generations.

Forests and Water Conservation

Water in theory is the most renewable of the natural resources. Yet, careless use, population growth, and increasing demand all mean that provision of adequate safe supplies of water is now a major source of concern, expense, and even national and international tension. Forests in catchments generally result in cleaner water downstream, thus significantly reducing the costs of purification. In addition, particular forests such as tropical moist forests appear to increase flow into catchments as well as ameliorate local flooding.

With the burgeoning water scarcity in many parts of the world, the importance of this link is being rapidly realized today. Twenty-eight per cent of the world's forests are located in mountains and these forests are the source of some 60-80 per cent of the world's fresh water resources. They are also natural barriers for landslides, torrents, and floods. However, nearly 30 per cent of the world's major watersheds have lost more than three-quarters of their original forest cover.

Recognizing this problem, some countries have already started protecting or replanting trees on degraded hill slopes to safeguard their water supplies. Generating more knowledge on this forest environmental service, and developing appropriate payment or compensation mechanisms between upstream watershed service providers and the downstream beneficiaries, will be a key challenge for the forestry sector in the coming years.

Forests and Carbon Sequestration

Climate change has emerged as one of the most important concerns of the twenty-first century. Sea level rise, warming temperatures, uncertain effects on forest and agricultural systems, and increased variability in weather patterns are expected to have a significant impact in the developing world, where the world's poor are susceptible to the potential damages and uncertainties inherent in a changing climate. Since the inception of the Kyoto Protocol, the use of land use, land-use change and forestry (LULUCF) activities to combat climate change have been a topic of significant debate. Whether one is a protagonist or an antagonist on the issue, decisions taken within the UN Framework Convention on Climate Change (UNFCCC) have significant implications for the forest sector. Forests are both a source of carbon dioxide (CO_2) when they are destroyed or degraded and a sink when conserved, managed, or planted sustainably. Forest vegetation and soils currently hold almost 40 per cent of all carbon stored in terrestrial ecosystems.

However, in the tropics, forest clearance and degradation are together acting as a "net source" of carbon emissions. Though growth in plantations is expected to absorb more carbon, the likely continuation of current deforestation rates means that the world's forests will remain a net source of carbon dioxide emissions and a contributor to global climate change. However, there are also significant opportunities to develop innovative carbon sequestration forestry projects that generate positive synergies between forest restoration, mitigation of climate change and livelihood improvements for the poor. These need to be explored through mechanisms such as the Clean Development Mechanism of the Kyoto Protocol and the Bio-Carbon Fund of the World Bank. However, the success of such carbon trading initiatives will ultimately depend on the resolution of many outstanding issues, including clearly defining the legal ownership of the carbon, and also on the outcome of the negotiations for the next commitment period under the Kyoto Protocol. Nonetheless, in many countries, the prospect of trading carbon credits generated by the forestry sector has started influencing decision making in the forest industries of those countries and this can also have effects on future timber markets.

Integrating Conservation in Landscapes with Livelihood Security

In order to make Integrated Conservation and Development (ICD) (Raman *et al.*, 2003) approach meaningful a wider landscape approach is required. This will make the relationship between the conservation area and the wider people-influenced landscapes more linked, strong and definite.

Conservation areas can no longer be managed as "pristine" islands in "seas" of agriculture.

Conservation areas need to be seen as part of wider human influenced landscapes and ecosystems, where goods and services they provide are better and more widely understood.

Regarding forests purely in terms of conservation or production omits the vital role they play in securing and maintaining the livelihoods of many rural and urban people.

Thus forest landscape may be redefined as:

> *A landscape, that is, or once, dominated by forests and woodlands and which continue to yield forest-related goods and services. That those goods and services actively contribute to poverty reduction and livelihood security.*

This requires more than support of conservation agencies, but has to be integrated into mainstream development at local/national levels.

Forest landscape restoration focuses on restoring forest functionality, that is, goods, services and ecological processes that forests can provide at the broader landscape level as opposed to solely promoting increased tree cover at a particular location.

Landscape restoration recognizes the value of both biodiversity conservation and livelihood security. It also recognizes that trade-offs need to be made and agreed to.

We need to see conservation as a key component of improved land use planning and as part of human influenced landscapes-not isolated islands of conservation.

Planning Strategy

Some of the important concerns are:

- Conservation areas need to be seen as part of wider human influenced landscapes.
- Establishing common concerns on: efficiency, equity, sustainability and preservation of biodiversity.
- Sharing equitably and judiciously, responsibilities among the actors.
- Appropriate institutional structures (using existing institutions where available and building new ones where not) need to be empowered to take up the planning/implementation/monitoring processes. Such institutions will be at village/hamlet (Ecodevelopment/Forest Protection Committees or prevailing village institutions), PA (Protected Area level coordination/management committees).
- There should be complete transparency in functioning,

with full public access to information/documents, including public circulation of proposed action plans.

- Ensuring participation of villagers living around PAs .
- Creating livelihood options.
- Creating income generating activities.
- Improving cattle breed.
- Phasing out scrub cattle where possible.
- Improving agricultural resource base.
- Establishing sustainable harvesting of NTFP.
- Creating a fodder base for the wild animals in the forests and protecting it.
- Controlling population growth and encroachments.
- Promoting alternative energy use, like gas, biogas, bio-briquettes etc.
- Regulating eco-tourism which often have adverse impact on PAs.

Implementation Strategy

For the purpose of implementation the work programme may be divided into four broad categories. These are: Creating awareness, Conservation oriented Development, Community Development and Income Generation.

(a) Awareness Campaign

Carrying out awareness campaign is a prerequisite for proper orientation of the participating people in the landscape. This along with other measures discussed below will ensure establishing common concerns on: efficiency, equity, sustainability and preservation of biodiversity.

For this purpose grouping of villages may be undertaken in the following manner:

1. *Core villages :* Villages in and in the immediate vicinity of the PAs;
2. *Buffer villages :* Villages not in close proximity of the PAs but frequently used by wildlife;
3. *Fringe villages :* Those villages as are neither in the core nor in the buffer but in the fringes.

(b) Conservation Oriented Development

The ground vegetation in many places has been wiped out and the wildlife especially the herbivores have nothing to feed on inside the forests. They, therefore, come out and raid crop fields for survival. This is giving rise to frequent man-animal conflicts.

For a durable solution of the problem the wildlife habitats have to be restored. Attention, therefore, has to be refocused on renewal of the degraded forests, which can still be nursed back to health. Where even the rootstock is gone in vacant areas outside forests, agroforestry should be resorted to. Creation and maintenance of fire lines is another very important step proposed for restoration /conservation of forests, afforestation is suggested with a species mix simulating nature, as far as possible.

(c) Evaluation of Forest Services and the Need for Incentives

Forest conservation and sustainable forest management has to make tangible economic sense to all the groups whose activities have the potential to impact on forests. Being able to demonstrate the full range of ecosystem values and their economic benefits is one part of this equation. Another is to find ways of equitably capturing these values and benefits over the long term, so that they can put in place incentives for local communities, private sector actors and governments to promote sustainable forest management.

Forests receive little or no compensation or attention for the services that they provide from the beneficiaries of these services. Recognition of this flaw has encouraged the development of 'Payment for Environmental Services (PES)'. The PES approach suggests those who provide environmental services should be compensated for doing so and those who receive the services should pay for their provision. On the ground, this equates to downstream users such as urban water supply or hydropower companies paying upstream communities and institutions involved in forest conservation activities for watershed maintenance. Similarly, it can be viewed as forest protection communities or institutions being paid for the global carbon sequestration benefits that their forest protection results in.

(d) Community Development

Any community building programme should include *capacity building* as a basic step. A very special objective should be to foster and focus leadership capacity and multi-stakeholders coalitions to achieve tangible results early, while rebuilding institutional capacity for sustaining the efforts in the long run. Thus the key priorities can be identified as; (i) focusing leadership capacity building to achieve quick results; (ii) choosing strategic areas and forging multi-stakeholder coalition building around those; and (iii) building local institutions for sustainable capacity building.

To achieve results in the short run, capacity building efforts must define goals and results that matter and that people will strive to reach. Since capacity is limited all around, emphasis should be placed on forging coalitions to leverage scarce capacity as people working together can expand capacity. Organising stakeholders' workshop with state and non-state sectors will facilitate this process.

In view of limited capacities it is important to select a few feasible and visible entry points which may include among others : (i) governance of resource use and extractions, budget management and procurement; and (ii) delivery of basic services.

Institutions devoted to capacity building should be established/

identified and supported. Ultimately, this may prove to be the only sustainable approach.

(e) Income Generation

Even with heightened awareness a scheme is unlikely to succeed unless peoples' livelihood needs are met. Sustainable harvesting of NTFP where possible may partially supplement these needs. Apart from sustainable harvesting, value addition and marketing will also be important in the case of NTFP. Storage facilities have to be created.

There is scope for improvement in all such activities for improved productivity and quality. Training in such activities is also suggested.

Income Generation programme includes among others: agroforestry, horticulture, livestock improvement, eco-tourism, pisciculture, piggery, poultry, apiary, broom making, floriculture, sustainable harvesting and marketing of medicinal plants etc.

(f) Research and Monitoring

Research and monitoring should be participatory in nature involving all stakeholders and covering new paradigms of research. Research and learning of the local communities should be used complementarily with the formal systems of knowledge.

Participetary Monitoring System is a self-monitoring system (Bhatia *et al.*, 1998). PAM should be designed by participatory groups for their own use. Participatory Evaluation (PAE) is an evaluation of a development programme, which is carried out by local participatory groups.

Regular monitoring of the impact of the livelihood strategies on the local communities as well as biological monitoring for their impact on the PA needs to be taken up against the base line data.

The whole idea is to help grassroots' beneficiaries monitor and evaluate the programme. This will help increase beneficiaries' commitment to and understanding of designing, planning and implementing a community-based programme. This will also promote self-help and self-reliance.

Conclusion

The Convention on Biological Diversity under Earth Summit Watch Programmes recognizes *the close and traditional dependence of many indigenous and local communities embodying traditional life styles on biological resources, and the desirability of sharing equitably benefits arising from the use of traditional knowledge, innovations and practices relevant to the conservation of biological diversity and the sustainable of its components.*

In its SUMMARY REPORT the World Commission on Forests and Sustainable Development has made two important recommendations. These are:

1. *Plan for the use and protection of whole landscapes, not the forest in isolation*
2. *The Commission believes that sustainable resource use is most likely to occur if local communities participate in managing the resources on which they depend. Participatory decision making is a prerequisite for community involvement in forest management :*

The success of Joint Forest Management in India largely depends on a participatory approach with the communities.

Periyar Tiger Reserve (PTR) in Kerala (Gubbi, 2006) is one among the seven PAs in India selected for the implementation of IEDP. In accordance with the tripartite agreement signed between the external donor agencies (World Bank & IDA), Government of India (GOI) and Government of Kerala (GOK), Eco-development Committees were constituted. The goal of the project is conservation of biodiversity through people's participation.

A review carried out by Sanjay Gubbi (2006) says that among the seven projects launched by the India Eco-Development Project (IEDP) for tiger conservation, Periyar Tiger Reserve (PTR) is generally recognised as a success and the communities are believed to have positive attitudes towards PTR and wildlife due to the implementation of the IEDP. It was implemented to reduce impacts of local communities on the PAs, and *vice versa*. The IEDP at PTR deserves considerable credit for addressing several concerns and issues such as failing to adopt participatory approaches, providing infrastructure without consulting local communities, equity, gender empowerment, and so on. The new approach as opposed to custodial policing is reported to have brought about considerable improvement in the protection status of the reserve.

Thus the key things that emerge from the above discussion are:

1. A landscape approach should be adopted for conservation of the protected areas where there would be multi-stakeholders.
2. The concerns as well as benefits should be shared by all such stakeholders.
3. There should be complete transparency and equity in the management.
4. The communities must perceive the conservation effort as beneficial to them both from economic as well as aesthetic point of view.

REFERENCES

Bhatia, A., C.K. Sen, G. Pandey, J. Amtzis, 'Capacity-Building in Participatory Upland Watershed Planning, Monitoring and Evaluation— A Resource Kit', Integrated Mountain Development (ICIMOD), Kathmandu, Nepal, 1998.

Fifth World Parks Congress, Durban, South Africa, 2003 —Recommendations, in, *The ARC Journal* 16, 2003.

Gubbi, S., 'Tiger habitats and Integrated Conservation and Development Projects: A case study from Periyar Tiger Reserve, India', M. Sc. dissertation in Conservation Biology, Durrell Institute for Conservation and Ecology, University of Kent, UK, 2006.

Krishnaswamy, A. and A. Hansoon, eds., 'World Commission on Forests and Sustainable Development, Summary Report', Produced by Darrag

Communications, Published by World Commission on Forests and Sustainable Development ISBN0-9685191-0-5, Winniepeg, Manitoba, Canada R3B0Y4, 1999.

Palit, Subhabrata, Forests, its Multiple Services and its Primal Roles in Climate Change Mitigation, *Green Earth,* Vol. 2, No.1, January. June 2011

Pradhan Sanjay, Building Capacity to Move Past Conflict and Fragility: An agenda for action, Development Outreach, World Bank Institute, October 2009.

Putz, F.E. "Jack", 'Tropical Biologists in Working Forests and Midlife Crises', Department of Botany, University of Florida, Gainesville, *TROPINET, Vol. 12, No. 1,* 2001.

Raman, T., R. Shankar and D. Mudappa, 'Bridging the gap: Sharing responsibility for ecological restoration and wildlife conservation on private lands in the Western Ghats', *Social Change* 33 (2 & 3):129-141, 2003.

The Convention on Biological Diversity 5 June, 1992. Sponsored by United Nations held in Rio Summit, 5th June, 1992.

7

Relocation from Protected Areas

Need for a Balanced Approach

P.B. Gangopadhyay and *H.S. Pabla*

Introduction

Indian forest is rich with floral and faunal diversity. However, there is competing demand on this forest land and natural resources due to increasing biotic pressure and developmental needs of a growing economy. To provide for safe breeding area for wild life and also to afford special protection to representative habitats a protected area network has been established across the country with the creation of 102 National Parks, 515 Wildlife Sanctuaries, 44 conservation reserves and 4 community reserves representing only about 4.90 per cent of land area. It is generally thought that these protected areas are devoid of human population and whatever biotic pressure is exerted on a Protected Area is due to the fringe population. The reality is much different. More than 5000 villages are situated inside these Protected Areas with approximately 30 lakh people residing in them. This is besides a larger number of villages in the 10 km. zone of these Protected Areas with significant dependence on these Protected Areas for fodder, fuel, Minor Forest Produce and also livelihood.

Co-existence Theory

It is generally understood that wildlife and forest dwellers have lived in harmony over years. But why it is necessary now to manage the National Parks/sanctuaries at the exclusion of the people who live inside it. It was true historically but with changing dynamics of increasing population and reducing forest area to depend on, the equilibrium has been upset. Man and wildlife cannot coexist in high density. In the past low human population existed in harmony with high density wildlife. In present context wherever population density has increased, wildlife presence has dwindled. This has been very clearly brought out by the Wildlife Institute of India (WII) study of 2008 regarding habitat evaluation and prey predator population estimation. Hence there is a need to create at least some inviolate space for wildlife in exclusion of any biotic interference. How much that should be or could be, is a matter of consideration. Whatever this extent might be, there will still be enough number of villages to practice the coexistence theory and make it a success by collective efforts.

Rationalization of Protected Areas Boundary

Initially the protected areas have been notified with a boundary that enclosed an important wildlife habitat, eventually including a large number of villages also. It was expected that during the process of settlement these boundaries will be rationalized after deciding the claims of the villages. However, this has not happened for large number of protected areas. Hence, there is an urgent need to rationalize the protected areas so that in the process a good number of villages can be excluded from the protected areas which are not ecologically integral to it.

Present Approach – A Case Study of Madhya Pradesh

In Madhya Pradesh there are 732 villages inside 34 Protected Areas. The total population is 4.3 lakhs. Even if it is decided to relocate all these villages, a huge sum of Rs. 16000 crore will be needed for Madhya Pradesh alone, besides the physical impossibility of finding alternative land to settle them and social and cultural trauma in relocating this huge population. Hence, a pragmatic approach has been adopted to critically examine the location of each and every village to select a village for relocation based on its cost effectiveness and ecological advantage with minimum social impact. If by relocating one or two villages from interior forest areas a big chunk of forest can be set free from biotic interference, then it will have great advantage from conservation point of view. But, if a group of villages are so situated that their relocation does not release a substantial habitat then it is not worthwhile. Hence, a detailed exercise was undertaken on the map and on the ground, for each National Park/sanctuary and the villages were grouped in the following three categories:

(1) Villages situated near the periphery of the Protected Areas, can be excised by marginal alteration of the boundary so that they are set free from the restrictions of Protected Areas.

(2) Villages situated in the core area with high ecological advantage are identified for relocation with consent of villagers.

(3) Rest of the villages which cannot be relocated nor can be excised, they will be excluded as enclave and treated not to be part of Protected Areas.

This exercise has resulted in identifying 114 villages out of 732 which are critical from ecological point of view 426 villages have been identified for excision by marginal alteration of boundaries. Rest 192 villages will be excluded from Protected Areas as *in situ* exclusion by creating enclaves within the Protected Areas.

This approach is a balance between both the extreme views and provides ample opportunities to practice both the theories simultaneously. This, however, requires Hon'ble Supreme Court's approval before State Government can notify the revised Protected Areas. Presently, the proposals of Madhya Pradesh and Himachal Pradesh are under consideration of the Apex Court after recommendation of the Central Empowered Committee.

Reality

However keen the wildlife conservation protagonist may be, as against

Rs. 3200 crore required for Madhya Pradesh only. Rs. 103 crore could be made available for relocation so far during preceding three years. At national level, for the project tiger areas alone against NTCA's estimation of Rs. 5000 crore for relocation of most critical villages, from Tiger reserves, no special grant has been available. Only annual routine budget of NTCA is being used to squeeze out urgent relocation needs.

Relocation Benefits Villagers

The new relocation package of Rs. 10 lakh per family has been a very big motivating factor for villagers to move out voluntarily. Every family actually becomes 2 to 3 relocation units thus compensation amounting to Rs. 20 to 30 lakhs is available for each family as in most of the states adult children are considered independent family unit. The villages in interior areas are benefited by relocation due to the following counts:

- Liberal Package – Rs. 10.00 lakh per family (or 2 ha Land with Rs. 2.5 lakh cash); Extended families got Rs. 20-70 lakh.
- Every adult person/couple, orphan is a family.
- Relief from Restrictions on Development.
- Relief from Crop Damage, Cattle Lifting, Injuries/Death from Wild Animals.
- Access to Better Education, Health, Employment, Business Opportunities, Market, Communications.

The contrary view identifies the following factors, against relocation:

- Trauma,
- Social Disruption,
- Reduced Access to Forest Resources,
- Frittering of Cash by Beneficiaries on Luxuries and Indulgences, and
- Exploitation by Shopkeepers and Traders.

These apprehensions had been taken care of in Madhya Pradesh Model of relocation in a manner. After identification of critical villages, with informed consent of villagers, the following relocation process has been followed in Madhya Pradesh.

Total Allocation for a Village: No. of Adults @ Rs.10 lakh.

Three Options:

- All Cash : Rs.10.00 lakh per Adult/Couple.
- All Cash : Compensation for Assets Plus Rs. 7.00 lakh or More
  - 2 ha, plus Rs. 2.5 lakh (Remaining Money goes into Village Infrastructure Development Fund)
  - Most villagers want all cash.
  - Land Option is always difficult as the forest land for resettlement is almost 3 times the Land acquired. Also in this option all do not get good land.

Relocation Process

- Money is kept in Joint Account of the spouses.
- Park Managements try to ensure that money is used primarily for buying agricultural land and other assets.
- Interests on deposits adequate for household expenses until lands are bought.

A case study of one village 'Bori' in Satpura Tiger reserve shows how the villagers after relocation are better connected with the development (Table 7.1)

Conclusion

Hence, without disputing co-existence or exclusion theory, sincere efforts should be put in to practice exclusion theory for only small percentage of villages which are in crucial habitat while trying inclusive management for most of the villages which are not likely to be relocated.

Table 7.1 : Comparative account of facilities available to Bori villagers after relocation

Sl. No.	*Particulars*	*Pre-relocation period*	*Relocation period*
1.	Area of the village	118 ha	243 ha
2.	Distance from the main road	72 kms (Bhaura)	6 kms (Semari)
3.	Distance from the market	25 kms (Rampur)	6 kms (Semari)
4.	Primary health centre	83 kms (Sukhtawa)	6 kms (Semari)
5.	Distance from tahsil and block	Kesala –190 kms – main road and 84 kms pedestal	18 kms Babai
6.	Police thana	Sohagpur – 190 kms – main road and 84 kms pedestal	18 kms Babai
7.	Railway station	72 kms (Bhaura)	6 kms –Semari
8.	Drinking water facility	11 hand pumps	4 hand pumps
9.	Houses	Huts of mud and grasses	Cement/concrete
10.	Agricultural land	40 hac	234 hac
11.	Irrigation facility	Mostly dry farming	Irrigated with 25 tube wells, 2 stop dams, and 2 wells
12.	Electricity	no	Electrified
13.	Community hall	none	One
14.	Playground	none	One
15.	Motor cycle	1	15
16.	Colour television	none	30
17.	Dish Antenna	none	30
18.	Toilets	none	76
19.	LPG	none	76
20.	Tractor	none	One
21.	Solar lights	few	For all

This seems to a balanced and pragmatic approach to secure at least some inviolate habitat for survival of endangered wild life.

Part III

CASE STUDIES

8

Biodiversity Conservation and Utilisation of Natural Resources in the Biosphere Reserve Situation in India

Some Observations

Samit Ghosal

Biosphere Reserve Programme

The programme of Biosphere Reserve was initiated under the 'Man and Biosphere' (MAB) programme by UNESCO in 1971. Biosphere Reserves are protected areas with a wholistic and inclusive approach in Biodiversity Conservation. Biosphere Reserves are areas of terrestrial and coastal ecosystem promoting the conservation of biodiversity with its sustainable use. Biosphere Reserves (BRs) are designed locally recommended nationally and recognised internationally but remain under the sovereign jurisdiction of the states where they are located. Biosphere Reserves are ideally organized into three interrelated zones, viz. (i) Core zone, (ii) Buffer zone and (iii) Transition zone. Core zone is the fully protected area where biodiversity is preserved. In the buffer zone sustainable use of natural resources are permitted. Transition zone is the area where all the stake holders work and researches are carried on. Biosphere Reserves fulfil three basic functions, which are complimenting and mutually reinforcing – (a) Conservation Function – Conservation of biological resources and biodiversity. (b) Developmental Function – Promote environmentally compatible economic and human development which is socio-culturally and ecologically sustainable. (c) Logistic Function – Support environmental research, monitoring human activities and imparting education and training.

The programme recognises the local communities as an integral part of ecosystem and promotes ecologically compatible socio-economic development of the local communities. Nature of exploitation of the land and forest resources by the people living in the Biosphere Reserve is directly related to the sustainable maintenance of the bio-diversity of the Biosphere Reserve Ecosystem. The human dimension of the Biosphere Reserves make them special from other protected areas, interaction with local communities is essential to keep intact the ecological knowledge and cultural values of the communities living in the area. We have to conserve the natural resources of the Biosphere Reserve *vis-à-vis* addressing the material needs of the local communities through the sustainable use of natural resources. People living within the confinement of forest ecology have to support their subsistence economy by optimum utilisation of resources at their disposal. The balance between the material needs of the people and conservation of natural resources are to be maintained for the interest of the stake-holders in particular and the nation in general. Therefore, the indigenous and eco-friendly ways of managing the natural resources by the local communities within the Biosphere Reserve is an important issue. The indigenous knowledge in land and forest management which are present among the tribal people living inside the Biosphere Reserves are used by them in their practice of subsistence agriculture as well as in the nature of exploitation of forest wealth which needs to be urgently addressed because the bio-diversity present in the Biosphere Reserve is a big repository of the human traditional knowledge base. Anthropologists' interest in the study of Indigenous Knowledge (IK) has been growing in importance in development policy and practice and in academic research, especially after the Rio Conference in 1992. The indigenous knowledge and techniques of the people in the field of subsistence agriculture and forest exploitation can make valuable contribution to the modern and contemporary knowledge. Core areas in the Biosphere Reserves are to be seen as the areas where the traditional knowledge of the tribal people can be preserved and enhanced.

World Scenario and Indian Endeavour

At present there are in total 553 Biosphere Reserves in 107 countries all round the Globe. As the programme focus has shifted from simple protection of nature to areas displaying close interaction between man and environment, the dynamicity of the Biosphere Reserve programme has become apparent.

In India there are all together 15 Biosphere Reserves and the Gulf of Mannar is entirely a marine biosphere reserve.

Table 8.1 : UNESCO Biosphere Reserves Network in the World

UNESCO Region	*Total number of BRs*	*Number of Countries Involved*
Africa	52	22
Arab Nations	26	13
Asia and Pacific	113	22
Europe and North America	258	31
Latin America and Caribbean	104	19

To fulfil the UNESCO condition of zero population presence in the core area has been a difficult proposition for the Indian Biosphere Reserve. The core area of most of the BRs in India are inhabited by the traditional forest dwelling tribes since time immemorial, much before the establishment of the protected areas such as, the Reserve Forests, and in that matter even before the declaration of the Biosphere Reserves.

Biosphere Reserves in India

As a follow up action of UNESCO's Man and Biosphere (MAB) programme, Ministry of Environment, Government. of India, has identified 15 Biosphere Reserves (covering 68761.95 sq. km.) in India on the basis of their unique biodiversity and effectiveness as a conservation units. India has a network of protected areas in the form of 94 National Parks (covering 37591.75 sq. km), 502 Wildlife Sanctuaries (covering 118952.11 sq. kn), 2 Conservation Reserves (covering 42.44 sq. km) and 28 Tiger Reserves (covering 35747.68 sq. km) under the Indian Wildlife Protection Act of 1972. It may be mentioned here that many Biosphere Reserves' and Tiger Reserves' boundaries are mutually overlapping. Biosphere Reserves are protected areas with a difference. It takes into account the overall developmental activities and resolves conflicts between development and conservation and ensures increased and broad based local people's participation compared to the Wildlife Sanctuaries and National Parks' Programmes. Biosphere Reserves emphasise on overall biodiversity and landscape rather than some specific flagship species. In the following table we have delineated the basic differences of the three protected area, viz. National Parks, Sanctuaries and Biosphere Reserves.

Table 8.2 : Categories of Protected Areas

Names	*Objectives*	*Features*	*Zonation*
National Parks	Preservation of species of a habitat with minimal human interference	No human residence other than Public Servant on duty	Core
Sanctuaries	Conservation of species and habitats by manipulative management	No human residence other than Public Servant on duty	Core, Buffer and Restoration
Biosphere Reserves	Conservation of natural resources with a view to improve the relationship between man and environment	Both natural and human influenced ecosystem; substantial human settlement outside core area, ensure peoples' participation	Core, buffer and transition

Table 8.3 : Biosphere Reserves in India

No.	*Name of BRs*	*Year of Declaration*	*Area (Km^2)*	*States*
01.	Nilgiri	1986	5520	Tamil Nadu, Kerala, Karnataka
02.	Nanda Devi	1988	2236.74	Uttarakhand
03.	Nokrak	1988	820	Meghalaya
04.	Manas	1989	2837	Assam
05.	Sunderbans	1989	9630	West Bengal
06.	Gulf of Mannar	1989	10500	Indian Territorial water of Tamil Nadu coast of the Mannar Gulf.
07.	Great Nicobar	1989	885	Andaman & Nicobar Islands
08.	Simlipal	1994	4374	Orissa
09.	Dibru-Saikhowa	1997	765	Assam
10.	Dehang Debang	1998	5111.5	Arunachal Pradesh
11.	Pachmarhi	1999	4926.28	Madhya Pradesh
12.	Kanchendozonga	2000	2619.92	Sikkim
13.	Agasthyamalai	2001	1701	Kerala
14	Achanakmar Amarkantak	2005	3835.51	Madhya Pradesh Chhattisgarh
15	Katchchh	2007	12454	Gujarat

Tribes and Biosphere Reserves

By and large Indian tribes are forest dwelling people and the Biosphere Reserves in India are generally Reserve Forests, Sanctuaries and Tiger Reserves. So it is quite natural that Biosphere Reserves would be the areas with thick concentration of Tribal population. The core and buffer areas of the Biosphere Reserves are also the core areas of the Tiger Reserves, e.g. the core and buffer areas of the Pachmarhi Biosphere Reserve coincides with the core area of Satpura Tiger Reserve, likewise the core and buffer areas of Similipal Biosphere Reserve and Sundarban Biosphere Reserve are also the core area of Satpura Tiger Reserve and Sunderban Tiger Reserve, respectively. The core area of the Kalakad Mundanthurai Tiger Reserve in Tamil Nadu overlaps the core and buffer areas of the Agasthyamalai Biosphere Reserve. Many National Parks (NPs) are also Tiger Reserves and thus come under Critical Wild Life Habitat. Here, we come across a situation where human settlement is allowed at a particular location in the context of Biosphere Reserve but the same location when comes under Tiger Reserve or National Park, human intervention whatsoever is not permitted. Therefore, in India, by and large, the UNESCO's guidelines for Biosphere Reserves which advocate human role in a Biosphere Reserve are being suppressed by the more powerful principle of forest conservation. The people, who are mostly tribes, living inside the core as well as in the buffer areas of a Biosphere Reserve are the worst sufferer under the policy of relocation of human settlements from the core area and in some cases even from the buffer areas of the Biosphere Reserve. To understand the situation in totality it is pertinent to understand the forest acts and rules enacted from time to time, especially during post-independence period.

Genesis of Tribal Right to Forest

Various Acts and legislations contravening the right of forest enjoyed so far by the tribal people came into force for the development of forests. The main objectives of these regulations were commercial forestry and revenue earnings.

The forest department was established in 1864 and the Indian Forest Act was passed in 1865. Bori Sanctuary in Madhya Pradesh was the first reserve forest in India. Prior to this, there was no restriction on the use of forest resources for domestic needs and to earn some cash by selling the surplus. The British administration in India gave no credence to the traditional rights and customary use of forest resources by the local tribes. They put forward such arrangements that the customary use of forest resources by the tribes was their mere privilege and not a right.

In this regard, we may refer to 1894 National Forest Policy and its subsequent amendment in 1927 and 1935, even the post-independence National Forest Policy of 1952 considered Reserved Forest as National Forest. All the acts and laws were created for the colonist's need for timber by overriding tribal's customary rights and declaring forest as the state property.

The Wild Life Protection Act of 1972 gave primacy to conservation over exploitation and curtailed economic activities of the tribals by creating two types of protected areas, viz. National Parks and Wild Life Sanctuaries, where technically all human activities except tourism were restricted. It was primarily aimed to curtail the rights and privileges of the tribal communities on forest resources and only some concessions were made available to them in the form of 'Nistar' in respect of fuel wood, grazing, collection of leaves and litters and were mainly confined to the forest villages situated in and around the periphery of the forest areas. In 'Nistar' tribal people living inside or within 10 km radius of forest are allowed daily 20 kg head load of fire wood to collect from forest.

So over the years we see the changes in the relationship of the tribals with the forest, from Right to privilege and finally to mere concession in the use of forest resources. This had completely alienated the tribes from the affairs of the forests. This has also acted as a mental block in their participation in the forest management in future. But fortunately, much to the relief of both forest and forest dwellers, the planners and policy makers, the people who were at the helm of national affairs understood the situation. As a result, some commissions and committees were set up to strengthen the forestry based tribal economy, which were:

1. U.N. Dhebar Commission in 1961.
2. Hari Singh Committee in 1967 on tribal economy in forest areas.

4. National Commission in Agriculture in 1976.
5. Finally B.K. Roy Burman Committee in 1982.

The reports of these committees highlighted the following points:

(a) The importance of sharing the forest wealth with the tribal people.
(b) Recognition of the basic needs and demands of the forest resources by the local people.
(c) Advocating people's participation in the management, development, and regeneration of forests.

This has been the beginning of sustainable approach in forest development and management. Because forest is not merely a group of trees, rather, it is a whole habitat, an ecosystem, which accommodates various species of trees, shrubs, grasses, roots and tubers and a variety of animal life, all contributing something or the other to the tribal life by providing him with food to eat, minor forest product to gather, consume or sell, materials for his house and herbal medicines for his illness, fuel for cooking and warmth during winter, pasture for his cattle so much so that even the tribal culture is influenced by the forests.

Some acknowledgement of tribal rites to the forest came in the form of the people oriented National Forest Policy of 1988. The sustainable forest management, involving the tribal people living in the vicinity by their direct participation in the actual process has been started at an empirical level only after the 1988 forest policy, which states—

1. Tribal people should be associated in protection, regeneration and conservation of forests.
2. Meeting the basic needs of tribal folk by providing them fuel wood, fodder, MFP and timber.
3. Providing employment to the people living in the forest areas.
4. Protecting the rights and concessions so far traditionally enjoyed by the tribals.

On the basis of this, the Central and the State Resolution in 1990, ensured people's participation in forest management through Joint Forest Management (JFM).

Development of tribes in India is possible only through a political resolve, acknowledging the tribal right to the forest as a legitimate one and empowering the tribes with a decisive role in forest management in synergy with age old symbiotic relationship with the forest ecology. The Scheduled Tribes 'Recognition of Forest Right Act, 2006' has ultimately admitted the tenure and access rights of forest dwelling Scheduled Tribes in respect of forest land. The Act recognised tribal right on forest land, MFP etc. as their *bona fide* livelihood.

The provisions made in the PESA (Panchayats Extension to the Scheduled Areas) Act of 1996 are also an effective tool to the Gram Sabhas and the People living inside the Core areas of the Biosphere Reserves and many other protected areas as far as their developmental aspects are concerned as many of them would now come under this constitutional provision. The core areas of the protected areas, be it BRs or NPs or Tiger Reserve, are certainly devoid of any development schemes or programmes, like road, education, health etc., which are normally available to the areas under the control of village panchayats. Development of these protected areas are the absolute prerogative of the forest department.

Recently, there is a move by the MOEF by amending the 'Wild Life Protection Act of 1976' so that the right of forest dwelling tribes are denied in the existing 80 National Parks and 441 Sanctuaries covering 14 per cent of the geographical area of the country. Tiger Reserves are created by demarcating areas from National Parks and Sanctuaries with highest possible level of protection for the Big Cat. Tiger Reserves, Sanctuaries, National Parks and Biosphere Reserves are mutually overlapping and transgress each other's areas. The declaration of 'Critical Wild Life Habitat' in protected areas as envisaged in the Recognition of Forest Rights Act, 2006 will mitigate the positive approach of the FRA, 2006. A recent news (*Times of India*, dt. 3.3.2011) says that MOEF plans to relocate thousands of people out of 600 plus National Parks and Sanctuaries in the country by declaring them as 'Critical Wild Life Habitat' without following the guideline laid down in the Forest Rights Act (FRA) of 2006. The guideline requires the scientific evidence confirmed by an independent expert committee that the areas could only survive as Wild Life Habitat if people are relocated and local communities and Gram Sabhas should be involved in demarcating an inviolate area.

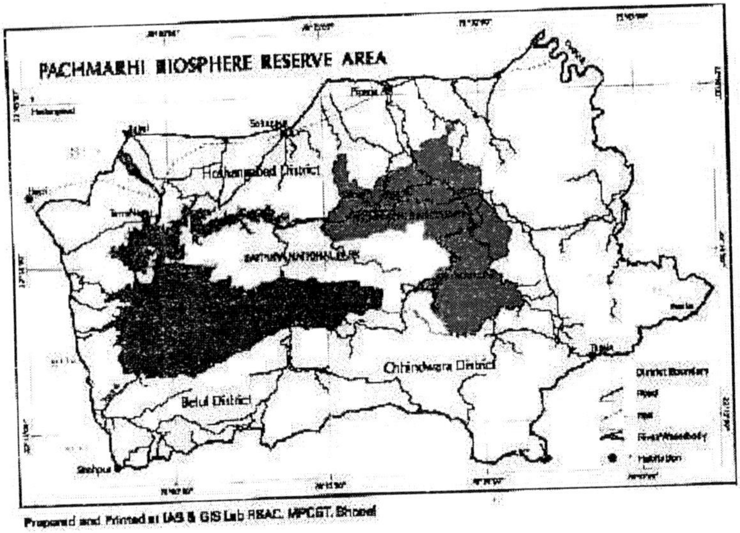

Map 8.1 : Pachmarhi Biosphere Reserve

Pachmarhi Biosphere Reserve

Let us take the empirical example of Pachmarhi Biosphere Reserve in detail to show the conflicting and contradictory conservation rules and acts *vis-à-vis* the forest dwelling tribes. The core area of the Pachmarhi Biosphere Reserve comes under Satpura Tiger Reserve where no human habitation is allowed which is also the area of Satpura National Park. As par Biosphere Reserve mandate there should not be any human habitation inside the core area, so the six villages located inside the core area of Pachmarhi Biosphere Reserve may be relocated or resettled. But the villages under the buffer zone of the Biosphere Reserve is also going to be evicted as these come under the Satpura Tiger Reserve even though BR mandate allowed human settlement there. Human right activists take this cause to fight against the forest department Pachmarhi area was designated as Biosphere Reserve by Government of India on 3rd March, 1999. Pachmarhi Biosphere Reserve besides being a vast natural resource with a unique topography, is also the home of a sizeable number of tribal population.

The total area of the Pachmarhi Biosphere Reserve is 4987.38 sq. km. It envelops three wildlife conservation units, viz. Bori Sanctuary (485.72 sq. km.), Satpura National Park (524.37 sq. km.) and Pachmarhi Sanctuary (417.78 sq. km.). All the three wildlife conservation units, Satpura National Park, Bori Sanctuary and Pachmarhi Sanctuary, comprising an area of 1427.00 sq. km., have been declared as Project Tiger Reserve in August 2000. In Pachmarhi Biosphere Reserve, the Satpura National Park (524.37 sq. km.) is considered as the Core Zone and the remaining area of 4525.93 sq. km. including Bori Sanctuary (485.72 sq. km.) and Pachmarhi Sanctuary (417.78 sq. km.), serve as the buffer zone. As such, so far there is no demarcated transition area in it (EPCO PBR Documents, 1(1), 2001). Bori Sanctuary is the oldest reserve forest in India. The Bori Reserve forest was declared as a Wildlife Sanctuary in 1977 under the Wildlife Protection Act of 1972 by the Government. of Madhya Pradesh. Pachmarhi Sanctuary was created out of Bori Sanctuary in the year 1977 and then Satpura National Park was created out of Bori and Pachmarhi Sanctuaries in the year 1981. The Pachmarhi Biosphere Reserve area comprises 622 villages (*Source*: EPCO 2001). There are seven villages inside the core area of Pachmarhi Biosphere Reserve of which only one is a forest village, rest of the villages are revenue village. There are two tribal groups found in Pachmarhi, one is Korku (Mawasi) and the other is Gond. Detail of the six villages situated inside the core area of the Pachmarhi Biosphere Reserve and their population figures are given in the following table:

Table 8.4: Population Structure of Core Villages of Pachmarhi Biosphere Reserve

Sl. No.	*Village*	*Nos. of Family*	*Population*	*Family Size*
1.	Dhana	23 (13 Mawasi,10 Gond)	127	5.52
2.	Ghodanar	17 (Mawasi)	114	6.70
3.	Badkachar	31 (Mawasi)	197	6.35
4.	Rorighat	45 (Mawasi)	256	5.68
5.	Kajri	29 (25 Mawasi, 4 Gond)	187	6.44
6.	Binora	40 (Mawasi)	239	5.97
7.	Chitor Pattan	47 (Gond)	237	5.04
TOTAL		232	1357	—

From the above table it is observed that 232 families with a population of 1357 are living in the seven villages inside the core area of the Pachmarhi Biosphere Reserve and it is needless to mention that all are tribes. They have 359.7 acre of agricultural land in their possession and they produced 957.3 quintal of crop. Paddy, wheat, maize and millet (*kodon/kutki*) are the main crops grown by them. The per capita land holding of all the villages taken together is 1.78 acre and their per capita production of crop is 4.72 quintal. The seven villages produce on an average 2.66 quintal of crops per acre.

Table 8.5: Per capita crop production and per capita land production in Pachmarhi BR

Sl. No.	*Village*	*Per capita land holding (in acre)*	*Per capita crop production (in quintal)*
1.	Ghodanar	0.23	0.64
2.	Dhana	0.19	0.42
3.	Badkachar	0.31	0.16
4.	Kajri	0.16	1.02
5.	Rorighat	0.10	0.65
6.	Binora	0.24	0.32
7.	Pattan	0.55	1.51

The forest department has annexed some sizeable amount of land from them in recent past which has negatively affected their livelihood and subsistence economy. These lands were occupied by them after clearing the forest due to population pressure. Now they have left with the lands for which they have patta or revenue document. In the changed scenario they require to maintain even more population, as population increases over time, with lesser amount of land. To cope with such a situation the people living in the core area have adopted some unique strategies in accordance with their indigenous knowledge. With this meagre land it has become very difficult for them to support their livelihood, as their main economy was land based subsistence agriculture. In response to this situation they have adapted various subsistence strategies to compensate the loss of land. However, these strategies are different in different villages, which are as follows :

Illegal re-encroachment of forest land for cultivation ; Bring under cultivation barren and high lands where no water is available and by using indigenous variety of seeds which can be grown even in such type of land and condition; Cultivation of *rabi* crop in the river bed when there is no water; Utilisation of vested revenue land with the help of an unique slash and burn type of cultivation; Intensify collection of forest produce for commercial use such as honey, *mahua* etc.; Providing services to pilgrims to promote religious tourism.

In spite of the fact that the forest department have redefined the village boundaries and demarcated it with pillar stones, the clearing of forest land remains to continue and unabated due to population pressure. They brought under cultivation hitherto uncultivable stony and high dry land, both own and encroached, and grew some special varieties of '*kodo*' and '*kuti*' seeds and also some types of dry rice. These indigenous varieties of seeds could grow even in harsh condition. In Pattan village they even used dry river bed during winter and early summer when there was no water in it. In Rorighat village they grew *lantana camera* plants in fallow lands and after a gap of two years, they cut the plants and put fire to the sun dried plants. The ash acted as fertilizer and helped to get a good production. This could be called a slash and burn cultivation in true sense because unlike the classical shifting hill cultivation they used the same field instead of moving elsewhere. In Binora and Kajri villages the land left with them after annexation to forest was so meagre that they had to intensify the collection of forest produce such as honey and mahua and used to sell them to the pilgrims coming for the Mahadeo fair during Siva Ratri. In one village they served as porter to the pilgrims who came for Nag Panchami Mela at the Nagduari cave.

Similipal Biosphere Reserve

Similipal Tiger Reserve was created in 1973 with an area of 303 sq. km as the core area in the Similipal Reserve Forest which was set aside as National Park and later the area was expanded to 845.75 sq. km with a buffer area of 1904.25 sq. km. In 1980 the core area of the tiger reserve was transformed into a National Park and the buffer area of the tiger reserve was declared as Sanctuary. The Government of Orissa imposed moratorium on tree felling in the Similipal since 1982. Similipal was declared as the 8th Biosphere Reserve of India with a total area of 4374 sq. km, of which 845.75 sq. km was the core area which was also the core area of the tiger reserve, and another 2128.25 sq. km

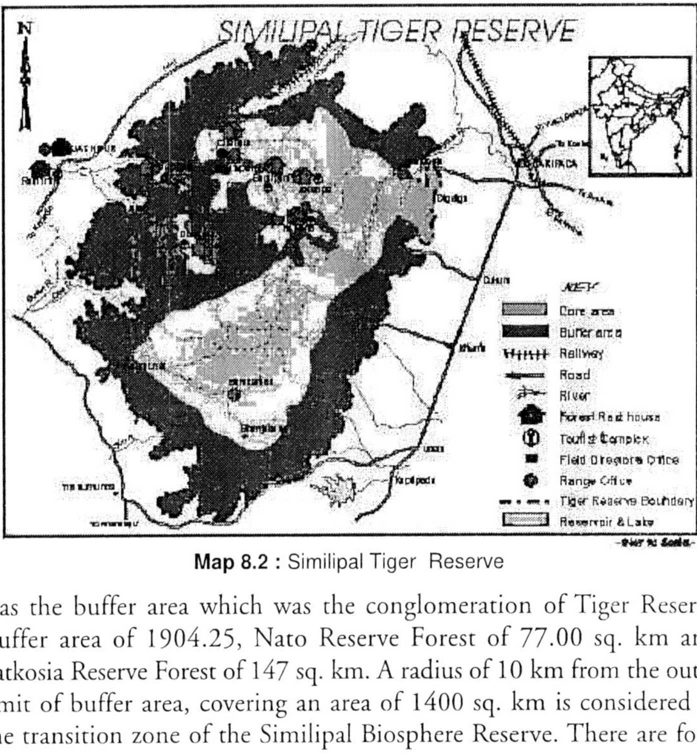

Map 8.2 : Similipal Tiger Reserve

was the buffer area which was the conglomeration of Tiger Reserve Buffer area of 1904.25, Nato Reserve Forest of 77.00 sq. km and Satkosia Reserve Forest of 147 sq. km. A radius of 10 km from the outer limit of buffer area, covering an area of 1400 sq. km is considered as the transition zone of the Similipal Biosphere Reserve. There are four villages in the core zone, 61 villages in the buffer area and 1200 villages in the transition zone.

Table 8.6 : Population Structure of Core Villages in Similipal Biosphere Reserve

Sl. No.	*Village*	*Communities*	*No. of Family*	*Population*		
				Male	*Female*	*Total*
1.	Kabatghai	Ho / kol	4	42	38	80
		Santal	13			
2.	Jamunagarh	Ho/ kol	18	39	47	86
3.	Jenabil	Ho/ kol	27	93	91	184
		Bathudi	1			
4.	Bakua	Ho/ kol	21	44	53	97
Total		84	218	229	447	

Let us compare the situation at Similipal Biosphere Reserves where similar eviction threats are looming over the four core area villages to fulfill the mandate of Biosphere Reserve as they have to be relocated. In the 845.75 sq.km Core area of the Similipal Biosphere Reserve there are four villages, namely, Kabatghai, Jamunagarh, Jenabil and Bakua. In these four core villages there are 84 families and the total population of these village are 447. These villages have 1061.14 acres of land of which 505.19 acres are under cultivation and the rest 555.95 acres are cultivable fallow. They have a very good production of agricultural crops like paddy, wheat, maize, millet and oil seeds. The core area land is very fertile with good facility of natural irrigation which gives them very good crop production. This is why they are mainly reluctant to move out of core area where they apprehend of not getting sufficient land for agriculture as well as pasture for their cattle. The Core area villages produce a good quantity agricultural crop with surplus to sell as most of their lands are capable of double cropping and their dependency on forest is limited to their self consumption only because they do not able to sell it to the market due to remoteness of the villages. In Similipal the high level of agricultural crop production is attained by adopting a somewhat different strategy from Pachmarhi. In Similipal they developed terraced and irrigated land and used high yielding variety of seeds to achieve a near surplus subsistence economy based on agricultural production.

Table 8.7 : Population Structure in Simlipal BR in 2006

Sl. No.	*Villages*	*Persons*	*No. of Family*	*Male*	*Female*	*Sex Ratio*	*Family Size*
1.	Kabatghai	80	17	42	38	904	4.70
2.	Jamunagarh	86	18	39	47	1205	4.77
3.	Jenabil	184	28	93	91	978	6.57
4.	Bakua	97	21	44	53	1204	4.61
	Total	447	84	218	229	1050	5.32

Table 8.8 : Per Capita Crop Production and Per Capita Land Holding

Village	*Per Capita Land Holding (in acre)*	*Per Capita Production of Crops (in Quintal)*
Kabatghai	1.97	5.91
Jamunagarh	3.59	10.21
Jenabil	2.37	7.66
Bakua	1.81	8.00

Story of Relocation of a Core Area Village at Similipal Biosphere Reserve

According to a report submitted by Pushpanjali Satpathy and Gunjan Jain on behalf of an Orissa based NGO, all the families (in total 69 at the time of displacement in March 2010) from the village Jenabil were relocated to Ambadiha, a village in Udala block of Mayurbhanj district. Ecology and landscape of the resettled village was in sharp contrast to the original villages. Jenabil was very very green with seasonal harvesting of crop and well irrigated land and the people were able to collect NTFPs from the forest for their livelihood subsistence. But in the new location where they were resettled there was hardly any green and the totally barren land with no water makes subsistence agriculture impossible. The people had no other alternative but to rely on the daily wage labour under NREGA or even more worst ending up as a migrant labour.

The displacement of the Jenabil tribals is a blatant violation of the Forest Rights Act, 2006 and the Wildlife (Protection) Amendment Act, 2006. Section 4(2)(d) of the Forest Rights Act, 2006 states the following as one of the conditions to be met prior to any relocation from a critical wildlife habitat :

> *"A resettlement or alternatives package has been prepared and communicated that provides a secure livelihood for the affected individuals and communities."*
>
> While Section 4(2)(f) provides that *"No resettlement shall take place until facilities and land allocation at the resettlement location are complete as per the promised package."*

Section 38(V)4 of Wildlife (Protection) Amendment Act 2006 states :

> *Subject to the provisions contained in this Act, the State Government shall while preparing a Tiger Conservation Plan, ensure the agricultural, livelihood, developmental and other interests of the people living in tiger bearing forests or a tiger reserve.*

Section 4(5) of the Forest Rights Act, 2006 states :

> *Save as otherwise provided, no member of the forest dwelling Scheduled Tribe or other traditional forest dweller shall be evicted or removed from the forest land under his occupation till the recognition and the verification procedure is complete.*

There are a large number of cases where forest officials have turned down FRA claims saying they are not applicable in the wildlife sanctuaries and national parks. In Similipal the forest department went a step further and barred NGOs and other organizations to intervene and help the tribals of Jenabil to file their FRA claims. The Village Level Worker (VLW) once managed to give the claim forms to the villagers but later there was no proper follow up. Hence, there was no filing of claims, verification and recognition of rights prior to the displacement of the tribals which is a clear violation of the Act.

Marine Biosphere Reserve and Marine Protected Areas

There has been a worldwide concern over the damage caused to the coastal areas due to man-made and natural changes. Various developmental activities which are being undertaken in the coastal areas and in surrounding seas have resulted in the degradation of marine biodiversity. Worldwide awareness for the creation of Marine Biosphere Reserves has increased considerably due to human depredation in many coastal areas because many important and unique aquatic plant and animal species have been extinct and whatever remains, need to be conserved and managed for posterity.

Marine Biosphere Reserves are, in a way, different from the terrestrial ones, but the priorities for their conservation are no less urgent than their terrestrial counter-parts. The preservation of marine ecosystems, otherwise destroyed by human activity, is generally less of an issue than it is for terrestrial conservation and the needs of marine conservation can not be readily addressed by models developed for terrestrial ecosystems, which are based on excluding or severely limiting human access in managed areas. This is in contravention to the philosophy of Biosphere Reserves developed as part of the UNESCO Man and the Biosphere Programme. UNESCO spirit of giving some space to the local people in biodiversity conservation appears particularly appropriate to Marine Biosphere Reserves, as it focuses on managing human activities and impacts within the sustainable capacity of the ecosystem.

The following are the aquatic eco-systems which are declared as Biosphere Reserves:

1. Gulf of Mannar Biosphere Reserve (Tamil Nadu)
2. Sunderbans Biosphere Reserve (West Bengal)
3. Great Nicobar Biosphere Reserve (Andaman and Nicobar Islands)
4. North Andaman Biosphere Reserve (Andaman and Nicobar Islands)
5. Little Rann of Kuchchh Reserve (Gujarat)

Apart from these five declared Marine Biosphere Reserves some more aquatic ecosystem along the Indian coast line have been identified as Marine Protected Areas (MPA). These are as follows :

(a) Malvan (Maharashtra)
(b) Gulf of Khambhat (Gujarat)
(c) Chilka Lake (Orissa)
(d) Lakshadweep (U.T.)
(e) Bhitarkanika (Orissa)

Gulf of Mannar Biosphere Reserve

The Gulf of Manner (GOM), the first Marine Biosphere Reserve in

India, is located at the southeastern tip of India off the coast of Tamil Nadu, extends from Rameswaram to Kanyakumari covering an area of 10,500 sq. kilometres in the Indian part of the territorial water of the Gulf of Mannar between India and Sri Lanka. The Gulf of Mannar Biosphere Reserve (GOMBR) coast is abutting 4 districts such as Ramanathapuram, Tuticorin, Tirunelbeli, and Kanyakumari. Starting from the southern tip of Dhanuskodi it extends up to Kanyakumari covering a shore line of 514 kilometres. The 560 sq. kms. of Core Area is comprised 21 tiny uninhabited islands ranging in size from 0.25 ha to 130 ha located offshore between a distances from one to four kilometres along the 140 kilometres stretch of coast line from Rameswaram to Tuticorin. Established in the 1980s, this 560 sq. km of Core area is the Gulf of Manner Marine National Park (GOMNP), the first marine national park not only in India but also in all of South and South East Asia. The Reserve has got the distinction of being a globally recognised Biosphere Reserve. The marine biodiversity in the shallow water of the reserve is noted for mangroves, sea weeds and sea grass which is s support system of a very complex ecosystem and provide an ideal breeding ground for a variety of marine animals including endangered marine Mammal Sea Cow or Dugong.

The Buffer Zone is comprised of gulf water to the south of the core area of the Marine National Park and an inhabited coast line to the north up to a distance of 10 km. inland along the 140 km. stretch of coast from Rameswaram to Tuticorin along the GOM National Park. The Transition Zone is not yet demarcated.

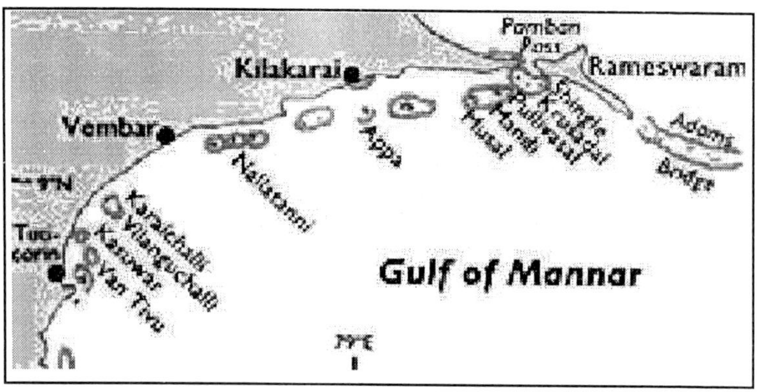

Map 8.3 : Gulf of Mannar

Table 8.9 : Marine District and Coast Length in Gulf of Mannar Biosphere Reserve

Sl. No.		*GOM Districts Coast Type & Length (in km.)*			*Total*
		Palk Bay	*GOM*	*Arabian Sea*	
1	Ramanathapuram	95.8	141.0	–	236.8
2	Tuticorin	–	163.5	–	163.5
3	Tirunelveli	–	48.9		48.9
4	Kanyakumari	–	11.5	60.0	71.5

Source: Fisheries Department, Government of Tamil Nadu

Marine National Parks:

There are twenty-one (21) tiny islands in the core area of the Biosphere Reserve situated within the Marine National Park. Primarily around these 21 islands the villages located on the shoreline carry out fishing activities.

Table 8.10 : Islands in the Gulf of Mannar Biosphere Reserve

Island Group	*Name of Islands*	*Area (Sq.Km)*	*Nearest Coastal Town*	*Distance from nearest Coast Line (Km)*
Mandapam	1. Shingle	0.13	Pamban	4
	2. Krusadai	0.66		3.5
	3. Pullivasal	0.30		3
	4. Poormarichan	0.17		3
	5. Manoliputti	0.02		5
	6. Manoli	0.26		5
	7. Hare (Musal)	1.29		7
Keelakkarai	8. Mulli	0.10	Keelakari	10
	9. Valai	0.10		9
	10. Thalairi	0.75		9
	11. Poovarasanpatti	0.01		8
	12. Appa	0.29		8
	13. Valimunai	0.07		9
	14. Anaipar	0.11		9
Vembar	15. Nallarthanni	1.10	Vembar	10
	16. Pulvinichalli	0.06		8
	17. Uppuchanni	0.30		8
Tuticorin	18. Vilanguchalli	0.01	Tuticorin	15
	19. Karaichalli	0.16		15
	20. Kasuwar	0.20		7
	21. Van Tivu	0.16		6

Table 8.11: Fishing Villages and Population of GOM Coastal Districts

Sl. No.	*Gulf of Mannar Districts*	*No. of Coastal Revenue Villages*	*Population*
1.	Ramanathapuram	184	145635
2.	Tuticorin	21	87381
3.	Tirunelveli	7	24966
4.	Kanyakumari	42	180841
Total254		438823	

Source: Tamil Nadu Marine Fisher folk Census 2008, Department. of Fisheries, Government of Tamil Nadu.

Alternative Livelihood Possibilities

1. Fishing Off Days

This is a cash incentive provided to the fishermen; GOMBRT has been paying a sum of rupees of Rs. 150 to each family per day for not going to sea during the peak fishing seasons. The maximum number of fishing off days that can be availed by a family is limited only to 10. This scheme is operational at the Ramanathapuram district only to preserve the pristine water biodiversity of the Gulf of Mannar.

2. Incentive to Agriculture

Practise of agriculture in the coastal villages of the buffer zone is still at a rudimentary stage due to salinity of soil. Proper irrigation facility and inducement of crop varieties suitable to the saline soil may be introduced to increase the production of agriculture. Reclamation of abundant salt pan by converting it to a cultivable land, especially in the Tuticorin district, may be taken up by the GOMBRT.

3. Horticulture and Plantation

Horticulture and Plantation based industries have got a huge scope of development in the area due to abundance of naturally available raw materials. The following types of products which are already in existence needs to be encouraged under the cottage industry scheme :

(i) *Palm Leaf Basket and Mat Making* : Palm leaf basket and mat are the two main community based industry in the middle and low threat villages where palm plantation is encouraged on a priority basis under the aegis of several Self Help Groups (SHGs).

(ii) *Palm Candy Making* : Palm candy making is another community based industry in the middle and low threat villages where palm plantation is encouraged on a priority basis under the aegis of several Self Help Groups (SHGs). Locally available Charcoal is used for heating in the process making the jaggery and palm candy.

(iii) *Coconut Coir Making Industry* : Coconut trees are abundantly grown in the plantation situated at the middle and low threat villages. Coir is produced from the outer husk of a coconut with the help of a small machine by the SHGs and is sent to other cities for making of mattress.

4. Sea Based Industry

(i) *Artificial Pearl Cultivation* : Cultured pearl is produced by cultivating marine mollusks in an artificial pond near the sea. Deliberately a small sand grain is inserted in the pearl oyster for a few months which in turn develops into a pearl.

(ii) *Production of Ornamental Fishes* : This is a new family based occupation with the help from the local fisheries departments. With the gradual increase of the demand for coloured fish for aquarium from the big cities, the business of ornamental fishes has become very lucrative.

(iii) *Development of Tourism and Water Sports (scuba diving, snorkeling etc.)* : The coral reefs of the Gulf of Mannar and calm sea surface is a very good space for various water sports and adventure tourism. If the infrastructure is properly developed by the tourism department for such venture it would attract tourist both from India and abroad. The revenue generated from such venture could be used in the development landscape and marine biodiversity conservation. The local people could be employed as guide and diving instructors after proper training.

5. Other Occupation

Charcoal Making : For making of charcoal they use an indigenous tree locally called 'karuvel' (*p.juliflora*) which is abundantly grown in the shores of Gulf of Mannar, especially in the Ramanathapuram district. The tree grows in the sandy fallow land where no other species could grow and as such has no timber value.

Conclusion

We observed that how in a Biosphere Reserve situation, the people living inside the core areas evolved their strategy of subsistence economy by adopting various mechanism which are ecologically sustainable and culturally suitable. The restriction on forest exploitation and land alienation leads to a situation of resource crunch, but the tribal folks living inside the core areas did not succumb to the traumatic situation imposed on them. Instead they outsmart the exogenous constraints and evolved and developed a stable agricultural economy based on their indigenous way of life.

In Gulf of Mannar marine Biosphere Reserve the situation is totally different since the core area, i.e. the Gulf of Mannar Marine National Park is situated in the sea and the islands in it are devoid of any human habitation. Only the buffer zone of 10 km from the shore line has the human habitation but the fishing communities who are living on the shore are dependent on the sea resource for their livelihood and they extensively utilized the marine resource at their disposal. Here the conservation challenge is not to displace the people but to restrict and gradually stop the exploitation of marine resource so that the marine biodiversity would be protected for the posterity.

It is imperative that conservation of forest and critical wild life (including tiger) habitat are essential not only for the animals but also for the humans. At the same time after the enactment of Forest Rights Act (FRA, 2006) which also has provision for Critical Wild Life Habitat and Panchayats Extension to the Scheduled Areas Act (PESA, 2006) the implementation of 'Yellowstone Model' (Pimpert and Pretty, 1995) which advocates that local people living inside the Parks need to be evicted for biodiversity conservation, has become toothless. Besides, this absolute protectionist approach would create 'conservation refugees'. Biosphere Reserves are the best approach to accommodate both the livelihood concern of the local people and the conservation of biodiversity. Biosphere Reserve Model promote integrated community based conservation by including local people in the decision make as a stakeholder in forest conservation. The inclusiveness of the BR approach with its zonation earmarked definitive space for wild life habitat, livelihood generation for the local people and for scientific research and monitoring.

REFERENCES

District Statistical Handbook. 2006-07. Ramanathapuram District, Directorate of Statistics, Tamil Nadu.

Ghosal, S., 'Management of Natural Resources in the core area villages of Pachmarhi Biosphere Reserve', in S. Sengupta. ed.., *Man-in-Biosphere : A case study of Pachmarhi Biosphere Reserve.* pp. 147-167. New Delhi: Gyan Publishers, 2007.

Mathur, P.R.G., *Ecology, Technology and Economy— Continuity and Change among the fisherfolk of Kerala,* Jaipur : Rawat Publications, 2008.

Melkani, V.K., *Conservation and Sustainable Utilisation of Biodiversity of the Gulf of Mannar Region,* GOMBRT Publication No. 5. Ramanathapuram, Gulf of Mannar Biosphere Reserve Trust, 2007.

Naganathan, V., *Marine Resesource Management through Peoples' Participation,* GOMBRT Publication No. 5. Ramanathapuram. Gulf of Mannar Biosphere Reserve Trust, 2007.

Pachmarhi Biosphere Reserve, Vols. I and II. Environmental Planning and Co-ordination Organisation (EPCO), Bhopal, 2001.

Patro, S.N. and M.K. Misra, eds., *Conservation of Similipal in its Wilderness,* Orissa Environmental Society, Bhubaneswar, 1985.

Patterson, J.A., *Vellapathi Fishing Village of Gulf of Mannar,* SDMRI Research Publication No. 2. Tuticorin, Suganthi Devadason Marine Research Institute. 2002.

Pimpert, M.P. and J.N.Pretty, *Parks, People and Professionals : Putting participation into protected Area : the law of mother Earth*. Geneva: United Nations Research Institute for Social Development, 1995.

Raychoudhuri, B., *The Moon and Net,* Kolkata : Anthropological Survey of India, 1980.

Satpathy, Pushpanjali and Gunjan Jain, *Tiger protection, Maoism and the Forest Rights Act: the story of Jenabil Out of the green, into the dust,* Unpublished report, 2010.

Singh, K.S. *People of India ; Tamil Nadu State*. Madras : Affiliated East-West Publication, 1997.

9

Biosphere Reserve Management in Similipal Biospheres of Orissa

Some Emerging Issues

D. Debnath, P. Bhattacharya and *K. N. Krishnakumar*

Researched Area : Simlipal Biosphere Reserve

The Similipal Biosphere Reserve (SBR), blessed with natural treasure, is located in the northern district of Mayurbhanj district. Similipal is in the eastern end of the Eastern Ghats and classified in the Chhotanagpur biotic province of the Mahanadian bio-geographical region. Besides its rich floral and faunal biodiversity, landscapes and waterfalls unique feature of Similipal is its densely forested hill ranges with sal trees. Its biological characteristics got international recognition as one of the first nine prime areas for tiger conservation programme and the sixth largest biosphere in the country. The SBR is also abode for many tribes like Khadia, Bhatudi, Kolha, Bhumija, Munda with rich culture with different dialects and festivals which are cynosure for attracting anthropologists and social scientists.

Government of India has notified the Similipal forest as biosphere reserve on the 22nd June, 1994. It comprises the entire Similipal Sanctuary (core and buffer together), the adjoining Nato and Satkoshia Reserve Forests forming additional buffer and a belt of approximately 10 km width all-around the entire buffer designated as the 'transition zone'. The total area is 5569 sq. kms. The Similipal hill ranges, a densely forested area, constitute the core and a part of the buffer zones of the BR. There are also 65 villages within these two zones including four in the core zone.

The transition zone of the Reserve has 1200 villages whose total population is about 4.5 lakhs. The tribals constitute about 73 per cent of this population. The forests and the biodiversity resources to a great extent sustain the livelihood of these people. The forest and wildlife in the sanctuary, and the human population and cattle living in close proximity impact on each other. The Management Action Plan for the BR seeks to put emphasis on suitable programmes of eco-development in the transition zone and also to a limited extent in buffer zone, to promote various alternative livelihood options, and thereby to reduce people's pressure on the forests (Government. of Orissa 1996, Census of India 1991). Against this backdrop the present study tries to assess the socio-economic conditions and development situations of the people living in the Reserve. It further tries to identify the emerging issues which are experiencing by local people as well as management authority of SBR with possible suggestion for future management. But to get a real picture on SBR, an historical analysis would be necessary before going to a detailed analyses on socio-economic status of local inhabitants as well as development situation within the reserve.

Forests and its Conservation History

Mayurbhanj was a feudatory state till 1949 and Similipal constituted roughly 5/8th of this ex-state area. Most of the forest-related activities of the ex-state were concentrated in this area. A preliminary working plan for the forests of Mayurbhanj state was prepared during the latter half of 1890s. By that time Similipal constituted 88 per cent of the total Reserve Forest area of this ex-state. The rulers of Mayurbhanj utilised the timber wealth of this forest for commercial purposes, and it was with this objective that they even established railway communication to exploit this wealth. However, there was always a pressure on their part for systematic exploitation of the trees and rampant cutting was not permitted. The rulers, like their counterparts in other princely states, were fond of gaming and used Similipal for recreation purposes. At that time, population was scarce and wild beasts used to create havoc in many areas. Members of the royal family took it as their responsibility to save the people from the dreaded beasts and besides shooting the latter themselves, also rewarded others who showed such kind of bravery (Das and Das, 1997). Besides, *kheda* or elephant-catching operations were also carried out by the authorities inside the forest. After the merger of Mayurbhanj in 1949, the Forest Department of the Government of Orissa took over the administrative control of the Similipal Reserve Forest. The strict administrative control of feudatory rulers was no more and people were given right on trees in their homestead lands. This created an opportunity for the local people as well as other stakeholders for indiscriminate exploitation of timber trees and Similipal also suffered its impact.

Simultaneously, encroachments in the forest increased and liberal issue of shooting permits also created a menace. Moreover, with increasing communication facilities, threats to the forest wealth of Similipal also increased significantly. In view of the wildlife management of this forest, the Government created a Forest Division at Jashipur under the name 'National Park Division', in 1956. However, the strength of this Division was insufficient to control and monitor the vast area. In 1973, Similipal was declared as a Tiger Reserve under 'Project Tiger'. The National Park Division merged into this project the regional headquarters of which has since then been located at Baripada (Das and Das, 1997).

Methodology Adopted

The methodology of the study was based on the following two broad phases: (i) Secondary data collection: The first phase was a review of the already documented studies on the subject. (ii) Primary data collection: Data collection from forest dependent households, traders and forestry institutions on livelihood of local people, village level institution, access to resources and level ownership as well as extent of dependency.

Sample size for the study varies according to zones. All the four villages in the core zone has been selected. In buffer zone, the total number sampled villages are wás 12 out of 61 villages. Out of 1200 villages in transitional zone, 120 villages were selected and villages were divided into eco-development and non-eco-development villages.

In core zone the sampling size is 20 per cent of the total number. of households in each village. In buffer zone the sampling size was 10 per cent of the total no. of households in the sampled villages. In transitional area the sampling size is 5 per cent of the total number of the households in the village where the number of households is more than 50 but in the case of village where the number of households is less than 50, 10 per cent of total households were selected.

To collect data on socio economic as well as development status, questionnaires have been prepared and administered in each sampled households in each zone. Personal interviews and group discussion, key informant interviews, workshops informal discussion has also been undertaken.

ANALYSES

Socio-Economic Conditions

In Core Area

The core area is inhabited by the tribal peoples with ethnic diversities within the natural surroundings and undulations. The people are living in the hutments made of the forest resources. Their average household size and sex ratio is comparatively higher than other two zones. The educational facility is poor and the literacy rate is very low (Table A.1). Only one village Kovatghai (out of four) has got a primary school which is up to third standard. The regularity of the teacher is almost nil in school. Only the male children are encouraged for education. The drop-out rate is very high. The basic educational support comes from the tribal residential school. Overall attendance is very poor due to extreme poverty. Most of the kids are involved in household duties, grazing of cattle and low parent motivation is also a factor for poor attendance. Their extreme poverty, unavailability of the schools, remoteness of the tribal inhabitation, lack of knowledge of government schemes and facilities and sense of self-satisfaction towards their present life-style are some of the basic causes behind the low literacy rate.

Villagers mainly depend on rainfed agriculture. Productivity of yields is very low. During lean season villagers migrate to different parts for wage employment. The inhabitants belong to small and medium categories of farmers. They depend upon the natural precipitation for their irrigation purposes. However NTFPs, mainly resin and honey, have been regarded as supplementary source of income. But only half of the population are involved in the collection of NTFPs. Villagers cannot able to sell their agriculture produce and NTFPs due to absence of network of transport and markets. Livestock has been increasing with the increase of the population. This degrades the grass land meant for wild herbivorous within the vicinity of core villages. Animal husbandry and wage earning (NTFP selling for few people) are the main sources of cash income for them. The problem of unemployment is also prevailing. The forest department gives them work for 15 to 30 days in year. They get better wage in the governmental jobs. But the private wage employers exploit them. They usually get employment for approximately 150 days a year and for rest of the time they remain unemployed. Such situation leads to low income and low purchasing capacity. The average annual income in most of the villages shows the abject poverty. Their habitual consumption of country liquor consumes the lion's portion of the income. Forest department (FD) provides employment for its infrastructure development works or repairing of existing infrastructure. FD is also assisting matric-passed adults to get driving licences by giving them training. All the households collect daily requirement of fuel-wood, fodder and small timber from the surrounding forest resources. The collection of the fuel-wood per household ranges from 50 to 75 kgs. The number of medicinal species collected by them are comparatively less.

In Buffer Area

The people are living in the same natural surrounding with undulations as found in the core zone. This area is predominantly inhabited by the tribals peoples with ethnic diversities in the same nature as we find in the core area (Table A.2). The people are living in the hutments made of the forest resources. Their average household size and sex ratio is comparatively higher. The educational facility is better and the literacy rate is medium. Fifty per cent of the villages have the schools. But the literacy rate is comparatively low. Only the male sections are encouraged for education. The drop-out rates is higher. The teachers are found irregular in school. So in one year the teacher/student ratio has been from 1:17 to 1:13. The basic educational support comes from Employment Guarantee School, Primary Schools, High Schools and Ashram Schools. Over all their attendance is very poor due to the school is far away from their habitation. Hence, most of the kids involved in household duties, grazing of cattle and low parent motivation and a factor for poor attendance. Their extreme poverty, unavailability of the schools in the buffer area, remoteness of their inhabitation is some of the basic causes behind the low literacy rate.

Most of the people engaged in agriculture. In the absence of irrigation facility villagers have to depend on rainfed agriculture. People usually migrate to adjacent areas for employment during lean season. The inhabitants are mainly marginal farmers. They depend upon the reservoir filled up by natural precipitation for their irrigation purposes. Sale of NTFPs is important source of income for villagers. The people are found to collect more species of medicinal plants in number and quantity than other area. Livestock increased with population increase degrading the grass land. Animal husbandry, wage labour and NTFP selling are the main sources of cash income for them. The selling rate of the livestock at the door-step is comparatively low. Hence they do not get much profit from animal husbandry. The problem of unemployment is also prevailing. Villagers get employment in forest departmental works. There is wage differentials in government and private engagement.The government rates of daily wage are Rs 55/- (revised by forest department) for both man and woman but local rates much less Rs.25 and Rs.20 respectively for male and female. All the villagers inside the buffer zone have been registered under National Rural Employment Guarantee Scheme (NREGS). Their sources of income ranges from agriculture, selling of cattle and poultry, selling of non-timber forest products (NTFPs) and wage earning. Their habitual consumption of country liquor spends the lion's portion of the income. FD is assisting matric-passed adults to get driving licences by giving them training. All the households are found to meet up the daily requirement of fuel-wood, fodder and small timber by collection from the surrounding forest resources.

In Transitional Area

The villages in the Transitional area are spread in the vast plain land. The populations are almost equally divided into male and female. The sex ratio varies in wide ranges from 527 to 1519, with the average of 974. The zone is predominantly populated by the Scheduled Tribes with very small percentage of Scheduled Caste and Other Backward classes. Housing pattern is the same as the two previous zones with the few houses are cemented. The literacy rate is better as the educational facilities are better compared to other zones. Hence the good percentages of the students are seen at all the educational levels, viz. primary, secondary, high school and college in the diminishing trend. Female literacy is much higher compared to other zones. Fifty six per cent villages have primary school facilities, which have been established by Tribal Welfare Department, District Education Departments. The children are seen to the Ashram Schools, but many children do not get the seats due to limited number of seats in the Ashram Schools. Due to transportation problems the school's authority does not supply regularly mid-day meals or the medicines to the school children.

The most interesting feature is that the average income in the household is comparatively less. The contribution of the earning from NTFPs to the household income is higher than other two previous zones. The majority of the populations are dependent on the wage earning. But the man-days created in the zone are comparatively less. As estimated they get in average 70 to 100 days. Hence there is a trend of seasonal migration to the nearest towns or cities. The per capita average land holding is lesser in comparison to other zones. The landless people in considerable numbers are observed. Majority of the farmers are coming in the category of small farmers. However, due to watershed activities the people of the transitional zone are getting better irrigation facilities. Though the animal husbandry is a good source of income due to market facilities, but the livestock they cannot domesticate the larger numbers due to lack of grass-lands or availability of fodder. They meet up the needs of the fodder from the jungle areas. The commercialization of some species like '*sal*' leaves, honey, '*kusum*' seed, resins are more profound due to proximity and accessibility of the local market and government traders. Hence the people are involved in the larger extent. The people earn a considerable amount in selling of fuel woods. The resource availability and the consumption of the small timber are in the decreasing trend in this zone. The awareness of the utility of medicinal plants is comparatively less, though the conservation of diversity of species is observed.

Development Level

The village institutions status and development situation discussed below:

In Core Zone

The villagers in the core area are not found in eco-development activities in the fuller extent. Their involvements in the community-based institutions are seen, but not uniformly in all the four core villages. Various diseases like malaria, anaemia and malnutrition are continued to decrease their work efficiency. Malaria is major concern inside the core area because each and every member of every household suffers from it every year. No primary health centre is found in the villages of this zone. But the medical facilities are provided by the anganwadi health workers and medical camps are organized by the Forest Department. The inaccessibility to core area is also the one of the reason for their present situation. The people in the core area are not satisfied with the drinking water facilities, sewage system and sanitation facilities. The various institutions such as bank, school, police station, health centre, post office are 20 to 65 kms away from the villages. Lack of education facilities often leads to their exploitation by different people like contractor engaged by Government, ration shop dealers and traders in market. FD has initiated some programmes for improvement of health conditions of tribal people by organizing health camps. Tribal people inside the core area are getting ration on subsidized rates through various schemes like BPL, Antyodaya, Anna Yojana and ration for aged people under BPL scheme. People get 16 kgs of rice and 4 litres of kerosene whereas they get 32 kgs of rice under Antyodaya, Anna Yojana. All the people are registered and some got cards under employment guarantee scheme but yet to get employment. This scheme guarantees the job for 90 days for one member of each household. Tribals are expanding their agricultural land by encroaching and cutting of trees on the plain area of village forest which come under jurisdiction of Panchayat.

It is interesting to note that the tribal people are now concerned with the better health, infrastructure, better education facilities, employment and capacity building. The people in the core area now realize the role potential agents for awareness generation, knowledge sharing and imparting information. The survey shows that forest officials are most effective in this regard. Lack of awareness and knowledge of local families residing within the park area about their entitlements create various conflicts and issues. The people can identify the factors responsible for the changing perspectives of livelihoods from local tradition to current stage.

In Buffer Zone

The villagers in this area are not found in eco-development activities to the fuller extent. Their involvements in the community-based institutions vary. They also participate in the Panchayat and School executive committees. Some Civil Society Organizations (CSOs) or Non-Governmental Organizations (NGOs) are working in the watershed management, herbal cultivation and rural employment through SHG formation. The people express their satisfaction with the forest conservation due to employment and micro-credit. Various diseases like malaria, diarrhoea and malnutrition are continued to decrease their work efficiency. More than 80 per cent of the diseases are caused by the lack of sanitation facilities. Excepting very few villages no medical facilities in the village itself are available. People have to walk down considerable distance (i.e 3 to 60 km). But the medical facilities are provided by the anganwadi health workers. FD has initiated some programmes for improvement of health conditions of tribal by organizing health camps. Tribals inside the buffer area are getting ration on subsidized rates through various schemes like BPL, Antyodaya Anna Yojana and ration for aged people under BPL scheme. Children are given polio drops and vaccination of the diseases like measles, diphtheria and T.B. They get the drinking water from hand pump, open well and river. No village has sanitation facilities, though villagers express the willingness to have these in the house premises. Excepting in one village no villages have the post office. The various institutions such as bank, school, police station, health centre and post office are far away distance from the villages. Lack of education led to their exploitation by contractor of government ration shop (PDS system) and traders in market. Fuel-wood head loading and cycle loading from STR is a huge business in the buffer area and a large number of families are involved in the same.

The tribal people are now concerned with the better health, infrastructure, better education facilities, employment and capacity building. The people in the buffer area can realize the potential agents such as Non-Governmental Organizations, Teachers, Women groups, SHGs, Forest or Panchayat Officials for awareness generation, knowledge sharing and imparting information etc. The people can identify the factors responsible for the changing perspectives of livelihoods from local tradition to current stage. Tribal are expanding their land by encroaching and cutting of trees on the plain area of village forest which come under jurisdiction of panchayat. During the focus group discussion in village Barheipani villagers said that a teacher has given contract for performing his job to teach the students by involving a person.

In Transitional Zone

The people are involved in forest conservation activities. One member from each household is the member of forest conservation committee, wherever the committee exists. In this zone like other zones the malaria is a prevalently occurred, which followed by the malnutrition among the children and anemia among the women. Due to poor personal hygienic conditions, the leukoria and cough and cold are found in larger frequency. Most of the villages in this zone are deprived of medical facilities. The children are benefited from the vaccination facilities provided by the health and forest officials. Most of the villages have the hand-pump, but they prefer to drink water from open-wells. In some villages there are electricity and telephone facilities are available. As the data suggest that in the average household income the contribution of Wage earning is only 6 per cent. So the 90 per cent of the households give the thrusts on the employment generation, followed by better infrastructure development and skill enhancement. The potential change agents are same as observed in the buffer zone, but the contribution of Panchayat and Forest Officials in awareness generation, knowledge sharing and imparting information about their entitlements are significant and effective, which is followed by community-based organizations. Majority people in the transitional zone are interested for natural resource-based micro-enterprises and they give the importance of NTFP processing units, followed by kitchen garden and agro-forestry. For the enterprise development they suggest knowledge and skill development, mainly SHG formation, pest management, effective marketing and inputs for cultivation and so on.

Emerging Issues

From the comparative analyses of various management zones some major issues have been emerged which are as follows:

Park Management Issues: Core and Buffer Areas

1. There is an increase of cattle population in core and buffer area, which has been doubled since 1997.
2. The grass land is meant for wild herbivorous but over grazing by the increasing domestic livestock causes the food scarcity for the wildlife.
3. The forest land is converted into agricultural lands by the villagers, which is supported to be regularized by the Panchayat.
4. Lack of coordination between forest officials and the members of community institutions is observed.
5. Lack of interests and motivations of the local people occurs for management of the SBR.
6. The number of forest official are less in comparison to the vast areas, forest beats are spread over large areas. Within the sanctuary area vehicles are not provided to the forest officials. The forests officials are not very serious due to their lack of motivation in discharging responsibilities prolong stay in remote and malaria prone areas.

7. Loss of bio-diversity occurs due to cultural practices like *Akhand Shikar.*
8. The conflicts between the people and the forest departments emerged as the forest department are not allowing to construct canals for the irrigation purpose in the core zone.
9. There is a common practice of girdling of the trees in the sanctuary area for acquiring the forest land for agricultural purposes.
10. Relocation of the village in core area has been a great challenge for stopping and checking smuggling and poaching activities.

Socio-Economic Issues

1. Literacy level and educational level among the women is very low in comparison to their malefolks.
2. The low literacy rate is due to their extreme poverty, remoteness, lack of awareness of government scheme.
3. Rain-fed agriculture with traditional technology do not provide sufficient yield required for daily need. This forced local people to migrate other areas for employment during lean season.
4. The problem of unemployment is also prevailing. The FD gives them work for 15-30 days per year and private farmers provide them work for 30-50 days per year which is not sufficient to sustain daily needs.
5. The lion's portion of their income was spent on their habitual consumption of country liquor.
6. High incidences of various diseases like malaria, malnutrition, anaemia, leukemia etc. reducing their work efficiency.
7. Health centres are comparatively less in number in all the three zones.
8. They do not get any access to various institutions like, bank, post office, schools and police stations. Lack of

awareness and knowledge of local people residing within and the fringe area about their entitlements which create various conflicts and issues.

9. Lack of education leads to their exploitation by contractor of government, ration shop dealers and traders in market.
10. Lack of personal hygienic condition and unavailability of toilet and sanitation facilities.

Livelihood Issues

1. Agriculture is the main occupation but there is lack of application of modern technology in all the three zones. That is why agriculture produces are only for their own consumption and not for sale.
2. Animal husbandry and wage employment are the two main sources of their subsistence. They are not getting the profit by selling their product due to absence of linkage with market in core and buffer areas whereas in the transitional zone fodder and grazing problems are prevalent.
3. Most common NTFPs for sell are '*sal*' leaves, '*kusum*' seeds, '*mahua*' seeds and flowers and honey but people of only transitional area and some villagers of buffer area are able to sell due to market access.
4. The villagers have the habit of collecting the species of medicinal plants but due to lack of processing and value addition they are not generating income by marketing the product.
5. Wage earning in the private sectors exploit as they are paid very nominal wage.
6. Most people depend on sale of firewood. As the income level very low alternative livelihood strategies is difficult to achieve.
7. In the transitional zone NTFPs have good contribution in the household income but there are no initiatives for enhancement of resources by cultivation.
8. Awareness of the utility of medicinal plants is comparatively

less, though the conservation of diversity of species is observed.

Policy and Legal Issues

1. The forest officials manipulate the laws for the protection of the sanctuary areas to harass local people which are potential source of conflict.
2. Lack of dissemination of policy in connection with Park Management and Biosphere is found.
3. Most of the EDC are defunct due to the lack of funds, awareness, knowledge and dissemination of information
4. There is lack of 'real participation' as they are not engaged in the planning, implementation and monitoring, evaluation of the programme in the SBR.
5. Officials of Panchayat make underpayment to villagers in various emploument generation schemes like NREGS.
6. The fund allotment for livelihood generation amongst the members of the SHGs for the upliftment of the women is always meagre.
7. The women representation in the formal organization is less in number as suggested by the policy of women empowerment.
8. Women are not engaged in protection, management and development of the BR due to cultural barriers.

Ways Ahead

To address the above mentioned issues for better management of BR and enhancement of livelihood to reduce dependency on forest resources the following recommendations have emerged for active consideration of SBR management.

Perspective Planning and Management Action Plan

Different types of programme under eco-development and social welfare activities should be framed in accordance with the five-year perspective plan would be prepared through the participatory process by conducting village meetings in three zones. Accordingly Management Action Plan should be evolved instead of taking up of activates on piece-meal as found at present.

Attitudinal Development and Confidence Building

To make all such programmes viable and sustainable, the proper attitude would be developed among local communities to enhance their interests and keenness to run. This can be achieved by providing them with the knowledge on modern technology. For example, bee-keeping and honey processing programme may not be viable in SBR because the participants have little knowledge about technical part. In addition, the beneficiaries are not able to keep bees in boxes due to careless attitude. Besides, it is also seen that distribution of boxes are also uneven and people are not interested to do this activity because of their collection habits of straightway from forest as customary practices and also they earn by selling without any investment. The SBR Management should take initiative in micro-enterprise development for their regular income generating activities. In addition, the attitude of forest authority should be changed from authorative to cooperative and local people should be treated as partners of management.

Capacity Building

The SBR management is providing financial support to EDCs for trainings, raw materials and machineries etc. But in many cases, it was found that master trainers hired by these groups were not so much capable to impart good training. FD should take some initiatives in this regard like arrangement of good capacity building instead of giving them money for trainings.

More Effective Institutional Process

More awareness and motivation programmes for active participation of local people by the institutional functioning, i.e. committee activities are required to achieve desired goals instead of mere formation of these committees. Meeting of members of these committees with forest officials at range level should be organized regularly at least in a month, so that their problems and needs could be assessed. These meetings could be served as a major tool to win the confidence of local people. It is very difficult for higher authorities to go to each and every village to identify the issues. Hence various issues or problems can be resolved by inviting them at one place.

Formation of SHG

The number of SHGs should be increased for providing more options in subsidiary and alternative livelihoods and consequently it would give benefits to womenfolks.

Multi-stakeholder Approach

FD should take advice from other developmental departments, NGOs or CSOs in the Mayurbhanj district while planning and implementing the projects so that number of failure projects could be reduced.

Marketing Facilities

The department of forests had taken some very good steps for marketing of products made by SHGs or EDCs. Some more efforts are required for better arrangement for marketing of these products like growers association, so that producers could sell their products in bulk and under one brand name. This can be done in multi-stakeholder participation while motivating other agencies like schools and department of education to give tailoring orders to SHGs which got sewing machines and trainings for this purpose.

Dissemination of Information

For betterment and achievement of the programmes in Similipal, various attempts and approaches are to be made to disseminate programmes to the target groups. Achievements should also be displayed in the form of hoardings and circulating posters and pamphlets.

ANNEXURE

Table A.1 : Comparative Assessment of socio-demography and socio-economic conditions in three zones

Sl. No.	*Criteria*	*Core*	*Buffer*	*Transitional*
1.	Sex ratio	1076	994	974
2.	Average Household	7	5	6
3.	Social Category	ST-100%	ST(majority)	ST-90%,SC-3%, OBC-7%
4.	Housing Pattern	Mud-100%	Mud-100%	Mud-92 per cent ; cemented house-8%
5.	Literates	16.51%	44.79%	42.77%
	Non-literates	83.49%	55.21%	57.33
	Literates: Male	34.47%	18.39%	44.69%
	Literates: Female	3.53%	6.19%	40.8%
6.	Educational Status			
	Primary	77.77%,	47.03%	53.52%
	Secondary	5.5%,	30.81%	29.82%
	High School	11%,	16.76%	12.62%
	College	5.5%	5.41%	4.04%
	School going children out of total	24%	65%	85%
	School going children —Male	86%	65.18%	50%
	School going children —Female	14%	34.84%	50%
	School facility	25%	50%	56%
7.	Agri Productivity	3.18/Acre	3.01/acre	4.7/acre
8.	Average Land Holding	8.4 Acre	3 acre	2.7%
9.	Land Holding Pattern	Semi-medium-33.3% Medium 55.55% Big 11.11%	Land less-0, Marginal 0-1 acre-11.11, Small 1-2 acre-47.22, Semi-medium 2-5 acre-13.89, Medium 5.1-10 acre-13.89, Big >10 acre-13.89	Land less-8.63 Marginal (0-1 acre) -9.96 Small (1-2 acre) -44.25 Semi-medium (2-5 acre)-22.79 Medium (5.1-10 acre) -9.62 Big >10 acre-4.74
10.	Irrigation Sources	Pond, canal, river, monsoon	Pond, River, canal, stop dam and monsoon	Monsoon-37% River-25%, ponds-15%,canal from forest hill/dam-12% and stop dam used by 11 per cent villages.
11.	NTFP Species	Sal -10% Kusum-10% Resin-40% Honey -40%	Sal leaves-68.06 % Kusum-29.17 % Mahua-45.83 % Honey-23.61 % Dhoopa-5.56 % Sawana-1.39% Mahula Fruit-8.33% Resin-5.56%	sal leaves-88.90 kusum-33.29 mahua-46.93 honey-2.40 sawana-1.00 mahula fruit-3.00 Resin-21.00 Chara-43.57 Tula-34.37 Harida-33.29

(Contd...)

Table A.1 :(Contd...)

12.	NTFP collection	50 per cent people collect NTFPs	83%	77.56%
13.	Market availability	Not available	Not available (local haat)	Near by urban and suburban areas
14.	Animal Husbandry			
	Avg. cattle/household	27.87	16.19	11.19
	Selling rate	100/poultry Goat-800-1500 Buffalo-2000-3000 Cow-2000-3000 at doorstep	100/poultry Goat-800-1500 Buffalo-2000-3000 Cow-2000-3000 at doorstep	100/poultry Goat-800-1500 Buffalo-2000-3000 Cow-2000-3000 at doorstep
15.	Wage rate	Rs. 25-30 on private farm & Rs. 52 from govt. per person	Rs. 25-30 on private farm & Rs.52 from govt.	Rs 25-30 on private farm & Rs 52 from govt.
	Nature of work	Agri, Forest infrastructure	Agri, Forest infrastructure	Agri, Forest infrastructure and contact labour in nearby urban and suburban areas
	Availability of work	15 days for govt. & 30-50days on private farm	15 days for govt. & 30-50 days on private farm	100 to 120
16.	Average Annual Income	10180	13607	6950
	NTFP	8%	13%	65 %
	Animal husbandry	11%	10%	10%
	Agriculture	73%	37%	19%
	Wage earning & other sources	8%	40%	6%
17.	Forest Utility			
	Small timber	87.5%	84.25%	60%
	Fuel Wood	100%	100%	100%
	NTFP	50%	83%	77.56%
	Fodder & Cane	Fodder-100% Cane - 25%	Fodder - 88% Cane - 6.66%	48%
	Collection of Medicinal Plants	78% Bhuichampa, Agnijal, Patalgarud, Gutkodika	Agnijal-44.44 per cent Patalgarud-18.51% Gangasiuili-55.55%	Gangasiuili-37 % Patalgarud -26% Kalibahu-10.% Tulsi-10 %

Table A. 2 : Comparative Assessment of Development situation in three zones

Sl No.	*Criteria*	*Core*	*Buffer*	*Transitional*
1.	Forest Protection and Conservation	EDC-55.5% FPC- 30.5% SHGs-11%	EDC-50 per cent Panchayat 1.5% FPC-5% SHGs-8%	-CFM Committees-(29.22%) EDC Committees-(40%) NGO-(3.38%) SHG-(6.76%)
2.	Prevalent Diseases	Malaria 100% Body ache-11% Stomach Pain-11% Malnutrition-11%	Malaria-93% Fever-13.89% Malnutrition-15.28% Iron Deficiency-4.17% Diarrhea-9.72% Leukoria-2.78%	Malaria-90 Brain fever-1.22 Diarrhoea-10.27 Fever-11.37 Malnutrition-36.40

(Contd...)

Table A.2 :(Contd...)

	Medical Facilities	Not available(only health camps)	8.33% villages get medicines from aganwadi workers with in their villages	6% villages have facilities
	Drinking water sources	River and spring	River, hand-pump, spring	Hand pump-88.33% Open well-83.33% River-35.83% Kuccha wells-18.33% Spring-12.50%
	Closed community sanitation	Not available	Not available	In some villages
	Electricity	Not available	Not available	Electric 25 villages & telephone 13 villages
	Institutions	Not available exept one EGS school		
3	Development on priority	Better health facility-29%, infrastructure-28, education-25%, employment-18%	Better health facility-35%, Infrastructure-32%, education-17%, employment-9%	Better infrastructure-23% better health facility-18% better education facility-17% skill enhancement-18% employment generation-24%
4	NRM based Enterprise	Kitchen garden-45%, Development horticulture-33%, agro-forestry-11% and herbal garden-11%	Kitchen garden-26%, horticulture-16%, agro-forestry-5% and herbal garden-13% any other-36%, not interested-3%, Goatary-1%	Kitchen garden-19%, horticulture-15%, agro-forestry-19% and herbal garden14% Nursery-13% NTFP processing unit-20%
Facility required		Source of QPM-59 %, pest mgt-33% & input for cultivation 8%	Source of QPM-49 %, pest mgt-5% & input for cultivation-36%, SHGs formation skills-3%, marketing skills-7%	Source of QPM-7%, pest mgt-7% & input for cultivation-23%, SHGs formation skills-40%, marketing skills-23%

REFERENCES

Census of India. Mayurbahanj District Gazetteer, Government of India, 1991.

Das, S. and B.P. Das, *Similipal Biosphere Reserve: Genesis of a Historical Reality,* Bhubeneshwar: Orissa Environmental Society, 1997.

Government of Orissa, *Management Plan for Similipal Biosphere Reserve,* December, 1996.

Kumar, P., 'Socio-Economic Conditions with Special reference to common access resources', in *Indian Forester,* 139 (9) pp. 918-988, 2004.

10

Livelihood Concerns and Conservation Prospects in Biosphere Reserves of India

Umesh Kumar

Introduction: Emergence of Biosphere Reserve

The environment, which is rich in biological diversity, offers the broadest range of options for people to rely on for the fulfilment of human survival. Loss of biodiversity influences the local area and its economic bases and social fabric. The experiences of the past few decades have shown that as industrialization and economic development take place in the society, the patterns of production, consumption and the needs change and accordingly changes people's responses to ecosystems. Conservation and sustainable use of biodiversity, hence, are fundamental to sustainable development. This aspect is important as an assessment of biological diversity at world level reveals that Asia is the most threatened continent (Hannah & Lohse, 1993; Mittermeier, 1988). The best approach to understand biodiversity is to look at it in a hierarchical manner in which biological organisms are organized. The smallest unit starts from the diversity contained in the genetic material of individual organisms and then goes on to encompass the biological communities in which species are organized and then to cover the wider ecosystem in which they exist.

Biodiversity is recognized at three levels, viz. genetic, species and ecosystem levels (Fig. 10.1). In all these levels of biodiversity, the components are dynamic in space and time. The genetic composition of species changes over time in response to natural and human induced selection process. The ecosystems strongly respond to external dynamics and internal stresses.

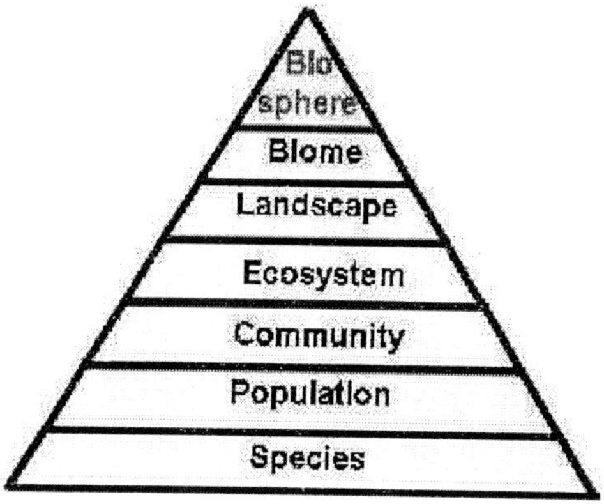

Fig. 10.1: Hierarchy of Biological Organization

Source : Based on IIRS Report (2002) on Biodiversity Characterisation at Landscape Level in North East India.

Ecological systems do not exist as discrete units but represent diverse parts of a natural continuum in the form of landscapes. While biodiversity is usually measured at the species level, maintenance of biodiversity requires management at higher levels of organization, particularly at the landscape scale, which effectively includes human beings also. The ideal is to preserve overall ecosystem vigour, including species diversity. It can be best accomplished by integrating it into the fabric of social, environmental and economic contexts (Marzluff and Hamel, 2001). Here lies the immense implication of the concept of the sustainable development where the issues of the man and environment are integrated together, for a better future for all the living being.

This viewpoint of man-environment linkage needs to be critically seen in the milieu of the Biosphere Reserve. The commencement of Biosphere Reserves goes back to the "Biosphere Conference" organized by UNESCO in 1968. This was the first inter-governmental conference organised to resolve the conservation issue and need for judicious use of natural resources, thereby predicting the present-day notion of sustainable development. This Conference resulted in the launching of the "Man and the Biosphere" (MAB) Programme of UNESCO in 1970. It aimed to facilitate resolution of increasing conflict between the people and the Protected Areas.

The UNESCO's agenda stipulates that Biosphere Reserves should be representative of a bio-geographic province and should have appropriate zoning system with legally constituted and minimally disturbed core zone. In addition, the site should conserve unique and pristine biodiversity, ecosystems and landscape suitable to explore and demonstrate approaches to sustainable development and should be of appropriate size to serve three crucial functions, viz. conservation, development and extension of logistic support. It is proposed to bring at least one representative site within each bio-geographic province of any given country under the network of Biosphere Reserves. All the more, Biosphere Reserves are designated to deal with important questions of reconciling the conservation of biodiversity, the pursuit of economic and social development and maintenance of associated cultural values. Consequently the Government of India, through the Ministry of Environment and Forest, launched in 1986 the Biosphere Reserve Programme. At present there are 14 recognised Biosphere Reserves in India.

Forest Dwellers *vis-á-vis* Biosphere Reserve Management

In the context of India, human populations living within the Biosphere Reserves have always been seen as a permanent threat involving conflicting interests and debate. The continuous discord on the issue at international level, prompted the UNESCO in 1996 to move away from the earlier held view of concentric rings of core, buffer and transition zones, and to adopt a more flexible way of looking upon the local needs and situations. Thus grew the approach of flexibility and creativity within the Biosphere concept, which was suitably widened particularly in view of the constraints posed by the need to see both biodiversity as well as the cultural diversity symbiotically. The advantages of cultural diversity at societal level are felt to be comparable to those accruing from the biodiversity. However, the question remains that while the issues of biodiversity have been addressed at length and caught attention widely, the important theme of cultural diversity has not been touched upon for serious analysis.

The Biosphere Reserves of India are the abode of many indigenous/ traditional communities who remain integral part of the ecosystem, living close to the nature. Living in the areas rich in natural resource, indigenous/traditional communities fulfil many of their livelihood requirements from the rich biodiversity around them. The ecosystems such as forest not only meet a variety of livelihood needs of the forest dwelling societies, through products such as timber and non-timber forest products, but also sustain traditional shifting cultivation and other agricultural practices contributing to the food security of the people within the Biosphere Reserves. In general, included within the management efforts of the Biosphere Reserves are protection of natural resources within Biosphere Reserves from the outside intrusions, and also restricting the use of its resources by the local communities, residing in the Biosphere Reserve and nearby. The concept of sustainable use of resources is being introduced in some areas but due to lack of information and appropriate regulations and also on account of location specific misunderstanding there are obstacles to handle the issue of resource utilization.

Of late emphasis is laid on the involvement and cooperation of the local forest dwellers in eco-development by way of community participation in forest eco-system management/rehabilitation programme (Mishra, 1999). In this respect there has been thinking for linking eco-development issue with the traditional institutions and customary system of land/forest-based activities based on the traditional value system of local communities (Kothari, 1998). The Biosphere Reserve management, therefore, necessitates not only understanding of ecological issues but also the social customs and economic practices including the cultural patterns. In order to achieve this, conservation-linked development strategy has to be based on a value system that people can understand, appreciate and accept. Therefore to ensure peoples, participation properly there is need to employ a 'bottom-up approach'.

The description below is devoted to comprehend the impediments faced in the Khangchendzonga Biosphere Reserve, mainly on account of the anthropogenic pressure around it and also to depict the present status of the forest resources, including the responses of the people and their attitude in the context of conservation efforts.

The Study Area

The present study pertains to the Khangchendzonga Biosphere Reserve in Sikkim (Figure 10.2), where 14 revenue villages lie in the periphery of the Reserve zone in West District. Out of these fourteen villages, two villages — Yuksam and Dubdi — were selected for collection of data. Further, for comparative purposes, Lachen, Gnon-Samdong and Lyngzah villages were selected from North District, for investigation. There is preponderance of Bhutia community in Yuksam while the Nepalese are a major community in Dubdi revenue village. The Lachen village is inhabited primarily by Bhutia, who call themselves Lachenpa. The other two villages, namely Gnon-Samdong and Lyngzah fall within the Dzongu reserve area and are uni-ethnic, inhabited by the Lepcha community.

The principal occupation of the people living in these villages is agriculture supported by animal husbandry. The agricultural pursuit is of subsistence level. With flourishing of tourism in Yuksam and Lachen some people have been engaged in this industry. There is also increasing involvement of local people in the hotels and transport sectors. As a result today only a few villagers pursue traditional occupation.

Objectives

The human population have been living in and around Khangchendzonga Biosphere Reserves since long time. However, in recent year the need to meet the forest dependent requirements of the ever-increasing population has begun to tell on biodiversity health of the Biosphere Reserve. Keeping in mind the above mentioned facts, the following are the main objectives of the present study:

1. To understand and analyses the anthropogenic pressure on biodiversity with reference to fuel wood and timber.

2. To elucidate the people's attitude towards conservation in relation to their willingness to accept and pay for the conservation.

Research Questions

The present study endeavours to answer the following questions:

1. Since the people residing in the core and periphery of Khangchendzonga Biosphere Reserve meets their fuel wood and timber requirements from forest around them, it is, therefore, crucial to find out which plant species are under stress?
2. People's participation is essential for the success of any conservation linked management strategy. Hence, it is essential to know the factors which play critical role in shaping the people concern for conservation in terms of willingness to accept and pay the cost of conservation?

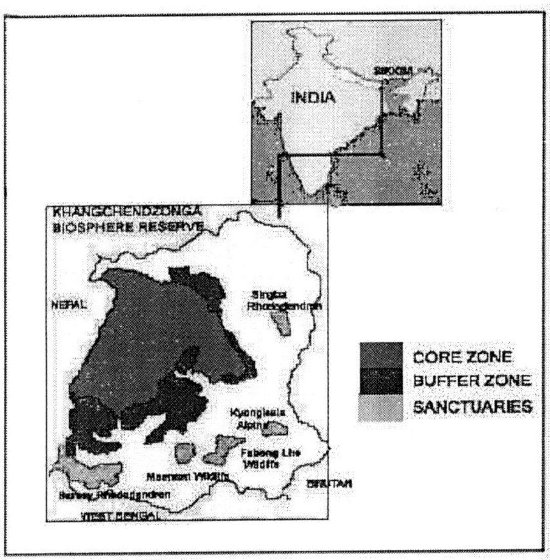

Fig.10. 2 : Khangchendzonga Biosphere Reserve

Research Methodology

Both primary and secondary data have been used to fulfil the objectives of the study. In order to gather the primary data field investigations were carried out in two phases — November to December 2006 and April to May 2007. The data pertaining to fuel wood consumption was culled by adopting a weight survey method based on fuel consumption over a period of 24 hours. In all 55 households were intensively surveyed. During the survey the each sample stakeholder was visited and the head of family was requested to monitor the amount of fuel wood that would be burnt during that particular day. The wood was weighed by spring balance before its use. On the next day, the remaining wood was weighed and deducted from the original bundle to calculate the actual consumption per day. Time spent for fuel wood collection was noted when the members of the households went to the forests. Participatory Rural Appraisal (PRA) technique was used to get information on availability and preference of natural resources. The resources were ranked following pair resource ranking method.

Based on observation on human needs and interference in Biosphere Reserve, a conservation attitude survey (CONVT) was conducted in some of the important fringe area settlements falling in the North and West Sikkim. Contingent valuation method (CVM) within the ambit of ecological economics with emphasis on willingness-to-accept (WTA) and willingness-to-pay (WTP) approach was adopted for these settlements located crucially in respect of Khangchendzonga Biosphere Reserve. This was done to understand the level of concerns of population or the stakeholders pertaining to the environmental conservation activities. The basic premise of the this valuation is that the environmental conservation costs of enforcing Biosphere Reserve principles through restrictions of the use of natural resources shall also be borne by the local population or the stakeholders within their socio-cultural milieu and economic framework of subsistence. To organise the data and to interpret the possible underlying issues, the entire responses to the questionnaire were further categorized into: conservation driven concern, socio-economic driven concerns, willingness-to-accept (WTA) and willingness-to-pay (WTP) concerns and participatory concerns in the Biosphere Reserve concepts. In addition, some qualitative information was gathered on the roles of NGO in conservation efforts through observation and discussion.

Availability and Preference of Species

The land use and land cover data as inferred from the interpretation of the satellite imagery (Chhetri *et al.*, 2002) shows that 30.55 per cent of the area is under snow cover. It is followed by Fir-Rhododendron forest, dense mixed forest and alpine pasture, which occupy 20 per cent, 16 per cent and 12.49 per cent of the area respectively (Table 10.1).

Table 10.1 : Areas under Biosphere Reserve and land use/cover of Khangchendzonga Biosphere Reserve

Sl. No.	*Land use/cover*	*Area*		*Normalized Difference Vegetation Index (NDVI) values*
		%	*Km²*	
1.	Dense mixed/conifer forest	16	419.19	more than 0.2
2.	Open mixed/conifer forest/silver fir-Rhododendron forest	20	523.98	0.2-0.27
3.	Degraded mixed/conifer forest	7.14	187.06	0.12-0.19
4.	Scrub land/forest blank	2.63	68.9	0.05-0.11
5.	Alpine scrub/pasture land	12.49	327.24	
6.	Alpine barren land/barren land	9.92	259.9	0.01-0.04
7.	Snow cover/glaciers	30.55	800.38	
8.	Rivers/streams/lakes/exposed soil	1.27	33.27	less than 0.01
	Total	100	2619.92	

Source : Based on Report of Maharana, I., Rai, S.C., Chettri, N., and Sharma, E. (2000).

Population living close to Biosphere Reserve is highly dependent on forests in the buffer zones, mainly for non-timber forest products (NTFPs), including extraction of medicinal herbs, litter, wild edible fruits, and other minor forest products (MFPs). Although the timber cutting is strictly prohibited, it seems difficult to stop the collection of fodder and fuel wood such as rhododendrons — a keystone species acting as biodiversity indicator of the region. Keeping in mind the aforementioned need of the villagers, a study on the availability and preference of resources for fuel and timber was carried out in the month of November-December, 2006 in Yuksam and Dubdi villages while in Lachen, Linzah and Gnon-Samdong it was carried out in the months of May and June, 2007. Analysis of data and interpretation are provided below.

Species used for Fuel Wood

Fuel wood provides the major proportion of household's energy consumption in the domestic sector, while commercial alternative energy sources contributed very little. The consumption of fuel wood varies amongst stakeholders with respect to different physical and economic factors. Pair-wise ranking of species used as fuel wood in Yuksam and Dubdi villages have been presented in Table 10.2. There are altogether 12 species used as fuel woods. The availability of status of these 12 species suggests that *Alnus nepalensis* (uttis) is most widely available fuel wood followed by *Dendrocalamus sp.* (Bans), *Quercus lamellosa* (Bajrant), *Engelhardtia spicata* (Mahua), and *Viburnum cordifolia* (Assare). The other species are available less widely. But preference-wise, *Quercus lamellosa* is the most preferred fuel wood species followed by *Castanopsis hystrix* (Jat Katus), *Quercus lineata* (Phalanth), *Eurya acuminata* (Jhinguni) and *Viburnum cordifolia*. The least preferred species is *Prunus cerosoides* (Panyun). A corelation between the availability and preference shows that except *Quercus lamellosa, Viburnum cordifolia* and *Eurya acuminata,* the other species, which are high in preference list, are not abundantly available. Moreover, *Castanopsis hystrix* is the second most preferred fuel wood species but is least available in the open forest. The above analysis reveals that except *Quercus lamellosa,* the other preferred species are less in number. It means in order to procure these species they have to depend on the reserve forest. Secondly, the excessive exploitation of this species is expected to reduce their availability in the open forest.

In Gnong-Samdong and Linzah villages of Dzongu area there are altogether eleven species identified by villages as fuel wood (Table 10.3). Interestingly *Schima wallichii* (Chilaune), *Alnus nepalensis, Spondias axillaries* (Lapsi) and *Engelhardtia spicata* are among the most preferred

Table 10.2 : Pair-wise ranking of species used as fuel wood in Yuksam and Dubdi Villages

Sl. No.	*Local Name*	*Scientific Name*	*Availability*	*Preference*
1.	Bajrant	*Quercus lamellosa*	10	12
2.	Jat Katus	*Castanopsis hystrix*	1	11
3.	Phalanth	*Quercus lineata*	4	10
4.	Jhinguni	*Eurya acuminate*	6	9
5.	Asare	*Viburnum cordifolia*	8	8
6.	Bans	*Dendrocalamus sp.*	11	7
7.	Mahua	*Engelhardtia spicata*	9	6
8.	Uttis	*Alnus nepalensis*	12	5
9.	Pansi	*Sorbus sp.*	2	4
10.	Kharane	*Symplocos ramisissima*	3	3
11.	Argali	*Edgeworthia gardeneri*	7	2
12.	Panyun	*Prunus cerosoides*	5	1

Table 10.3 : Pair-wise ranking of species used as fuel wood in Dzongu

Sl. No.	*Local Names*	*Scientific names*	*Availability*	*Preference*
1.	Chilaune	*Schima wallichii*	11	11
2.	Phalant	*Quercus lineata*	6	10
3.	Katus	*Castanopsis hystrix*	7	9
4.	Saur	*Betula cylindrostachys*	3	8
5.	Panisaj	*Terminalia myriocarpa*	5	7
6.	Uttis	*Alnus nepalensis*	10	6
7.	Mahua	*Engelhardtia spicata*	8	5
8.	Lapsi	*Spondias axillaries*	9	4
9.	Malato	*Macaranga pustulata*	4	3
10.	Tooni	*Cedrela toona* roxb.	1	2
11.	Kaulo	*Machilus edulis*	2	1

species. Among the least available species are *Cedrela toona roxb.* (Tooni), *Machilus edulis* (Kaulo), *Betula cylindrostachys* (Saur) and *Macaranga pustulata* (Malato). Other species are moderately available. Seen from the view of the preference, the *Schima wallichii* ranks the first followed by *Quercus lineata*, *Castanopsis hystrix*, *Betula cylindrostachys*, *Terminalia myriocarpa* (Panisaj), *Alnus nepalensis* and *Engelhardtia spicata*. A correlation between availability and preference shows that *Schima wallichii* is most widely available as well as most preferred fuel wood species. But other species, which though rank high in the preference list, are either moderately available or poorly available.

Fuel Wood Consumption Pattern

In order to find out the consumption pattern of fuel wood, 45 households were taken as sample, and the data collected from them, details of which are given in Table 10.4. In the Yuksam village only those settlements were considered which were dependent on Khangchendzonga Biosphere Reserve for fuel wood consumption. These settlements are Tshoka, Geychen, Norbugang, Khongtay and Yuksam. The settlements, which are not dependent on Khangchendzonga Biosphere Reserve, are Kopchey, Mantabong, Topsing, Gofa Danra, Dostang and Mangsabong.

Table 10.4 : Fuel wood consumption pattern in different villages

Settlement	*Number of households*	*Total Population*	*Sample Size*	*Fuel wood consumption pattern*	
				Kg/capita/ day	*Tonnes/ year*
Yuksam	364	1951	15	4.73	3368.3
Dubdi	69	402	10	3.5	513.6
Lachen	1609+12	2955	5	5.0	5334.5
Linzah	80	397	5	3.8	550.6
Gnon-Samdong	66	401	10	3.6	527.0

The study conducted in four villages (Table 10.4) shows that the average fuel wood consumption for four villages is 4.1 kg/capita/day. However, compared to the villages of Dubdi, Linzah and Gnon-Samdong, the average fuel wood consumption is high in case of Yuksam and Lachen villages. The average consumption of fuel wood in Yuksam and Lachen is 9.73 kg/capita/day while for other three villages it is 10.9 kg/capita/day. In terms of population also, Yuksam and Lachen are the large villages. Consequently, the anthropogenic pressure on biomass is high. The average yearly consumption of fuel wood in Yuksam and Lachen villages together is 4351.4 tonnes while for the villages of Dubdi, Linzah and Gnon-Samdong, it is 530.4 tonnes.

The inventory of resources used for fuel wood at low and high altitudes shows that the trees surrounding the village vicinity, irrespective of species have the maximum pressure of fuel wood extraction.

Nevertheless certain species are preferred over others for the fuel use because of their better burning quality. *Quercus lamellosa, Schima wallachii, Castanopsis hystrix, Quercus lineata, Eurya acuminata, Castanopsis hystrix* and *Viburnum cordifolia* are the most preferred species at low altitude. At high altitude *Rhododendron sp., Quercus lineata, Quercus lamellosa, Betula alnoides* and *Magnolia sp.* are the preferred species, which are used as firewood. But the availability of these preferred species in the forest is facing tremendous pressure. The settlements at high altitude, viz., Tshoka, Lachen and Thangu are the major consumers of fuel wood. Many species from natural forests especially *Rhododendron arboretum, Rhododendron barbatum, Magnolia sp.* are used as fuel by these settlements.

Species Used for Timber

The PRA conducted in Yuksam and Dubdi villages with respect to the timber used by the villages reveals that there are eight species of timber woods, which are preferred by the villagers. Of these preferred species *Alnus nepalensis, Albizzia lebbeck* (Siris), *Castanopsis hystrix, Juglan regia* (Okhre) are abundantly available while *Machilus edulis, Cedrela toona roxb., Beilschmiedia sikkimensis* (Tarsingh) and *Michelia champak* (Champ) are least available. Though the *Michelia champak* wood species is least available but it is the most preferred one. *Castanopsis hystrix, Juglan regia, Machilus edulis, Alnus nepalensis, Cedrela toona roxb., Albizzia lebbeck* and *Beilschmiedia sikkimensis* follow it. Thus we find that except *Castanopsis hystrix, Juglan regia* and *Alnus nepalensis* other species are not available in abundance. As such, in order to procure these species the local people depend on the buffer forest of Khangchendzonga Biosphere Reserve.

In case of the two villages of Dzongu, namely Gnong-Samdong and Linzah there are eight timber species preferred by the villages. These are *Michelia champak, Cinnamomum cecidodaphne* (Malagiri), *Morus indica* L. (Kimbu), *Juglan regia, Castanopsis hystrix, Machilus edulis, Alnus nepalensis* and *Cedrela toona roxb.* Among these species the *Alnus nepalensis* is most widely available followed by *Machilus edulis, Cedrela toona roxb.* and *Castanopsis hystrix.* The least available species are *Cinnamomum cecidodaphne* and *Michelia champak.* Interestingly the least available of species like *Michelia champak*, *Cinnamomum cecidodaphne*, *Morus indica* L. and *Juglan regia* are the most preferred ones. This co-relation between availability preferences suggests that in the want of preferred species in the open forest, the people depend on the buffer forest of Khangchendzonga Biosphere Reserve.

Attitude towards Conservation

People's participation in conservation efforts related to Biosphere Reserve is very important. Equally important is sticking to some disciplines including some obligations, which need to be enforced by the people themselves, as certain actions of the people are unfavourable to preservation of the eco-system. Imposition of Biosphere Reserve's regime in terms of conservation entails certain restrictions on the use of Biosphere Reserve resources ultimately get translated into some costs, which people have to bear. In order to know the people's response towards such restriction, a conservation attitude survey (CONAT) of approximately 20 per cent of the households was carried out in the selected fringe settlements of West Sikkim to determine how local communities and stakeholders perceive the situation and express their concern about environmental conservation. Contingent valuation method (CVM) within the ambit of ecological economics with emphasis on willingness-to-accept (WTA) and willingness-to-pay (WTP) approach was adopted for some of the settlements located crucially with respect to Khangchendzonga Biosphere Reserve. This was done to understand the manner through which the related population or the stakeholders express their environmental conservation concerns. The issues, which are important both for the policy makers and stakeholders, were considered for CONAT. The basic premise of the this valuation was that the environmental conservation costs of enforcing Biosphere Reserve principles of restrictions on the use of natural resources shall also be borne by the local population or the stakeholders within their socio-cultural and economic framework. To interpret the possible underlying issues, the entire responses of the query were further categorized into: conservation driven concern, socio-economic driven concerns, willingness-to-accept (WTA) and willingness-to-pay (WTP) concerns and participatory concerns in the Biosphere Reserve concepts.

Table 10.5a : Conservation Attitude Survey of people of study villages

Village name	*Conservation Concern (%)*	*Socio-economic fuelled concern(%)*	*WTA/ WTP* driven Concern (%)*	*Participatory Concern (%)*
Yuksam	90	80	100	100
Norbugang	67	30	85	90
Khongtay	85	57	100	100
Tsong	76	62	95	100
Mangtabong	73	56	90	100
Khecheopalri	85	71	100	100
Rambyathang	60	20	84	90

* WTA/WPA – Willing-to-accept and willingness-to-pay

Table 10.5b : Statistical derivation of Conservation Attitude Survey of Study villages

Sl. No.	*Response Category*	*Mean*	*Variance*	*Std. Deviation*
A	Conservation concern	76.57	116.94	10.81
B	Socio-economic Concern	53.71	396.27	19.91
C	WTA / WTP Concern	93.43	047.95	06.92
D	Participatory Concern	96.43	033.67	05.80

Table 10.5c: Correlation of responses of different categories of Conservation Attitude Survey of study villages

A.	WTA / WTP and Participatory Concern	– 0.9090
B.	WTA / WTP and Socio-Economic Concern	– 0.9341
C.	WTA / WTP and Conservation Concern	– 0.9751
D.	Conservation and Socio-Economic Concern	– 0.9313
E.	Conservation and participation Concern	- 0.8465
F.	Socio-Economic and Participatory Concern	– 0.9180

The socio-economic status and the ecological indicators of the settlements covered in this study were ascertained through the survey (Table 10.5a). The six settlements selected for the study positioned in the close vicinity of Khangchendzonga Biosphere Reserve. CONAT interviews were carried out at random sampling framework in these settlements. For covering a total of approximately 433 households belonging to these settlements, 102 households were actually surveyed. Settlement-wise overall positive conservation responses in the categories A, B, C and D were derived (Table 10.5b). The average positive ratings obtained ranged from 40 to 100 per cent. The general positive responses were observed to be high except within the category B (Table 10.5B) with high standard deviation (19.91) and variance value (396.27). This points to the fact that the "socio-economic driven concern" expressed by the respondents are weaker compared to responses under other categories. The reasons for weak socio-economic concern flows from the fact that tourism is emerging as a dominant sector in studied villages and the people are engaged in various capacities in this promising sector. Further, the correlations of responses of different CONAT categories were established and compared. The best correlation was observed between WTA/WTP and conservation concern (Table 10.5c).

The results show that the people are aware of the dangers to the eco-system and they are willing to 'accept' and 'pay' as well for the sake of the conservation. It also depicts that socio-economic conditions of the people play a crucial role in shaping the conservation attitudes of the community living close to Biosphere Reserve area.

Discussion

The study shows that the people living close to Khangchendzonga Biosphere Reserve are highly dependent on forests to meet their fuel wood and timber requirements. The forest cover in close proximity to the settlement and camping sites is experiencing maximum pressure because the people tend to collect fuel wood repeatedly from the same patch of the forestland. As the supply from the closer points decline, people penetrate further and further into the forest widening the area of impacted zone. In addition, the other factor that has put continuous pressure is the selective use of specific species as choice for fuel and timber woods. In recent years, therefore, the availability of firewood and timber trees have become sparse. Consequently, the people have resorted to the alternative variety but the quality of which is poor compared to previous ones. In other words, the shortage of good quality has led to widespread switching over to inferior quality fuel and timber wood. Chhettri and Sharma (2007) have made similar observation that the present practice of fuel wood and timber extraction is injurious to the eco-system.

Although the extraction of plant species by preference as firewood, fodder and timber is within the carrying capacity, there has been a visible change in species composition, and regeneration status of many high-quality firewood species is at risk near the Khangchendzonga Biosphere Reserve (Chhettri *et al.*, 2002). If this practice continued, it would adversely affect the ecosystem structure and function.

Extraction of fuel wood was slightly reduced after the intervention of Sikkim Biodiversity and Ecotourism Project, but the negative impact of extraction would still be substantial because much of the extraction is concentrated in the forest surrounding settlements and trekking corridor. It is presumed that promoting use of alternative fuel resources can minimize the impact of fuel wood extraction on biodiversity. However, Barber *et al.*, (1995) have cautioned against any assumption that alternative livelihood necessarily lead to better conservation.

Presently the Sikkim Biodiversity and Ecotourism Project promotes alternative use of firewood through various awareness programmes and capacity building training. It has been observed that several Lodge operators in Yuksam are now using alternative energy like kerosene and LPG for tourist purposes. Porters are now able to hire blankets while on treks to minimize use of firewood for heating. A code of conduct has been developed by a Yuksam based NGO named Khangchendzonga Conservation Committee (KCC) for visitors. The travel agents association of Sikkim has also adopted a code of conduct whereby alternative energy utilisation on treks has become mandatory.

The study shows that the people are aware of the adverse impact of the degradation of biodiversity on their livelihood pattern and are willing to participate in the conservation linked management strategy of the government. Maharana *et al.*, (2000) has also observed that the social and economic driven concerns are worth correlating to the people willingness to accept and pay the cost of conservation. It is because despite best of conservation attitude initially, socio-economic conditions of the people play a crucial role in shaping and maintaining the conservation attitudes of the community living close to Biosphere Reserve area.

The study has revealed that conflicts of interest do arise particularly when the real pressure of conservation restrictions begin to affect socio-economic conditions of people living in fringe area settlements, in the absence of viable alternatives to their traditional dependence on forest resources. The key to resolution of all conflicts over biosphere reserve resource use lie in the social, economic and environmental agendas prepared by keeping the people's basic concerns in mind. Discussions and observations recorded in the field situations suggest that the policies for Khangchendzonga Biosphere Reserve should give careful attention to the participation of stakeholders as well as their perceptions, in the sphere of recently implemented joint forest management strategy. Krishna *et al.*, (2002) suggests that a participatory approach involving stakeholders is essential for effective management of natural resources and ecosystem conservation in Biosphere Reserve zones. Such an approach should involve recognition and appreciation of the people's traditional knowledge and traditional ecology-preservation strategies in the management of Biosphere Reserve resources. It, in turns, will help to ensure that stakeholders do not become antagonists, instigating conflict in Khangchendzonga Biosphere Reserve areas.

In different context, Singh (1997) suggests that there should be conditional phasing out of people's dependence on forest resources. People now realize the need to consider the alternative economic avenues. People are happy that at least the growing tourism industry has come as a respite, and more and more villagers are now revolving their economic activities around tourism.

Conclusion

Enfolded within the Himalaya, the Khangchendzonga Biosphere Reserve Zone requires appropriate management in terms of both natural ecology and cultural landscapes. The communities living in and around Biosphere Reserve zone do not necessarily damage the environment. However, the increasing population and demands of livelihood sometimes prompted the people to overuse the surrounding regions, rather unintentionally. The people pursue agriculture at subsistence level. They are highly dependent on forests in the buffer zones, be it for timber or non-timber forest products. This situation indeed calls out for an effective conservation strategy based on provision of alternative livelihood options and additional resources, to reconcile the pressure and dependence in the Biosphere Reserve resources in appropriate manner. The efficient management of the ecological resources is expected to lead to conflict prevention, at various levels. This can be achieved by creating capacity building amongst the local communities. Increasing the awareness and introducing the alternative livelihood options will ensure reducing dependence on biosphere resources that are necessary for the ecology conservation. Nevertheless, the most important initiative to be implemented concurrently for ecosystem protection has to be based on participatory approach wherein community is given responsibility for effective monitoring and exercising judiciously their traditional rights of resource use. The ideal is to preserve overall ecosystem vigour, including species diversity. It can be best accomplished by integrating it into the fabric of socio-religious and economic system. Here lies the immense implication of the concept of the sustainable development where the issues of the man and environment are integrated together, for a better future for all the living beings.

Acknowledgement

The author is thankful to the Director, Anthropological Survey of India, for making the research work possible in Sikkim, under the national project, wherein the author collected data, at individual level. This is the shorter revised version of the report submitted to the Anthropological Survey of India. The views expressed here are of the author alone.

REFERENCES

Barber, C. V., S. Aliff, and A. Purnomo, *Tiger by the Tail? Reorienting Biodiversity Conservation and Development in Indonesia.* World Resource Institute, Washington, DC, & WALHI and the Pelangi Institute, Jakarta, 1995.

Champion, H.G. and S.K. Seth, *Revised Forest Types of India.* Government. of India Publications, New Delhi, 1968.

Chhettri, N. and E. Sharma, 'Firewood value assessment: A comparison on local preference and wood constituent properties of species from a trekking corridor, West Sikkim, India', in, *Current Science,* Vol. 92 (12) June, 2007.

Chhettri, N., E. Sharma, D.C. Deb, and R.C. Sundrial, 'Impact of firewood extraction on tree structure, regeneration and woody biomass productivity in a trekking corridor of the Sikkim Himalaya'. *Mountain Research and Development,* 22(2) pp.150-158, 2002.

Hannah, L. and D. Lohse, *Annual Report.* Conservation Institutions, Washington DC. 1993.

Hoovengel, R., *The CV Method: Scope and Validity,* Amesterdem: Free University, 1994.

Indian Institute of Remote Sensing, *Bios-diversity Characteristics at Landscape Level in North-East India using Satellite Remote Sensing and Geographic Information System,* IIRS, Dehardun, 2002.

Khoshoo, T.N., 'Biodiversity in India: Reality and Myths', in U.R. Rao, ed., *Science and Technology for Achieving Food, Economic and Health Security,* Bangalore: Prism Books Pvt. Ltd. 1993.

Kothari, A., 'Ecodevelopment and Joint Forest Management of PAs: Legal and Policy Implications', Paper presented at National Workshop on Ecodocumentation, November 1998, Wildlife Institute of India, Dehradun. 1998.

Krishna, A.K., S. Chhetri, and K.K. Singh, 'Human dimensions of conservation in the Khangchendzonga Biosphere Reserve: the need for conflict prevention', in *Mountain Research and Development,* Vol.22 (4), pp. 328-331, 2002.

MacKinnon, J. and K. MacKinnon, 'Review of the Protected Areas System in the Indo-Malayan Realm', in *International Union for the Conservation of Nature and Natural Resources,* Gland, Switzerland and Cambridge, U.K. p. 284, 1986.

Maharana, I., S.C. Rai, N. Chhettri, and E. Sharma, 'Fuel wood pressure on the national forests of Khangchendzonga National Park of Sikkim Himalaya', in A. Arunachalam and M.L. Khan, eds., *Sustainable Management of Forest,* International Book Distributor, Dehradun, pp. 279-295, 2000.

Marzluff, J.M. and N. Hamel, 'Land use issues', in, *Encyclopaedia of Biodiversity,* Vol.3, San Diego, California : Academic Press, pp.660, 2001.

Mishra, B.K. 'Sustainable Wildlife Conservation and Community Development through Integrated Ecodevelopment in India', Paper presented at the International Training Workshop on Sustainable Agriculture in an Environmental Perspectives, at Svalov Weibull, Svalov (Lund), Sweden, 1999.

Mittermeier, R.A., 'Primate diversity and the tropical forest: Case studies from Brazil and Madagascar, and the importance of the megadiversity countries', in E.O. Wilson, ed., *Biodiversity,* National Academy Press, Washington, D.C. 1988.

Singh, S., 'Biodiversity conservation through ecodevelopment planning and implementation lesson from India', *South-South Cooperation Programme on Environmentally Sound Socio-Economic Development in the Humid Tropics, Working Papers,* No. 21, UNESCO, Paris, 1997.

UNEP, *Global Biodiversity Assessment,* Cambridge : Cambridge University Press, 1995.

UNESCO, *Biosphere Reserves: The Seville Strategy and Statutory Framework of the World Network.* UNESCO, Paris. 1996.

11

Participatory Forest Management in Himachal Pradesh

Benefit Flows and Equity

Anirban Ganguly and *Adrian Lopes*

Introduction

Paradigms of forest management in India have undergone a major change since the early 1990s. The Indian Forest Policy, 1988 explicitly talks of creating a "people's movement" towards managing forests – an approach which can be referred to as Participatory Forest Management (PFM) as distinguished from management by state control. A Government Order issued in 1990 laid the foundation of the currently prevalent institutional form of participatory approaches through the mechanism of Joint Forest Management (JFM).[1] JFM is essentially a "co-management approach" where the state and forest fringe communities jointly manage forest patches. In return, communities earn the right to a share of the benefits from timber harvest, as well as various intermediate returns. Besides, communities also get a "first charge" on other forest products such as medicinal plants and grasses as per locally worked out regulations.

The application of such approaches in areas of significant biodiversity has been contentious to some degree. There is one view that such areas should be kept totally out of bounds for any human use whereas there is another view that controlled human use should be allowed (Terborgh, J. and van Schaik, C. 2002). However, if communities receive sufficient benefits over the short-run to be able to sacrifice certain kinds of forest uses, there could be possibilities of reconciliation of the two approaches. The concept of eco-development attempts to strike a balance between the two approaches by trying to ensure that sufficient livelihood opportunities are created for communities in the fringes of protected areas so that pressures on resources within the protected areas get reduced while development needs of the communities are met.

The practice of JFM rests on ground rules set by the appropriate local level committee, variously called JFM Committee, Village Development Committee, Forest Development Committee and in case of Protected Areas, Eco-development Committee. These committees usually have a General Body comprising members of all village households, and an Executive Body comprising fewer members, and with a local Forest Department official as the Member-Secretary. Evidently, formation of such Committees requires an initial mobilization effort, since most forest areas have been traditionally managed directly by the Forest Department. An inherent feature of JFM programmes is, therefore, Entry Point Activities (EPAs), which are non-forest activities (such as road construction, or repairing of a local structure) that could potentially act as a binding force, and induce communities to undertake forest protection efforts collectively.

In essence, JFM is thus an incentive measure that provides local communities necessary stakes to take part in forest protection in the short-run, in anticipation of benefits in the longer run. The underlying assumption here is that local communities have inadequate stakes to undertake forest protection or restrain unsustainable resource extraction due to limited livelihood options. JFM is expected to provide an escape route out of this imbroglio — with communities gaining even in the short-run through enhanced livelihood options or returns from a basket of forest products on an annual basis.

At the same time, JFM has been viewed as an equity-enhancing development intervention, both at an inter-village as well as at an intra-village level. Thus, in several states, poorer villages or those with a higher proportion of backward classes are preferentially selected for JFM interventions. Also, while planning village level interventions, efforts are made to promote activities that benefit poorer groups, or women, or other disadvantaged groups. As an example, several states promote the development of fuelwood species in JFM interventions so that women are relieved of the burden of collecting fuelwood from distant forest patches.

Of late, JFM is also being seen as an integrated village development programme in forest-fringe areas. In other words, the focus is no longer exclusively on forest protection, but on broader land-based development activities. Specifically, in villages adjoining Protected Areas, access of local communities needs to be restricted for meeting wider (global) objectives, such as biodiversity conservation. As mentioned earlier, the typical mode that is followed in these cases is that of eco-development, where emphasis is placed on developing (alternative) livelihoods in the fringe areas of Protected Areas.

JFM -- in all these connotations – is intensely context-specific. The most early experiments with this approach were carried out in degraded *sal* (*shorea robusta*) forests of West Bengal in the early 1970s, and gradually the approach has spread all over India in various institutional modes, guided mainly by the 1990 Government Order. These modes have varied according to degrees of forest dependence, background levels of degradation, and past trends of people's involvement in managing forests or other natural resources.

Himachal Pradesh – the state where the present study was carried out - is among the most forested states of the country (with forest cover of 26%) (FSI, 2009). The state has a large rural population comprising 90 per cent of the total, and expectedly a high degree of dependence on forests. The state also has a long history of people's participation in forest management, which started with the introduction of village cooperative forest societies in the district of Kangra before Independence. After Independence and till about the early 1970s, the emphasis was on consolidation of the Forest Department, establishment of forest-based industries and afforestation on all types of land. Subsequent to the National Agricultural Commission (1976) Report, a number of donor agencies started supporting the implementation of people-oriented programmes through targeted forestry projects. In all of these projects—Indo-German Dhauladhar Project, National Social Forestry Project, Integrated Watershed Development Project – Village Development

Councils (VDCs) were formed with the aim of involving local communities in development. PFM, in its current form was introduced through the Indo-UK Himachal Forestry Project launched in 1994. Under this programme, Village Forest Development Committees (VFDCs) were formed to share responsibility in managing forests. All these projects essentially represent a partnership approach, and the sustainability of this approach largely depends on short term and long-term incentives for communities (and individuals) to join and benefit from this partnership (Bahuguna *et al.*, 2004).

The evaluation of benefits of such partnership approaches is a challenging task. Such evaluation, on one hand, requires adequate baseline information on the nature of forests and community dependence at the beginning of the programme, and on the other hand, needs context-specific indicators of performance evaluation. There have been several attempts to characterize the performance of JFM programmes, notable among these are the studies conducted by the Ecological Economics Research Network (EERN) as part of a long-term research and monitoring programme (Ravindranath and Sudha, 2004). The Himachal Pradesh case represents a special challenge in this context, since the background levels of forest dependence is typically high, and the usufruct-sharing system is among the most progressive among all Indian states (100 per cent of forest produce, including NTFPs, with all intermediate harvests accruing to Village Forest Development Societies). In effect, this means that communities are entitled to get all benefits out of forest products, though a percentage of this (40%) needs to be ploughed back for forest management and conservation activity. Thus, the PFM programme in theory has relatively stronger incentives built into it, though the community response to such incentives may vary based on volumes and time horizons over which the benefits accrue.

The issue, therefore, is to identify the volume and distribution of the benefits so that the degree to which the incentives work can be assessed. Though there is a large body of work on social and institutional analysis of JFM in various social and geographical settings, there has been relatively less work on quantification of benefits in an economic sense. Conventional Forest Department data is usually inadequate to conduct such analysis. In some cases, micro-plans prepared at the start of an intervention do contain some baseline information; however, institutional arrangements to track future benefits are rarely in place.

Sporadic efforts have been made at quantitatively assessing benefit flows in the context of JFM. Studying forest-fringe communities in the states of West Bengal and Gujarat, Hill and Shields (1998) try to assess the incentives for community participation in JFM by looking at the income accruing to various groups of forest users (such as head-loaders or fuelwood collectors, NTFP collectors, livestock owners and wage earners). This is carried out by comparing the incomes of each group in a JFM village with that of a control or non-JFM village over a thirty-year time horizon. The study finds that in the state of Gujarat an average household stands to gain from JFM, while the opposite holds true in the state of West Bengal[2]. While this study assesses how harvesters or users of different forest products are affected by JFM, it does not, however, ascertain the equity implications of distribution of forest benefits to different socio-economic groups. Kumar (2002) quantifies the net benefits accruing to income-stratified households in JFM and non-JFM villages in the state of Jharkhand, looking at the impact of JFM on the extraction patterns of forest products, and assessing equity aspects of the benefit patterns over a forty-year time horizon. The study concludes that while JFM does help in sustainable forest regeneration, it is at the expense of the poorer households. He argues that the gains to different socio-economic groups cannot be assumed to be uniformly distributed, and that the institutional design of JFM needs to include suitable compensation schemes to alleviate the poverty of the poorest groups.

Clearly, such issues require deeper exploration in various geographical contexts, if JFM needs to serve its multiple purposes as discussed earlier. The present study represents an attempt at such exploration through micro-level (village ward) estimation of incremental increases in forest income due to PFM and their distribution across economic classes in three "paired sites" (PFM/non-PFM) in the state of Himachal Pradesh.

Method

Study Area

The study was conducted in the north Indian state of Himachal Pradesh in the western Himalayas. The sites were located in three Forest

Divisions — Paonta (low altitude), Solan (mid-altitude) and Seraj (high altitude). The high altitude site was in geographical proximity to the Great Himalayan National Park (GHNP) where a community-based biodiversity conservation approach has been tested. In each Division, two panchayat[3] wards were selected, one with a PFM intervention and the other without, the latter serving as a "control". These are shown in the map below (Figure 11.1).

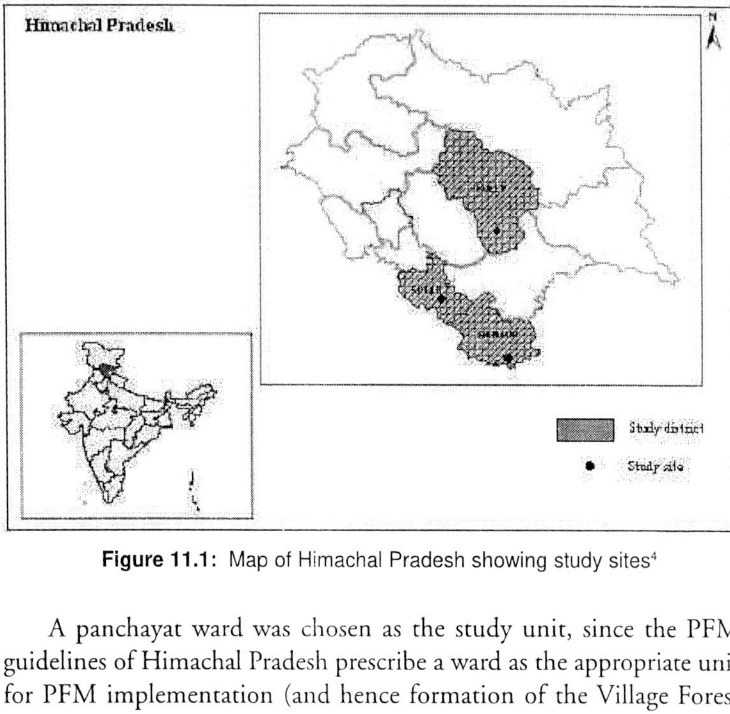

Figure 11.1: Map of Himachal Pradesh showing study sites[4]

A panchayat ward was chosen as the study unit, since the PFM guidelines of Himachal Pradesh prescribe a ward as the appropriate unit for PFM implementation (and hence formation of the Village Forest Development Committee, through which the programme is implemented). Village level data were collected through household interviews (complete enumeration as per VFDC list) and PRA methods. The profile of the wards is provided in Table 11.1.

Survey

Primary data for this study were collected during field surveys carried out during February–July 2005. 273 households were surveyed in the

Table 11.1: Profile of study sites

Division	*Main forest species*	*Altitude (m)*	*Panchayat ward*	*PFM (Y/N)*	*Population (adult equivalent)*[5]	*per cent SC/ ST*[6]	*Population density (per km²)*	*Per capita forest availability (km²)*	*Live-stock units*[7]
Solan	Chil, oak	1500	Kolthi-Kanyara	Y	162	91.3	82.8	0.002	90.8
			Jadli	N	257	50.0	138.3	0.001	184.5
Seraj	Fir, spruce, deodar, oak	3000	Hirab	Y	211	38.9	17.0	0.056	133.5
			Kulwari	N	255	37.5	20.7	0.044	152.5
Paonta	Sal	350	Pilhodi	Y	257	100	13.4	0.064	223.1
			Sainwala	N	262	90.0	20.6	0.041	159.0

6 villages through structured questionnaires. The data collected covered (a) basic household level information such as caste, education levels, occupation, monthly expenditure and income; and (b) details of forest products harvested (fuel-wood, green grass, NTFPs, tree fodder and leaf litter). Price data were collected from nearby markets/traders.

Income Sources

There are a variety of sources from where households in these villages generate income. These include harvested forest products, daily wage labour, government services and private services, and agricultural income. Accordingly, household incomes are classified into two broad categories — *forest* income and *other* income.

Households harvest forest products for domestic use. Fuel wood is used for cooking and space heating. Leaf litter is also harvested from the forests and is used for bedding of livestock — cows, buffaloes, goats and sheep. NTFPs are harvested mostly in the higher altitude zones and fetch high returns when sold by villagers in nearby wholesale markets[8]. Fodder grass and tree fodder are used as inputs for livestock. These are consumed by livestock during grazing and stall-feeding[9].

Annual flows of forest products into the household economy were estimated using the household survey data. The market prices were used for valuing products and annual benefit flows. Due to surplus labour availability, the value of labour-time for harvesting forest products was assumed to be zero. To estimate the quantity of grass consumed during grazing, a method adopted in a research study (Gatenby *et al.*, 1989) on buffalo grazing practices in the Koshi Hills of Nepal — a broadly similar ecological region — was used. This study estimates that for each additional hour of grazing, a buffalo needed on average, 1.3 kg less of grass during stall feeding. Based on an average grazing day of 5½ hours, the saving is thus 7 kg of grass[10].

Under the category "other income", the following kinds of income were considered:

(a) *Net agricultural income:* This was calculated on a household basis using market prices after netting out input costs. Where price data were not available, government minimum support prices for the concerned crop was used to value agricultural produce. In arriving at estimates of net agricultural income the following costs were deducted from the gross output value: seed costs, fertilizer costs, pesticide/insecticide costs, depreciation and repairs, and interest on working capital. The input costs were based on estimates made by the Commission for Agricultural Costs and Prices (MoA, 2005)[11].

(b) *Income from employment :* This includes wages paid by the Forest Department for plantation activities (in PFM villages) at the rate of Rs. 65 per day; income from employment in government and private services; and income through remittances from outside the village.

Income Distribution

The population of each village was divided into quartile classes for the analysis of income distribution. Incremental incomes accruing to each quartile class was used to assess the equity effects of the PFM programme.

Data Analysis

Forest Dependence

We first plot per capita income in each village against forest dependency, measured by the proportion of forest income in total income (Figure 11.2). The plot shows that the relationship is negative, implying that poorer villages have a higher degree of forest dependence (correlation coefficient (r) = -0.81). It is also seen that the PFM villages (P) have lower total per capita incomes than the non-PFM (N) ones, which is expected, since the Forest Department of Himachal Pradesh preferentially selects poorer villages for implementation of the PFM programme.

Income Accruing from Forest Products

The per capita (adult equivalent) forest incomes (broken down into forest products) are depicted in Figure 11.3. In general it is noted that, across sites, the forest products can be arranged in decreasing order of per capita income as follows: cut grass, fuelwood, tree fodder, grazing, leaf litter and NTFPs.

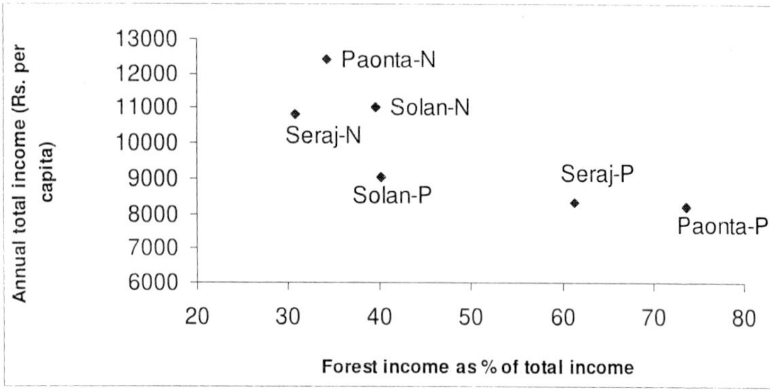

Figure 11.2 : Income and forest dependency

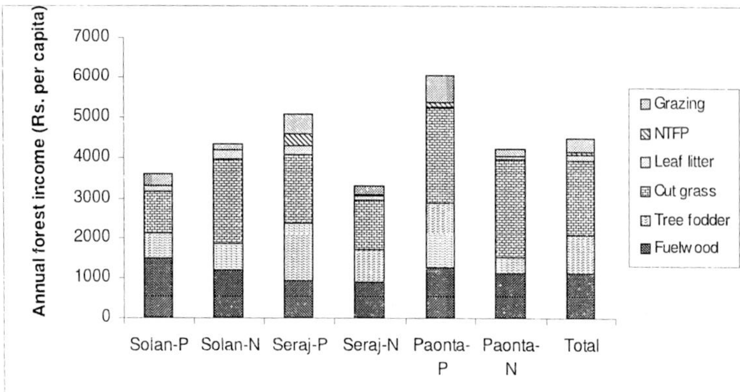

Figure 11.3 : Forest income per capita

It is observed that in Seraj and Paonta, the PFM villages have substantially higher forest incomes per capita than the corresponding non-PFM villages (the opposite is observed in Solan Division). The PFM village in Solan also has a much lower dependence on forests than the other two PFM villages as seen in Figure 11.2. Both the PFM and non-PFM villages in Solan have the same proportion of income accruing from the forests, displaying a very similar forest livelihood pattern. This is due to the following reasons: (a) The two villages in Solan are relatively more accessible by road, and hence they are relatively more connected with external markets; and (b) The PFM village in Solan has a relatively recent history of PFM intervention as compared to other two sites. (The PFM programme in Solan formally started with Forest Department interventions in 2002-03. In the other two Divisions, there has been a longer history of PFM activity beginning in the mid-1990s).

Fuelwood is a necessary commodity that is used for cooking and space heating. In rural Himachal Pradesh the practice of using dung-cakes is not prevalent, and only a few rich households can afford to use LPG stoves for cooking. Hence it is not surprising to note that per capita income derived from fuelwood is approximately the same in each of the three Divisions.

It is observed that income derived from tree fodder is greater in the PFM village as compared to the respective non-PFM village in Seraj and Paonta (the opposite is observed in Solan). This is because the number of goats and sheep in the former set of villages is greater (goats and sheep are fed more on tree fodder than cows, bulls and buffaloes, which are fed more on grass). Also, the PFM villages of Seraj and Paonta and the non-PFM village in Seraj derive a considerable amount of income from tree fodder as compared to the remaining three villages. A plausible reason for this is that former three villages are located within or next to heavily forested areas, thus facilitating easier access to tree fodder species at the time when herders take livestock out to graze/ browse in the forests and grasslands.

Cut grass, as mentioned earlier, contributes the greatest proportion to forest income across the three Divisions. The highest per capita income from cut grass is seen in Paonta Division. This Division is characterized by a high number of hybrid cattle, from which more milk is derived as compared to cattle in the higher regions[12]. In order to produce more milk, it was noted, that these cattle require more fodder than cattle in the hillier regions.

Leaf litter was used more in Solan and Seraj Divisions as compared to Paonta. The reason for this is that in the latter Division, most of the households have cemented floors for their cattle sheds. In the former two Divisions, the floors of cattle sheds are made of mud and the weather remains moist and cold during most of the year, which necessitates the daily use of leaf litter.

NTFPs contribute to income in greater amounts in the higher altitude regions, as can be seen in Seraj Division. The PFM village in Seraj derives higher income per capita as compared to the non-PFM village. This is because the PFM village is located within a more densely forested area (see Table 11.1), thus facilitating easier access to valuable NTFPs, which are usually harvested by cattle herders at the time of grazing.

Income Distribution and Equity

PFM as a development programme in Himachal Pradesh is meant to be pro-poor by enhancing livelihood options for forest-fringe communities (Gouri *et al.*, 2004). Therefore, we need to understand the nature of distribution of incremental benefits from PFM across various economic classes. As a first step, we look at the distribution of total income in each site. The following set of graphs (Figure 11.4) show the total (annual) income distribution in each village, using smoothed histograms. The distributions are positively skewed.

Fig. 11.4 : Total income distribution (Rs./year)

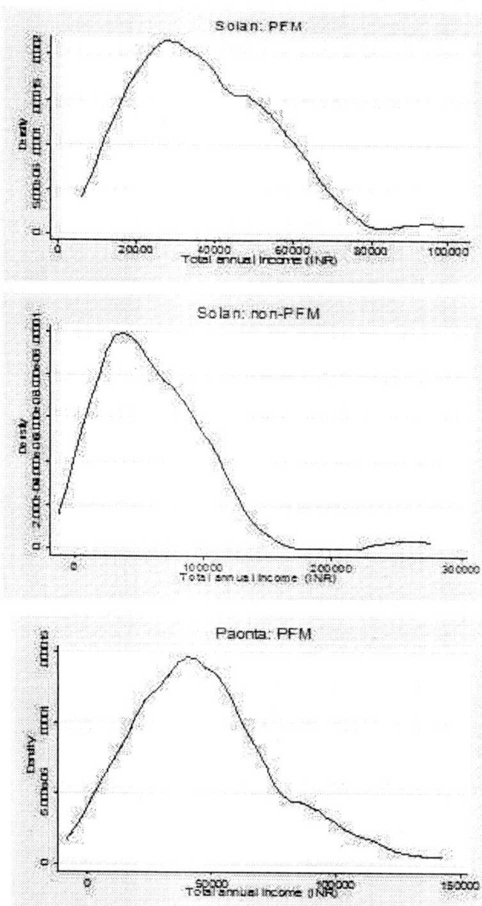

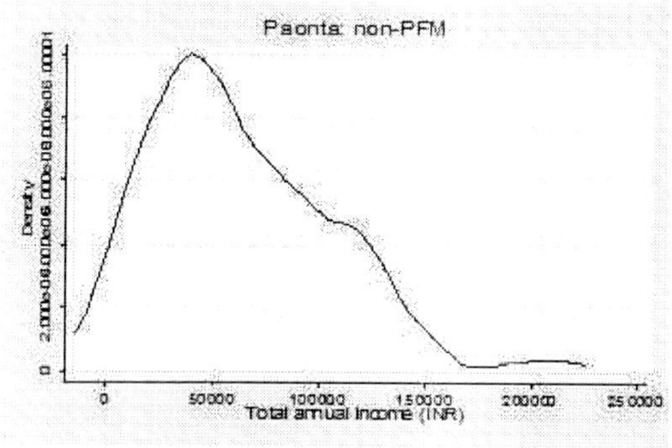

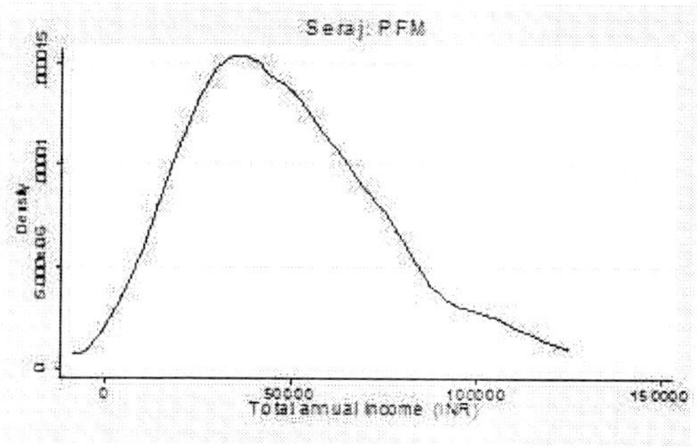

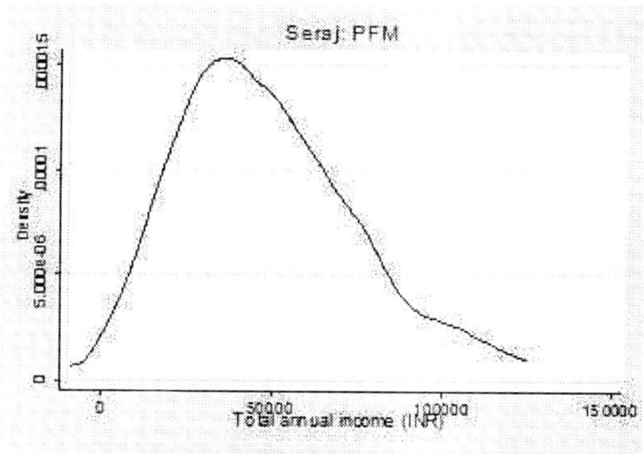

Next, we construct Lorenz curves (Figure 11.5) for each pair of sites to see if the PFM intervention has resulted in enhanced equity in terms of forest income. These curves do not reveal a clear trend. We then construct quartile income categories and compare incremental incomes for each quartile across PFM and non-PFM villages.

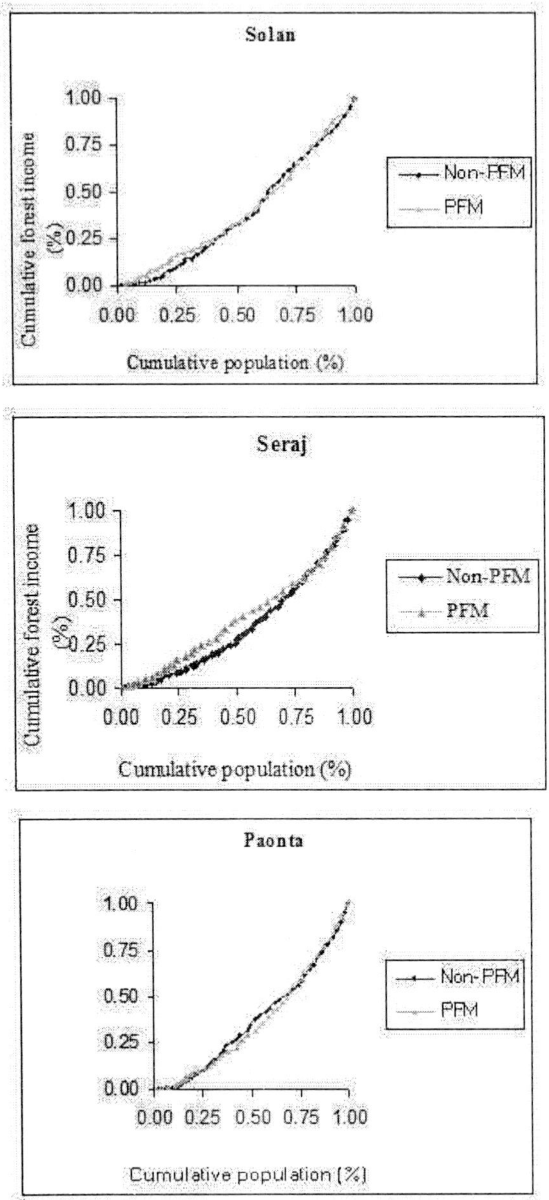

Fig. 11. 5 : Lorenz curves showing distribution of forest income

The following table (Table 11.2) shows the degree of forest dependency (ratio of forest income to total income) for each quartile class (1- poorest, 4- richest).

Table 11.2: Forest income per capita (Rs.) and dependency (%) by income category

Division	*Income category*	*Forest income: PFM*	*Forest income: non-PFM*	*Forest dependency: PFM (%)*	*Forest dependency: non-PFM (%)*
Solan	1	4194	2087	65	51
	2	4028	5474	57	70
	3	4340	6108	48	45
	4	2999	5118	21	25
	Average	**3877**	**4667**	**42**	**41**
Seraj	1	3626	2152	90	68
	2	4341	3732	66	51
	3	5607	4063	59	33
	4	7225	4155	47	18
	Average	**5200**	**3526**	**59**	**30**
Paonta	1	2887	2299	72	48
	2	5367	6460	74	60
	3	6377	3783	69	25
	4	8838	4658	70	22
	Average	**5867**	**4310**	**71**	**33**

Table 11.2 shows two general trends across the villages. First, forest income per capita increases with income, i.e. the economically richer households derive more income per capita annually from the forest resource as compared to the poorer households within each village. The PFM village in Solan is the only exception, where per capita forest incomes remain relatively uniform across income categories. Second, forest dependence decreases with a rise in income, i.e. the economically poorer groups depend more on forest products than economically richer groups. In other words, the negative relation between total income per capita and forest dependence, as was seen in Figure 11.2, holds true both at the inter village and intra village level. The only notable exception is the PFM site in Paonta where forest dependence remains constant across economic groups, the reason being that this village has a relatively homogeneous population (with all households belonging to the *Gujjar* community[13]) with almost identical resource use patterns.

These observations have relevance for policy. On the one hand, a PFM programme tends to improve inter-village equity by enhancing the livelihood options of the economically poorer villages as a whole. Thus, the PFM programme appears to work favourably on this count.

But on the other hand, a PFM programme tends to reduce equity within a village. The economically advantaged households stand to corner most of the benefits of the programme in two of the three Divisions. This is also depicted in Figure 11.6, which shows the *incremental* per capita forest income accruing annually to a PFM village over the corresponding non-PFM village in the Division, for each respective income category.

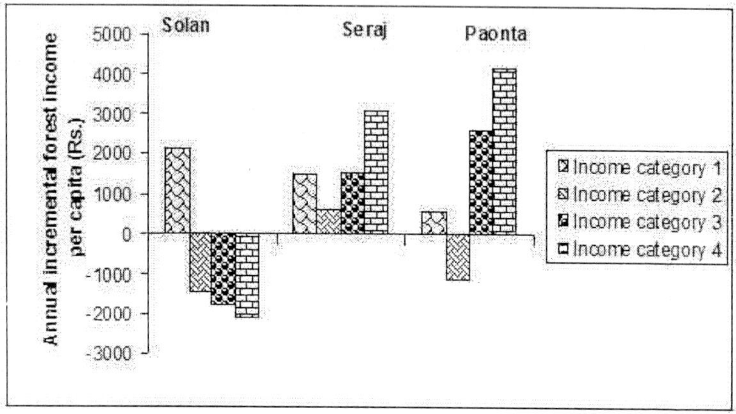

Fig. 11.6: Incremental forest incomes per capita (Rs.) accruing to PFM villages annually

While a general positive trend is observed between per capita forest incomes and total incomes in two of the three Divisions, this needs to be disaggregated into income derived from the individual forest products. Table 11.3 depicts the incremental per capita annual income accruing from each forest product, in the four income categories.

The general positive trend observed in Figure 11.6 does not carry forward to each forest product. In Seraj and Paonta most of the forest products do depict a positive trend. An exception is noted in income category 2 in the latter. A possible reason is the same as mentioned earlier in the context of the villages of Paonta – the non-PFM village relies to a larger extent on milk from livestock and thus more per capita income is derived from grass fodder here. As mentioned earlier, the PFM programme is relatively recent in Solan, and hence it may be too early to expect any short run tangible benefits.[14]

Table 11.3: Incremental per capita incomes (Rs.) from forest products accruing to PFM villages annually

Division	*Income category*	*Fuel-wood*	*Tree fodder*	*Cut grass*	*Leaf litter*	*NTFP*	*Grazing*
Solan	1	1015	662	172	22	-2	239
	2	392	22	-1920	29	0	29
	3	-152	-663	-973	-135	10	146
	4	-365	-114	-1715	-168	5	236
	Total	231	-9	-1116	-62	4	162
Seraj	1	-358	603	634	109	156	329
	2	19	-350	509	51	186	194
	3	51	97	463	186	364	382
	4	120	1771	441	167	371	200
	Total	-43	530	512	129	269	277
Paonta	1	273	169	57	-8	40	57
	2	-589	614	-1257	-121	40	218
	3	426	1496	103	-6	157	418
	4	543	2132	389	-14	119	1011
	Total	161	1101	-181	-38	89	425

Taking note of trends in each forest product has important policy implications in that the Forest Department can target their interventions more specifically. Clearly in the PFM village of Seraj, interventions should be targeted at the development of grass, tree fodder and NTFPs. This makes economic sense also because the village has large number of livestock (cows, buffaloes, goats and sheep), and it is located at a high altitude at which several valuable NTFPs thrive.

In the PFM village of Paonta, interventions should be targeted at developing tree fodder species and fuelwood. This too makes economic sense because the PFM village has a larger number of livestock that browses on tree fodder (goats/sheep). Secondly, the people in this village are poorer than in the non-PFM village and thus LPG may not be very affordable to them, which makes the case for developing fuelwood to assist in daily livelihoods. In this village, the PFM programme has involved a group of women to develop *bhabar* grass *(Euliopsis binata)*[15] that can be used to make ropes. Quite clearly this particular intervention has paid dividends in the short run, thus making a case for its continuance.

In Solan the highest returns are generated by fuelwood and grazing. An intervention targeted at developing fuelwood makes economic sense since the people of the PFM village are poorer than in the non-PFM village and hence may not be able to afford LPG.

Conclusion

The effectiveness of a PFM programme hinges crucially on the short-run benefits to forest-fringe communities. The study observes that benefits do start accruing in the short-run where forest dependence is high. In the Himachal Pradesh context, this is of particular significance due to its relatively high forest cover and high proportion of rural population. At the same time, the PFM intervention does lead to enhancement of forest incomes in two of the three sites. However, the gains within PFM villages are not evenly distributed across income categories. Thus, while the income enhancement objective of PFM is not in question, its distributive impacts are uncertain. The need, therefore, is to address interventions more directly at poorer economic groups, and dovetail these with non-forest livelihood options.

Finally, the degree to which the PFM programme serves as an incentive to better manage forests depends on the extent to which benefits sustain in the long run. In other words, one needs to assess long-term forest flows, and its impacts on various socio-economic groups. The present study is based on one-point estimates and does not attempt to do this. Clearly, these estimates need to be projected to a reasonably distant time period to obtain long term flow values. This requires periodic monitoring of benefits across groups through suitable processes, such as micro-planning. To this end, there is also a case to incorporate such information into Working Plans so that this becomes an integral part of management planning systems within the Forest Department. In the process, there needs to be explicit recognition of potential trade-offs between maintenance of ecosystem services like biodiversity and the availability of sustenance (and livelihood) benefits of forests. While this study does not directly address this issue, it draws attention to the fact that if participatory management of forests are to be considered a means to enhance the quality of forests in broader (long term) 'public' interest, a significant share of the benefits must flow to local communities in the short run to achieve the desired longer run goals.

FOOT NOTE

1. The Forest Department of Himachal Pradesh (where the present study is based) has preferred to use the term "Participatory Forest Management" in its Executive Order formalising this arrangement. In this section, JFM has been used due to its wider currency at a national level, and its use in the national level Government Order. However, in later sections, we will be using the term PFM to refer to the specific Himachal context.
2. The result for West Bengal is clearly counter-intuitive. The reasons for this include the following: (a) Head-loaders stand to lose due to closure of forest patches; (b) There is a reduction in NTFP production in plantation areas.
3. Unit of local governance comprising one or a few villages.
4. The map of Himachal Pradesh shows districts (administrative units within a state) rather than Forest Divisions. These two categories are not necessarily coterminous. Solan, Seraj and Paonta Forest Divisions lie within Solan, Kullu and Sirmaur districts respectively.
5. According to the National Sample Survey (NSS) classification in India, 1 adult = 1.56 child, where a child is someone below the age of 10.
6. Scheduled Castes/Scheduled Tribes.
7. 1 buffalo = 1 unit; 1 cow = 1 unit; 1 goat or sheep = 0.1 unit (Qureshi and Kumar, 1998).
8. Key NTFPs in the Seraj study site include Gucchi (*Morchela esculenta*), Banafsha (*Viola serpens*), Singli mingli (*Doscorea deltoidea*), Mehendi (*Lawsonia inermis*), Chora (*Angelica glauca*) and Dhoop (*Jurenea dolomiaea*).
9. In estimating grass consumed during stall-feeding, we assume that 60 per cent of the total stall-fed diet is green grass while the rest is dry fodder, which consists of crop residue from farmlands, and is thus not considered as forest income.
10. Domestic livestock were then converted into a common unit using the classification: 1 buffalo = 1 unit; cow = 1 unit; 1 goat or sheep = 0.1 unit (Qureshi and Kumar, 1998).
11. When using this data, it was observed that in some households the net agricultural incomes were negative. This is clearly a data problem; the very fact that agricultural activity is being carried out implies that there is a positive return. The reason for negative values could be : (a) input costs used for the calculations, as obtained from government data, are greater than actual input costs in the study area and (b) output was under-reported by the respondents at the survey stage. For the purpose of analysis, negative values were treated as zero.

12. This information was gathered during PRA exercises held in the villages
13. The Gujjars of Himachal Prdaesh are predominantly graziers belonging to the Muslim community.
14. We, however, do note that forest incomes per capita depict a declining trend with rising income in the Solan site. Thus we expect that the PFM programme would be equity enhancing in the longer run..
15. Bhabar is a tufted perennial grass growing in mountainous and sub-mountainous regions. Harvesting bhabar grass is a common livelihood option for poorer people of this region.

Acknowledgements

This paper is based on a study funded by the DfID-assisted Himachal Pradesh Forest Sector Reforms Project. The views expressed are those of the authors.

REFERENCES

Bahuguna, V.K., D. Capistrano, K. Mitra, and S. Saigal, S., ed., *Root to Canopy:regenerating forests through community-state partnerships.*,Winrock International India. 2004.

FSI, *State of Forest Report 2009.* Ministry of Environment and Forests, Dehra Dun. 2009.

Gatenby, R., S. Neopane, and P. Chemjong, *Traditional Feeding Practices for Buffaloes in the Koshi Hills.* Pakhribas Agricultural Centre Technical Paper 99. Kathmandu, Nepal, 1989.

Gouri, Mudgal S., E. Morrison and J. Mayers, *Policy Influences on Forest-based Livelihoods in Himachal Pradesh, India,* London. : International Institute for Environment and Development, 2004.

Hill, I., and D. Shields, *Incentives for Joint Forest Management in India: analytical methods and case studies.* World Bank Technical Paper No. 394. 1998.

Kumar, S., 'Does "Participation" in Common Pool Resource Management Help the Poor? A Social Cost-Benefit Analysis of Joint Forest Management in Jharkhand, India', in *World Development* 30 (5): 763-782, 2002.

MoA. *Reports of the Commission for Agricultural Costs and Prices: 2004-05.* Ministry of Agriculture, Government of India, 2005.

Qureshi, M.H., and S. Kumar, 'Contribution of Common Lands to Household Economies in Haryana, India', in *Environmental Conservation* 25 (4): 342-353, 1998.

Ravindranath, N.H., and P. Sudha, *Joint Forest Management in India – spread, performance and impact.* Universities Press, Hyderabad, 2004..

Terborgh, J. and C.P. van Schaik, 'Why the world needs parks', in J. Terborgh, C.P. van Schaik, L. Davenport, and M. Rao, eds., *Making parks work: Strategies for preserving tropical nature.* Washington: Island Press, 2002.

12

Sustaining Livelihoods under Eco-development Initiative in Kalakad Mundanthurai Tiger Reserve in Southern Tamil Nadu

Key Results and Future Challenges

V.K. Melkani

Background

The positive role the local resource dependent communities can play in natural resource conservation planning and action was neither acknowledged nor given a genuine consideration in past. This resulted in developing a feeling of alienation among the local communities living in and around these areas towards the need for conservation and lack of their crucial support for the conservation efforts. This was not helpful to the welfare of both the conservation and the local communities. The conflicts between the management and the local communities were of common occurrence (Kothari *et al.*, 1989). The National Forest Policy 1988 duly recognized this and envisaged a larger role of local communities and their involvement in forest conservation, regeneration and protection. The Convention on Biodiversity (CBD) of which our country is a part also reiterated the role of local communities and their involvement in such initiatives for sustainable forest management and biodiversity conservation. The National Wildlife Action Plan, 2002-2016 categorically provides critical focus among its 13 Strategies for

Actions on involving local communities in wildlife conservation and restoring the degraded forest areas outside the Protected Areas. These global and national obligations and understandings paved way for emergence of a new era in conservation management both in the Forest and the Protected Area (PAs) systems. The exclusive approaches for conservation, hitherto followed in the country were converted to an inclusive approach where involvement of the local communities was planned and insured and various workable approaches, viz. Joint Forest Management (JFM), for participatory forest protection, regeneration and conservation efforts and Eco-development processes for participatory biodiversity and wildlife conservation were attempted. These processes contributed significantly in tilting the situation and reducing the rising conflicts between the management and the communities. The levels of achievements during field implementation of these initiatives might vary from site to site, yet the learning's obtained provide clues for refining the strategy and the protocols of these approaches to build in equity, both in participation and benefit sharing and securing long term sustainability of these efforts.

About the Area

Kalakad Mundanthurai Tiger Reserve (KMTR) located in the districts of Tirunelveli and Kanyakumari of Tamil Nadu state falls between 8° 25′ - 8° 53′ North Latitude and 77° 10′ -77° 35′ East Longitude. Established in 1989, it is the 17th Tiger Reserve in the country with undulating terrain with altitudinal range varying from 40m MSL to 1800m MSL forming the southernmost tiger habitat in the country. The Reserve is comprised Kalakad, Mundanthurai and part of newly established Kanyakumari Wildlife Sanctuaries and extends over 895 sq. km. representing tropical wet evergreen forests worldwide and also represents Type 1 Tiger Conservation Unit (Annamalai, 2004). The Reserve is part of Agasthyarmalai Biosphere Reserve and receives rains during both monsoons (750mm on eastern outer slopes to 3500mm in the western higher reaches).

The Reserve has rich floral diversity in 10 distinct forest types. Part of southern Western Ghats is one of the global biodiversity hot spots and Agasthyarmalai region is one of the 5 centres of plant biodiversity and endemism in India. The rich evergreen forests of the Reserve are the source of 12 rivers and tributaries giving birth to holy Tamirabarani – the lifeline of Tirunelveli, Tuticorin and part of Kanyakumari districts. This unique product from the intact catchment forests of KMTR sustains 10 major reservoirs and 3 hydroelectric power plants. The Reserve is known for its rich floral diversity – 2,254 Angiosperms (448 endemic); 58 Red listed species; 601 medicinal plant species; 90 species of wild relatives of cultivated plants; 3 Gymnosperms; 156 Pteridophytes and faunal diversity containing – 47 species of fishes; 47 amphibians; 89 reptiles; 337 birds and 79 mammals in addition to its rich religious and cultural values (Annamalai, 2004).

Problem Profile

The reserve is well buffered in the west, north and south sides with forests in Tamil Nadu and Kerala States. The Eastern boundary (approx.110 km.) is open and abuts many villages which interact with the fringe forests and put pressures on the resources – fire wood collection ; livestock grazing ; NTFP collection ; removal of small and large timbers etc. Before the initiation of eco-development efforts the local people's support towards conservation was generally lacking and majority of poor people depended on Reserve's resources for livelihood. They did not relate themselves as having a permanent stake in the conservation of the resources of the reserve. The conflicts with management and local communities were occurring quite often. To the people, the management was an enemy and *vice versa.*

- 145 villages/hamlets (about 35,000 households) within 5 to 7 km of the eastern boundary of the Reserve. 2 large townships and 7 small towns, 2 important factories employing about 3,000 people and one multinational tea company on leased forest land in the core of the reserve which has 3 tea factories (about 10,000 workers). In addition 3 colonies of state Electricity Board staff and five habitations of one tribe (Kanis), about 650 people were residing inside the Reserve. Forest fires during summers were quite common. Illegal timber felling, interstate border problems, huge local/religious tourism pressure and shortage of front line staff were other aspects of the problems to which the reserve was exposed.

Participatory Biodiversity Conservation in KMTR

A pilot project under World Bank aided FREEP (Forestry Research, Education and Extension Project) focusing on eliciting the local people's support for biodiversity conservation in the Reserve was initiated between 1995–1999 (with 2 time extensions, the project period closed on 31.12.2001). With an initial budget of Rs. 9.14 crores (however, with two time extensions the budget was also enhanced to Rs.11.80 crore). The project consisted of three main components (Project Document – FREEP, 1994) :

- Eco-development – securing local people's support for biodiversity conservation
- Park management – improved management with respect to both infrastructure and capacity
- Research, monitoring and evaluation – developing base line data on the Reserve and its monitoring

Eco-development is defined as a site specific package of measures derived through people's participation, which addresses all aspects of land use and other resources in order to promote sustainable land use as well as off-farm activities (income) which are not deleterious to PA values (Panwar, 1992), as a package of programmes that will demonstrate PA manager's concern for socio-economic development of fringe villages and will result in greater cooperation of residents of villages in the conservation and management of wildlife in the PA (MOEF, GoI, 1991) and as a strategy for protecting ecologically valuable areas from unsustainable or otherwise unacceptable pressure from the needs and activities of people living in and around such areas (IIPA, 1993).

The eco-development initiatives were attempted in the 5 km zone along the eastern boundary of the Reserve and all the villages/hamlets that showed willingness towards the initiatives were systematically covered. 133 grassroots organizations called the Village Forest committees (VFCs) registered under the Tamil Nadu Registration of Societies Act, 1975 were established in the participating villages/hamlets. Two members were allowed to become members in the VFC (one male and one female member) on payment of a membership fee of Rs.1 per month. The General Body of the VFC comprised of all members with a meeting once in three months and to pass resolution with a two third majority. The Executive Committee comprised of seven members, fifty per cent of whom were women and that ensured women's participation in the participatory working and decision making. The executive members were choosing their leader, the VFC chairperson with consensus holding the position for two years. The eco-development Forester, a staff of the Tiger Reserve was the *ex-officio* Member Secretary of the VFC. The VFC has a joint account in the nearest branch of a bank wherein the funds for implementation of micro-plan activities will be deposited and the VFC will withdraw the funds as per the approved micro-plan and the decision of the Executive Committee. A group of two to four villages/hamlets depending on the size of the village were provided services of a field worker (NGO representative) to facilitate the functioning of the VFC. The development of rapport among village people, assisting in micro-planning, conductance of VFC meeting and recording of proceedings, collection of repayment of loan amount from the beneficiaries and its deposition in banks as well as to undertake various capacity building and awareness programmes in the villages were the important functions and contributions of these workers who were predominantly from the participating villages only were the real link between the Reserve management and the participating villages. Majority of the workers were women and that helped to secure very high level of women participation in the eco-development initiatives undertaken in KMTR. The role played by the young local people as field workers is creditable and contributed to the project success in a very big way.

What is Eco-development and what is it not?

As evident from the definitions the Eco-development is a site specific package of measures for —

- Promoting a healthy and positive interaction between management and public, specially the local people,
- Aimed at two way reduction of park – people and people – park interactions and arising conflicts, and
- Therefore, *a tool and a methodology for effective* conservation;
- However, it not a substitute for policing and patrolling and also not;
- Not a revenue sharing arrangement and not; and
- A "panacea" for all ills of management of a PA.

The eco-development is a truly participatory process and exercise where people's needs and conditions are respected and responded in best possible and feasible manner; bottom up approach with a strong belief that people can do and make a change and is process driven and evolving mechanism. Eco-development essentials include — open dialogue and sensitive learning; comprehensive and action stimulating monitoring and refining approaches; sincere and genuine implementation and taking such opportunities with pride to serve both the people and the nature.

Partners in the Process

The KMTR management, local villagers (Village Forest Committee's [VFCs] – 133 as on December 2001 at the time of project closure ; and 204 in October 2010; 70 VFC's were established after the project closure from Government of India's funding support), NGOs and their workers (9 Local NGOs and 55 field level workers who were representatives of NGO's). The project has separate staff for Eco-development and protection works of the Reserve. The fines and fences or the carrot and stick policy was the soul of the programme as it was the first initiative of its kind and to start where the dream of success was in dilemma, however as time passed and relationship grew strong, the fence became a social fence for conservation and fines initiated to gradually reduced and KMTR became a joint and proud possession of the management and the local communities and the attachment has not broken since then.

The Process

Securing people's participation in conservation and developmental action is painfully slow process to start with and gains momentum when the rapport and relationships grow. The initial micro-plan preparation took somewhere around 8-9 months which subsequently reduced to 2-3 months when the philosophy of the programme, its vision and do's and don'ts started becoming clear to vast sections of the society as the process slowly and steadily progressed. The following sequence of major steps constituted the participatory conservation process attempted in the Reserve under the World Bank aided pilot project —

- Building rapport and nurturing relationships (through entry point activities).
- Forming village forest committees – VFCs – the grassroots level organizations committed to conservation and self-development and their registration under Societies Registration Act.
- PRAs and PLAs, involving understanding and assessing the village level resource and need surveys, the Strengths, Weakness, Opportunity and Threat (SWOT) analysis, situational analysis and participatory village specific micro-planning where, for affecting differential treatments to various resource dependent people the categorization of people in Red, Yellow and Green Groups — where the Red Group denoted the high level of dependence on Reserve's resources for livelihoods and first priority was accorded to them in providing alternate livelihoods so as to gradually reduce the pressures from the Reserve was attempted.
- Preparation of micro-plans and their approval in consultation with the VFC's. The revision of micro-plans was flexible so as to incorporate appropriate changes based on the reflections of the changing ground realities over time.
- Implementation of planned activities by the VFCs and its facilitation by the management

- Joint monitoring of activities by the VFCs and the Reserve management.

Basic Components of the Micro-plans

A pro-rata of Rs.1250/= (later enhanced to Rs. 1600/=) per household was the guiding factor to fix the budget lines of the micro-plans depending upon the number of house-holds in the participating villages. The following broad categories of inputs were focused in the micro-plans for which the consensus from the local people was available. Further based on the field realities flexibilities were permitted in the quantum of the three broad categories of in-puts —

- Biomass generation (about 25 per cent of budget) — homestead plantations, avenue plantations and community land plantations.
- Reduction and efficient use of wood (about 25 per cent of budget) – reducing consumption, improving efficiency, trying alternatives materials and methods for replacement of wood as energy material, viz. LPG, kerosene stoves, bio-gas, pressure cookers and husk *chullas*. The yellow group members in the village who used to purchase fire wood from wood cutters were motivated to opt for other materials and methods for energy use and that helped to wean away the wood cutters from cutting and removing firewood and the prospective purchaser was also targeted simultaneously which made a congenial situation for the programme to establish itself among various categories of people and winning their support.
- Alternate employment for forest dependent and enhancing incomes (about 50 per cent of budget) – some 50 and odd minor enterprises were attempted which were socially acceptable, conservation compatible and cost effective. Some of these for which credit were made available on 12 per cent simple interest per annum with a provision that the identified beneficiary also contributes about 10 to 25 per cent of the costs involved based on the quantum of

the credit which in the initial period of the project implementation ranged between Rs. 500 to Rs. 8,000 only were — fish sale, purchase of milch cattle, tea and petty shops, poultry farming, tailoring, handicrafts, utensil sale, savarimudi, juice business, coconut leave mats, painting and carpentry works, idly *mavu* making, bullock cart, lime manufacture, hollow cement bricks, fire wood shops, mini plough machine, chairs and marriage arrangement articles business, public address system business, cycle and mo-bike repair shops, hair cutting shops, musical instruments etc.

The micro-planning approach, therefore, contained the following features which makes it unique—

- Dependence ranking,
- Categorizing activities,
- Low budget and confidence building style,
- Care for less privileged,
- Provisions for review and amendments, and
- Listing beneficiaries at planning stage.

The Ideological Setting

Development actually depends upon a natural resource capital, and the goods and services for human beings are constantly created and consumed from the natural resource base, thereby making it a shrinking capital that need constant enrichment. This requires serious attention so as to ensure that the quantity and quality of resource exploitation is within the limits of delivery and not beyond which is crucial man's own survival and future. The Protected Areas on the other hand serve as critical habitats and the management focus is primarily for the optimization and sustenance of wildlife, therefore, the extraction of natural resource which impact the quality of habitat is curtailed to a great extent. This throws a hidden cost to local communities as much of their dependencies on the natural resources in these areas are legally not permitted. For a larger cause of biodiversity conservation and ecological service support mandated from these areas genuinely requires that the losses on the part of local dependent communities are compensated by way of alternatives be it a new skill or a new livelihood. Precisely this is what the process and practice of eco-development aims for. The legal provision as applicable to the Protected Areas in the country emphasizes on growing acceptance of the fact that the protected areas which are part of the larger repositories of the wild biodiversity, the support to human societies by way of ecological support services are of paramount nature. However, for the poor and marginal communities for whom the livelihood needs depend upon the extraction of some of the marketable goods and resources from the protected areas are unavoidable, it throws an intricate challenge to protected area managers to devise ways and means to ensure that the livelihood needs of these disadvantageous people are met through alternative means and judicious land uses in the surroundings where the productivity is optimal and conservation friendly. And the understanding and skills of dependent communities are developed in an appropriate manner and this is the real challenge of the eco-development.

Design Features of Eco-development Initiative in KMTR

- Separate wings with dedicated teams for Reserve protection and facilitating people's participation for conservation through eco-development.
- Financial empowerment to local communities (for the first time in the country the funds for implementing the micro-plan activities were kept at the disposal of the VFCs in the joint bank account of the VFCs).
- NGOs worked as partners and not as contractors.
- Very high and priority focus for providing required space for evolving awareness generation among the local people and equal space for continuing dialogue that shapes discussions and participatory learning.
- Building strong and developing relations, ensuring gender equity, respect for all, simplicity and sensitivity.
- In built evolving capacity building efforts for enhancing knowledge and skills among the local people and Reserve staff to understand the intricacies of the new efforts and to shoulder new roles and responsibilities.

- Strengthening stakeholder ownership and establishing credibility and trust among the local people and their institutions for long term sustainability.

The Implementation Approach of Eco-development in KMTR

The very important point of KMTR model of eco-development was the fact that biodiversity conservation initiatives focus on the catchments value of KMTR's forests – the holy Tamaribarni river – the life line for people, where people could feel stake and relate themselves to the values of the Reserve. The following equally priority focal areas which could make people to view the initiative as a unique initiative (Melkani, 2001) and for which their support could be secured continually were—

- Recognize inputs of the unrecognized and avoiding undue political colour and considerations;
- Careful monitoring of unhealthy trends meticulously in the initial stages and rewarding good participation;
- Maintaining conservation agenda and making community to shoulder responsibility and feel proud of themselves; and
- Inculcate and encourage local conservation leadership qualities

Major Project Impacts

First model where people were empowered to implement a micro plan themselves and PA management genuinely facilitated the process leads to community participation in VFCs from about 50 per cent to now at 74 per cent average enrolment in VFC's.

The figures of various aspects of the eco-development initiatives in KMTR as on June 2009 are as below:

Total number of village forest communities —193 (133 during the project and 60 after the project)

Total number of families joined in VFCs – 34,902

Total number of village forest committee members – 50,475

Total number of VFC members benefitted – 29,837

Total number of VFC chairpersons – 193 (Male – 137; female – 56)

Total number of SHGs – 776 (Male SHGs –93; Female SHGs – 683)

Fund utilized for loan purpose (Seed money) – Rs. 4,33,10,570 (Rs. 3,13,10,570 during the project period)

Total amount so far revolved – Rs. 25,61,32,202

Total amount with members at present – Rs. 4,80,79,480

Amount available in VFC account – Rs. 2,07,97,362

Corpus fund – Rs. 6,88,76,842

Percentage of loan recover – 91%

Representation in VFCs:

Chairpersons - BC – 99, SC – 68, MBC – 10, OC – 3, ST – 2 (182)

VFC – Membership – BC – 19145, SC – 13948, MBC – 1025, OC – 411, ST – 103 (34,902)

Beneficiaries –BC – 17487, SC – 8342, MBC – 1023, OC – 246, ST – 80 (27,178)

Empowerment of women

Members in VFCs – 21,639 – 62%

Members in EC – 811 – 56%

Women Chairpersons – 56 – 30%

Women SHGs – 540

Beneficiaries – 6980

Loans – Rs. 93.68 lakh

Recovery per cent - 100%

Ecological Impact

- Reduction in cutting and collection of fire wood in head loads – 3215 (1995) to 114 (2009) – 95%
- Reduction in grazing (number of cattle heads) – 22123 (1995) to 1106 (2003) – 95%

- Near zero problem Protected Area
- 5000 households adopted alternate energy use
- Habitats in the fringe forest areas have restored significantly
- VFCs play active role in control and extinguishes the fire incidents/spreads
- Timely information to reserve officials and staff for better management
- The reserve staff now concentrates on remote areas

The reduced levels of resource dependency have made the degraded fringe forests habitats replenishing in their status and assisting rich biodiversity to flourish again. The status of vegetation both in terms of quality and cover has improved many folds with increasing sightings of wildlife in these areas. The ecological sustainability is visibly evidenced by forest recovery as a result of project initiatives. Improved catchment protection as a result of reduction in tree felling has contained degradation including soil erosion thereby improving aquifer recharge and availability of water. The non-removal of under growth, green manure, dried twigs; marked reduction in grazing now has facilitated natural regeneration. Increased food availability for herbivores due to improved status of nutrient cycling will help in optimizing the population of key predators. The conflicts between the local communities and the reserve management are stories of the past now. The involvement of local people in management and their support for conservation has made enhanced protection of floral and faunal diversity possible. There is considerable reduction in forest offences through timely information by local communities to the management. The project initiatives have very clearly established that the philosophy and practice of eco-development where local communities are involved in the management can compliment biodiversity conservation, reducing conflicts and enhancing economies of local communities.

Sustainability

- Growing revolving fund
- Vibrant institutions now under a federation

- Eco-development staff in place
- NGO workers are now supported by VFC's
- Change in mindset and attitude

Key Learnings

- Focus on a cause for conservation to which people can easily relate themselves is essential to be on right footing
- Sense of commitment is essential
- Villagers need constant guidance, support and touch
- Internal problems of community pose serious threat and affect implementation
- People needs to be encouraged, motivated and trusted to enable them to take charge of responsibilities
- Flexibility in micro-plans helps in evolving the process as per changing needs and circumstances
- Demonstration of a technique/method/skill first before multiplying in large scale is useful
- There is no end to capacity building and motivation
- Support from higher levels makes change to take place
- Dual role play by staff in implementing eco-development can be counter productive

Future Challenges

- Monitoring activities of VFCs – strengthening institutional linkages,
- Sustaining rapport and relationships – changing and evolving roles and process in changing times,
- Inter/intra caste/group conflict management,
- Ensuring a common vision for future,
- Investment in building capacity, awareness of younger generation establishing small scale enterprises to create jobs for local people,

- Ensuring conservation agenda,
- Redefining the roles and responsibilities; and
- Undertake appropriate and mutually agreed and to the extent possible, eco-development activities for the Electricity Board colonies, Kani tribal communities and the Tea factory workers as their dependence on the resources needs to be addressed for a much larger and wholesome outcome of participatory biodiversity conservation in KMTR.

Conclusion

A successful foundation has been laid for a vibrant functioning of participatory biodiversity conservation in Kalakad Mundanthurai Tiger Reserve under the World Bank Project (CCF&FD, KMTR, 2009). The very fact that the project initiatives are continuing with enhanced fervour even after more than eight years of the project close indicate its sustainability. The growing revolving funds at the disposal of the VFCs, the continued working of the field level working and remuneration of their honorarium by the VFCs and the fact that the status of the forests and biodiversity of KMTR today is in the best of their status and it is almost a near nil protection problem Tiger Reserve in the country today signifies the sustainability of the project efforts which is not that easy to achieve. Collaborative bonds have been developed and new relations are forged among the resource dependent community which today has a shared vision to conserve the rich biodiversity of KMTR and to continually improve the livelihoods and income levels of the local communities (PEACE, 2004). The efforts made have been duly appreciated by the World Bank and the Governments both at the Centre and the state level and is now recognized by the World Bank as a "Centre of Learning in Participatory Biodiversity Conservation" add to the argument. The long-term success, however, will depend on further refining and sustaining the efforts hitherto made and improving upon the relationship and understanding between the local communities. It will be of high significance now that linkages are forged among other key stakeholders for mainstreaming biodiversity conservation at a larger pedestal. The various agencies responsible for controlling, regulating and enforcing various provisions of law in the area and also those who undertake various developmental activities to support local people in their pursuit of conservation by keeping a sharp focus on conservation needs and realities in their programmes and activities to add value to these efforts and make it truly wholesome. A balanced approach to contain conflicting needs and aspirations of local communities and other stakeholders through improved understanding and a common vision among them for the cause and concern of biodiversity conservation will definitely safeguard the welfare of both the biodiversity and the local communities in KMTR.

Acknowledgement

The author wishes to acknowledge the CCF and Field Director, KMTR for providing the data and other information.

REFERENCES

Annamalai, R, Eco-development in Kalakadu – Mundanthurai Tiger Reserve – Status report. Tamil Nadu Forest Department, Government of Tamil Nadu. 2004.

CCF&FD, KMTR. Report presented in the Field Directors of Tiger Reserves meeting, Sariska, 25-26 July, 2009.

Indian Institute of Public Administration, New Delhi, Biodiversity Conservation through Ecodevelopment, A Priliminary Indicative Plan for Great Himalayan National Park, Himachal Pradesh and Kalakad Mundanthurai Tiger Reserve, Tamil Nadu. 1993.

Melkani, V.K. Involving Local People in Biodiversity Conservation in Kalakadu – Mundanthurai Tiger Reserve – an overview. Current Science. Vol. 80(3) 437-441. 2001.

MoEF, GoI, Detailed Guidelines of the Centrally Sponsered Scheme "Eco-development in and around National Parks and Wild Life Sanctuaries'. 1991.

Panwar, H.S., Guidelines for Planning and Implementing Eco-development Programs as a Means of Integrating Management of Protected Areas with the Concerns of People for Sustenance and Culture, Unpublished WII. 1992.

PEACE Lessons learned from eco-development experiences in India: A study report submitted to Project Tiger, Government of India, New Delhi. 2004.

Report on Conservation of Biodiversity in KMTR through Eco-development and Improved Park Management, FREEP, 1993, Appendix 4.

13

Cost Sharing is Essential to Create Belongingness

Experiences from Eco-development Project in a National Park of India

Bidhan Kanti Das

Introduction

Conservationists and social scientists are greatly polarized in their argument regarding conservation of depleted biological resources. The conservationists are in favour of protection of biodiversity without any kind of human interferences. On the other hand, social scientists argue the issue from human rights perspective, viewing local communities as an integral part of the ecosystems (Shah, 2007). Approach of conservation is predominantly colonial in nature by establishing protected areas (PAs) that essentially enforce forcible exclusion of local communities from the forest areas (Adams, 2004; Hutton *et al.*, 2005). In effect, creation of protected areas is increasing rapidly in developing countries. This isolationist approach of conservation inevitably leads to considerable conflicts between local communities and forest staffs in access to forest resources. Notably, it is seen that most of the local communities in forest landscapes, are facing extreme poverty with income less than 1 dollar per day, especially in developing countries (Sayer *et al.*, 2007). Under such backdrop, it is clearly unfair that poor, marginalized communities become further marginalized and impoverished due to creation of protected areas under global conservation programmes (Arjunan *et al.*, 2006). Recognizing the complex problems due to protectionist management strategy, it is widely acknowledged that successful conservation is hardly possible without participation and support of local communities (Arnold, 2002). So, participatory and people centered approach has been undertaken in development projects like 'integrated conservation and development' projects, 'ecodevelopment' to reduce poverty as well as to conserve biodiversity (Christensen, 2004). Like other developing countries, India is no exception. Forest authorities are creating a huge network of PAs across India debarring access to resources enjoyed over the years by local communities. This has led to tremendous conflict between resource users and forest managers and staffs.

To reduce impoverishment due to creation of protected areas and to increase positive attitudes towards conservation of forest resources, forest authorities launched eco-development project in seven tiger reserves of India with assistance from the World Bank and Global Environment Facility. Buxa Tiger Reserve is one of them. Under the project, village eco-development is the most important component to increase positive attitude of local population about biodiversity. One of the approaches of the project is villagers themselves will prepare and implement microplan for eco-development to ensure active commitment and participation. That constitutes the core of the project strategy. The most important characteristic of these micro-plans is that 25 per cent of the total investment is to be contributed by the beneficiaries themselves towards village common fund with the intention to create belongingness among members for assets created. The purpose of the chapter is to assess how far eco-development activities are successful after implementation in different forest protection committees. Most importantly, it tries to explore the nature of villagers' contribution in eco-development investments as well as how poor and marginalized people respond to the strategy of sharing cost for investments – an area of in-depth, micro level study which is not available in the existing literature of developmental intervention in conservation programme.

The chapter is structured in the following sections. The first section deals with the contextualisation of the present investigation in a conceptual framework. The second section briefly describes the study area, i.e. Buxa Tiger Reserve, and its biodiversity importance as well as people who reside within it. Section III describes how eco-development has been conceived in this project by donor agencies like the World Bank. Section IV concentrates on the assessment of eco-development investment and nature of contribution by beneficiaries themselves for investment followed by an analysis on how poor and marginalized people respond to the strategy of sharing cost for investments. A discussion will be done about the findings and possible future directions to improve the situation will be dealt with in the last section.

Contextualising the Study

From the diverse problems in exclusionary nature of conservation strategy (a detailed discussion in the first chapter), a participatory and people oriented approach had been adopted which was known as integrated conservation and development project (ICDP). The ICDPs were implemented to reduce poverty and increase income levels, nutrition, health care and education as well as to conserve biodiversity (Christensen, 2004). The central concern of ICDP was to promote social and economic development among communities adjacent to protected area boundaries. The basic assumption was that 'people who are made better off as a result of development project will refrain from illegal exploitation of a nearby protected area even in the absence of negative incentive provided by more effective penalties' (Wells and Brandon, 1992). This approach has become the standard approach in linking the conservation of biodiversity with community development in PAs without any field level experience (Wells *et al.*, 2004). However, this approach has been severely criticized by conservationists and social scientists. Social scientists have argued that ICDPs operate like the conventional development projects and result in 'highly inequitable outcomes that severely limit local peoples rights (Schmidt-Soltau, 2004) potentially becoming poverty traps, for local communities (Dove 1993). Researchers analysing ICDPs argued that identifying locals as the agents of forest degradation is itself a wrong assumption, disregarding the role of timber mafias, mining, industrial exploitation (Dove, 1993; Christensen, 2004).

In India, efforts to link protected area management with local social and economic developmental programmes are referred to as "eco-development" (Panwar, 1992). It recognises that people residing in and around PAs have to bear maximum opportunity costs while deriving little tangible benefits from conservation activities (Badola, 1999). So, conservation initiatives must provide alternative livelihood programmes for forest dependent communities. However, this assumption has been criticised as it has little evidence (Christensen, 2004).

It is beyond doubt that preservation of biodiversity is hardly possible without consideration of people's needs and aspirations. Criticising ICDPs, Christensen argued that success depends on explicit testable assumptions, clearly stated objectives and measurable conservation targets. They should promote simple and adaptive conservation and development intervention for strengthening protected areas (2004). In India eco-development project (IEDP), eco-development has been conceived as a strategy that enlists people's participation for biodiversity conservation through generation of ecologically sustainable employment opportunities for villagers. It categorically states that to achieve eco-development objectives under the project several strategies ranging from eco-development investment through local institutions, PRA based micro-plan preparation as per local people's own wishes and interests based on local resources, to ensure that women, tribal, landless labourers and other disadvantaged and marginalized groups participate in the planning process and getting benefits.

Perhaps the most innovative feature of this project is beneficiaries' contribution towards project investment. The World Bank document specifically pointed that village eco-development investments should be done as they conserve biodiversity by creating sufficient incentives for a consensus that commits people to specific, measurable actions that improve conservation. If the objective of an investment is to benefit local people (including poorest of the poor), it is essential to require some form of cost sharing. Without cost sharing, such investments are highly likely to fail. If the village eco development investments fail, local people will not continue to commit to the actions that improve conservation. Contribution of any type generally show increased sense of belongingness towards assets created and ensure sustainability of activities. For this, beneficiaries have to contribute 25 per cent of the total investment in each microplan for village common fund (SAR, 1996). Under this project, this strategy has been adopted to instill an increased sense of belongingness among members for assets created. Contribution could be in terms of cash, kind or labour.

Though some studies have been done in various watershed projects regarding beneficiaries' contribution leading to increased belongingness, there is hardly any study on conservation projects in national park environment. To fill this knowledge gap, an attempt has been made to assess how far eco-development activities are successful after implementation in different forest protection committees. Most importantly, it tries to explore the nature of villagers' contribution in eco-development investments as well as how poor marginalized people respond to the strategy of sharing cost for investments.

For this, micro level in depth study has been undertaken among sampled FPCs/EDCs who had already spent about 70 per cent or more of total budget (Table 13.1). Data on people's contribution for eco-development investments was also collected from members in sampled FPCs/EDCs. It was revealed that 31 FPCs/EDCs have fulfilled such parameter. Of them, 13 FPCs and 6 EDCs were selected (61.29%) for study. This number is one-third of total FPCs/EDCs, which are under various stages of implementation. Structured and open-ended questionnaires were prepared by the author for data collection. The data were collected through group discussion, interview of individual beneficiaries as well as members of concerned executive committees, records from FPC registers as well as concerned Beat and Range records. Physical verification of each eco-development activity has been done as far as possible. However, it is to be noted here that assessment of all eco development activities could not be done physically due to absence of some members during field survey, shortage of time, absence of records etc. Estimation of economic benefit has been done on the basis of data provided by concerned beneficiaries as well as concerned Executive committee members during field investigation.

Area of Study: Buxa Tiger Reserve

A. *Name, Location, Constitution and Extent*

Buxa Tiger Reserve (BTR) is situated in Alipurduar Sub-division of Jalpaiguri District, West Bengal, India. It stretches over a length of 50 km from West to East and 35 km from North to South. The total area of the Reserve is 760.87 km^2 of which 385.02 km^2 has been constituted as Buxa Sanctuary and National Park (Core zone of the Buxa Tiger Reserve) and the balance 375.85 km^2 area is treated as buffer zone. Buxa Tiger Reserve was constituted in the year 1983 and became the 15th Tiger Reserve of the Country. The legal status was Reserved forest, Protected forest and Un-classed state forest, the first reservation being made in the year 1879. The Forest Settlement Officer inquired into the rights during the years 1890 to 1896. The first Sanctuary Notification was made over an area of 314.52 km^2. This area has been settled for rights and concessions under sections 19 to 25 of Indian Wildlife Protection Act, 1972 by the Collector, Jalpaiguri District. The Collector declared that no right of anyone exists in 331.60 km^2 of Buxa Wildlife Sanctuary in terms of Section 21(b) and Section 19 of Wildlife Protection Act, 1972. An area of 117.10 km^2 of the Sanctuary was preliminarily declared as National Park under section 35(1)(2) of Wildlife Protection Act (1972). It was finally constituted as Buxa National Park on 5th December, 1997 (Management Plan of BTR -1999-2009).

B. *General Significance*

Buxa Tiger Reserve is biologically very rich. It is located in the confluence of 3 major Bio-geographic Zones, viz. Lower Gangetic plains (7B), Central Himalayas (2C), and Brahmaputra valley (8A). The project site supports vital population of tiger (*Panthera tigris*), the National animal. BTR represents several elements of bio-diversity of North-East India, one of the most biodiverse Indian Regions. Most of the floral endemic species of N-E India (about 60%) are encountered in BTR (Management Plan of BTR-1999 to 2009). The endemic Indo-Malayan species like Chinese Pangolin (*Manis crassicaudata*) and Reticulated Python (*Python reticulatus*) have been reported in Buxa Tiger Reserve. The rare Clouded Leopard (*Neofelis nebulosa*), Marbled Cat (*Pardofelis marmorata*), Black-necked crane (*Grus nigriocollis*), etc. (some of the endemic species of North-East zone) are present in B.T.R. Moreover, the Reserve acts as a carbon sink of the region. The mountain ranges intercept rain laden clouds and recharge ground water. It protects the catchments of several rivers and streams and thereby reduces soil erosion and maintains water regime. It sustains the economic prosperity of the region through down stream irrigation.

More than 50 per cent of the plant species of India are found in North-East India. Of these 60 per cent are endemic. BTR has many of those characteristics and the present check list shows 352 species of trees, 133 species of shrubs, 189 species of herbs, 108 species of climbers, 144 species of orchids, 46 species of grasses and reeds, 6 species of cane and 4 species of bamboo. Along with the floral diversity, the Buxa Tiger Reserve has a wide range of faunal diversity. There are 68 species of mammals, 41 species of reptiles, 246 species of birds, 4 species of Amphibians, 33 species of fishes identified within the Reserve. Study on entomofauna of BTR listed 500 species of insects belonging to 13 Orders, 65 families and 229 genera.

C. *The People and Economy*

BTR has 37 forest villages and 4 fixed demand holdings within its boundary with a population of 18,100 (1991 Census). Twelve forest villages and 2 fixed demand holdings are located within core areas of BTR. In forest villages, dominant ethnic groups are Rabha, Oraon and Nepali (Table13.1). BTR is also encircled by 34 tea gardens and 46 revenue villages on western and southern sides (considering 2 km from park boundary). The human population of these revenue villages is 95,049 (1991 Census). Predominant ethnic groups in these revenue villages are Rajbansi, Mech and Migrant Bengalees.

Table 13.1 : Distribution of ethnic groups in forest villages of BTR

Ethnic groups /community	*No. of households*	*per cent of total households*
Rabha	836	28.64
Oraon	334	11.44
Santal	119	4.08
Mech	127	4.35
Garo	121	4.14
Nepali	955	32.72
Dukpa	217	7.44
Mixed*	210	7.19
Total	**2919**	**100.00**

* includes mainly Munda, Asur, Bhutia etc.

Source: Das, B.K. (2000).

Rain-fed cultivation of paddy and maize is the principal economic activity of forest villagers of BTR owing to absence of irrigation facility. In revenue villages, about one-fourth of the villagers are landless or share-croppers and are largely engaged as agricultural or daily labourers. A bulk of families are small and marginal farmers. Irrigation facility is minimum. According to 1984 census, cattle population of forest villagers, revenue villagers and tea garden labourers is 18854, 41694 and 42428 respectively. These populations graze in forest areas daily, posing great threat to biodiversity of species and spread of infectious diseases among wild animals.

The areas fringing the reserve are either cultivable lands or tea estates. As a result, most of the population is engaged in cultivation or tea estate jobs. Due to expansion of Alipurduar Township towards the forest areas, a group of semi-urban population has also come into contact in fringes of forest areas. As a result, demand for timber and other forest products increased considerably for house construction and furniture.

About one-third of total members are landless in studied FPCs/EDCs of BTR. Generally, numbers of landless are less in forest villages in comparison to revenue villages. But, in forest villages, about 60 per cent have less than 5 bighas of cultivable land. This is mainly due to steep increase in population and break down of Joint family system (Das, 2000). In FPCs, landless population is more than 40 per cent of studied populations. The inequality of cultivable lands exists within FPCs and EDCs largely due to the fact that revenue villagers are members of FPCs.

Among landowners, members solely depend on rainfed agriculture due to non-availability of irrigation system, especially in forest villages before implementation of microplan. In revenue villages, about one fourth of total cultivable land is under minor irrigation system. In forest villages, people cultivate maize, marwa, millet, mustard, jute etc. Villagers from revenue areas cultivate paddy, potato, jute, mustard, some vegetables etc. Landless people engage as agricultural or daily labour at Panchayat works, firewood sale, and forest department works. Forest villagers are facing extreme hardship for income at present as clear felling coupes (CFC) and plantations reduced dramatically due to ban in CFC after declaration of protected areas.

Incomes from sale of milk, areca nut, bamboo, NTFPs are treated as supplementary sources for sustaining daily needs of families of villages especially in forest villages. Livestock assets act as emergency source of income especially during rituals and festivals, treatment, education etc. Some members sustain their livelihoods from small-scale businesses in vegetables, cattle, areca nuts. A fair number of youths have migrated to northern parts of India for work as daily labourers in Industries.

Conceiving Eco-development

To preserve biodiversity, Government of India acknowledges people's participation. Biodiversity cannot be conserved if people's needs and aspirations are not taken into consideration. From shifting isolationist approach of PA management, to participatory approach involving local communities, eco-development measures have been started since 1991 for conserving biodiversity. Eco-development is an initiative to reduce dependence on forest and to ameliorate hardships faced by local communities for resource use restrictions – in cash, kind and labour through alternative income generating activities.

Various definitions have been proposed including: (i) "site specific economic activities based on people's choice with the objective of promoting sustainable use of land and other resources as well as farm and off farm income generating activities which are not harmful to protected area values" (Panwar, 1992) and (ii) "limited rural development designed with the participation of local people for fulfilling genuine human needs with specific aims of protected area management" (Pabla *et al.*,1995).

To ameliorate hardships faced by villagers of BTR due to creation of Tiger Reserve, Forest Department of Government of West Bengal has launched massive developmental programmes under India Eco-Development Project in BTR since September 1996. The project has been simultaneously launched in seven globally important protected areas of India. The International Development Agency (IDA) and the Global Environment Facility (GEF) financed the 5-year project with a total outlay of Rs.35.71 crore for BTR.

The objective of the project is to protect and develop the bio-diversity in BTR through a two-pronged strategy. On one hand, it reinforces traditional strategies of protection and management of the Tiger Reserve. On the other hand, it aims at enlisting people's support for biodiversity conservation through generation of ecologically sustainable employment opportunities in fringe villages.

To reduce pressure on forests and negative interactions of local people on biodiversity, the project addresses the special issues regarding participatory management of protected areas through a strategy of Eco development. Here, *eco-development* is conceived as *a strategy, which aims to conserve biodiversity by addressing both the impact of local people on the protected areas and the impact of the protected areas on local people.* It deals with reducing negative interactions of local people on biodiversity and increasing collaboration of local people in conservation by (i) conducting participatory microplanning and providing implementation support; (ii) implementing reciprocal commitments that foster alternative livelihoods and resource uses to be financed by a village eco- development programme and that specify measurable actions by local people to improve conservation, and (iii) special programmes for additional Joint Forest Management, voluntary relocation and supplementary investments for special needs (SAR, World Bank, 1996). Eco development addresses the welfare and behaviour of local people and integrates these concerns into management of protected areas.

To achieve eco-development objectives, the following strategies were adopted. Firstly, all the eco-development activities should be undertaken among members of local institutions, e.g. Forest Protection Committees (FPCs) and Eco-development Committees (EDCs) exist in BTR. Secondly, Micro plans should be prepared by members themselves of various protection committees for eco-development activities as per local people's own wishes and interests and possibilities and resources of a particular area. Special emphasis should be given to ensure that women, tribal, landless labourers and other disadvantaged and marginalized groups participate in the planning process and benefit from the agreed programmes as far as possible during microplan preparation. Planned investments are to be judged from ecological, social and financial point of views. Thirdly, planned investments should have a community bias.

Fourthly, most important characteristic of these micro plans is that 25 per cent of the total investment is to be contributed by the beneficiaries themselves for village common fund. The intention of this is to instill an increased sense of belongingness among members for assets created. Contribution could be in terms of cash, kind or labour. Fifthly, beneficiaries have to comply reciprocal commitments to preservation of bio-resources.

Implementing Eco-development

Eco-development activities to be invested have been selected based on villager's priorities, local resources within financial allocation through PRA based microplan preparation by villagers themselves with the assistance of social, financial and technical experts. Authorities emphasized for community or large group asset creation as a priority status as this will instill community feeling among members as well as monitoring of asset creation will be easier.

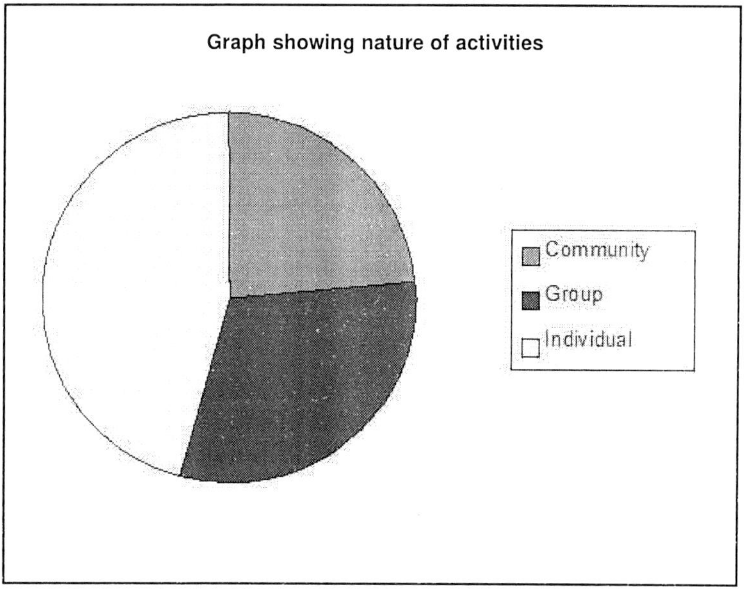

From implementation of microplans in studied FPCs/EDCs, it is revealed that about 46 per cent of total investments was invested in individual level assets in studied FPCs/EDCs, despite stress in community assets (see Graph). On the other hand, only 24 per cent of total budget was invested in community level assets. It is noteworthy that 100 per cent investment was invested in community assets in only 2 FPCs under study Similarly, 100 per cent investment was done on individual level assets in one FPC. As group level assets, 80 per cent of budget was invested in only one FPC. Moreover, more than 90 per cent of total budget as individual level assets was invested in three FPCs under study.

Selected activities can be broadly categorized into three level : (i) *Community level activities* like road improvement, agricultural implements e.g. tractor, power tiller, spray machine ; minor irrigation development, e.g. pumpsets, dug well, shallow well, deep bore tube well; dairy, poultry etc. ; (ii) *Group level activities* like agriculture, pisciculture, irrigation development, e.g. pumpsets, dug well, shallow well ; grocery, husking machine, areca nut garden, weaving etc. ; (iii) *Individual level activities* like piggery, goatery, milch cows, bullocks, rice and fried rice business, rickshaw/van, small shops and business, grocery, apiary etc. Generally speaking, successes or failures of activities largely depend on level of experience, training, motivation to work, as well as market demands of products. Overall, it is revealed that community cash crop cultivation through minor irrigation system by pumpsets and dugwells, use of tractor and power tiller and cycle rickshaw/van pulling are the most successful and profit making activities among the activities so far implemented. On the other hand, livestock and dairy activities, grocery are more or less loss making activities.

Community level activities that include village road development, social and farm forestry, provision smokeless chullahs, sausage works vary from one area to other areas. This type of labour intensive programme had been taken to arrange to villagers' own contribution for ecodevelopment activities. Most interesting observation is that forest managers tried to develop a model of asset creation, stressing most investments under 'community activities' in at least four protection committees under one range in the name of concerned beneficiaries' aspirations or wishes. These microplans have been prepared by beneficiaries without local needs and aspiration. The assets created like large scale dairy, poultry and piggery units, agricultural development in illegal land, tractor etc. with the hope of profits will be distributed among beneficiaries. Though initially productivity was higher and profits were more. But after some months yields declined but expenses for maintenance increased and eventually it became loss making (e.g. Nimti Domohoni FPC, Nimti FV). For these programmes villagers needs and aspiration hadn't been taken into consideration. They were forced to prepare such microplans under pressure from forest authorities leading to lack of support and involvement with the investments. Further, income from this type of investment does not even supplement the earning of beneficiaries that may lead to incentives creating lack of ownership of the assets.

Group level activities revealed that members have given topmost priority in cash crop cultivation with intervention of modern techniques by forming large groups within members. Development of minor irrigation is another major activity for multi crop system instead of mono crop as evident from members' choices.

Agriculture is one of the major activities of people residing in and around BTR. But irrigation facility for cultivation is less in these villages. So, people mainly depend on rain-fed agriculture. High yielding variety of seeds and improved method of crop cultivation was rarely practiced by villagers. Various FPCs have started community level crop cultivation with the interventions of modern techniques for awareness generation and increased productivity and employment generation for landless people. With the advent of minor irrigation facility, cultivation pattern of these lands changed to multiple cropping from mono cropping. Some small groups were formed ranging from 4 to 25 members for better management. FPCs centrally distributed high yielding seeds, fertilizers etc. Our calculations revealed that about 32 per cent of total budget was utilized for group level agricultural development. Improved agriculture has been undertaken – (i) to give an idea to cultivators about productivity of land which was not exploited much earlier; (ii) to increase sense of ownership, accountability and group solidarity through account maintenance; (iii) to give maximum employment to landless, marginal farmers as well as womenfolk who are mostly dependent on forests in agricultural fields and (iv) to help in 25 per cent contribution against micro plan activities under IEDP.

More than 13 per cent of total budget was utilized for renovation of pond and fisheries. Earlier, various small water bodies in the village remained unutilized due to financial problems. Members formed small groups for maintenance and management of ponds. From microplan, members renovated these water bodies. Members of concerned groups got labour for digging and renovation. FPC centrally has given small fishes, feed, fertilizers etc. Lands for fishery were leased for 5 years or so. This activity was undertaken (i) to utilize unutilized water bodies; (ii) to give maximum employment to landless, marginal farmers as well as womenfolk who are mostly dependent on forests in agricultural fields, and (iii) to help in 25 per cent contribution agáinst micro plan activities under IEDP. But, it is revealed that actual landowners became the owners of the ponds after one year implementation. Other members of the group are not getting benefits at present. Group members are helpless. Executive committees are not taking any step.

If we consider individual level assets, it is revealed that members, especially landless, marginal farmers identified goatery as most important individual activity which is about one third of total investment. Members regard goatery as a supplementary source of income. People opined that they have minimum investment in rearing and treat goat rearing as important cash income source during emergency /crisis period. Most poor members of STs have chosen piggery as it is socially acceptable. They are making profits. Person who are engaged in liquor business, are making maximum profits. They can provide fermented rice from liquor as feed for pigs. Beneficiaries opined that rearing of more than 2-3 pigs is difficult as they are unable to purchase feed for pigs. So some members sold additional pigs and engaged in other activities from the amount.

On the other hand more than 100 families especially from Rajbansi community initially engaged in fried rice/rice business under studied village. But only 50-55 per cent families are still continuing this business. Others left the business due to loss. However, some have purchased goats and some have leased agricultural lands as alternative activities. It is highly profitable. This type of business is confined to revenue villages.

In fact most of the individual activities are successful. It is felt that beneficiaries themselves believe that they are the owners of activities. They know that they have to earn money for sustaining daily requirements from those activities. As a result, they maintain or nurture activities more efficiently or judiciously.

But almost all the dairy activities failed due to improper maintenance, less feed availability, less availability of veterinary care etc. As an individual activity, hybrid milch cows also failed. It is also revealed that members, who sustain their daily needs from daily income, were not able to spend money for feed continuously. Without feed and lack of knowledge of maintenance, milch cows either died or did not give much yield. It is also revealed that though activities were insured, some members did not get insurance benefits due to lack of knowledge about system, lack of coordination between EC and agents etc. Generally speaking, only those members are making profits in activities who have some knowledge about those activities. Items failed due to lack of entrepreneurial skills, lack of knowledge and training and less demand for the product within the village. For example, a large number of groceries opened within FPC localities. Most are not making profit owing to excessive credit to locals as well as non-recovery of credit. In effect, some members shifted to other businesses, e.g. vegetable business.

People's Contribution

One of the most important eligibility criteria of village eco development investments is that they should conserve biodiversity by creating sufficient incentives for a consensus that commits people to specific, measurable actions that improve conservation. If the objective of an investment is to benefit local people (including poorest of the poor), it is essential to require some form of cost sharing. Without cost sharing, such investments are highly likely to fail. If the village eco-development investments fail, local people will not continue to commit to the actions that improve conservation. The project design specifies that members will contribute at least 25 per cent of total village eco-development investment in cash, kind or labour to instill more sense of belongingness among members for assets created (SAR, WB, 1996). This 25 per cent contribution of total investments in a FPC/EDC will create a village development fund in future.

In fact, this measure was the most problematique component of the project. Initially members were not interested to contribute. This is somewhat different measure from other conventional welfare measures undertaken by FD and civil administration. According to villagers, 'It is another Government programme for our development. Why should we want to contribute for this programme? Moreover, we have no avenues to arrange such contribution.' Forest authority had to spend most of the time to convince people about the necessity of contribution. As economic conditions vary, nature and ways of contribution naturally varied from FPC to FPC and EDC. Poor, marginal members found it very difficult to arrange the said amount.

Table 13.2 shows that one-fourth of the total beneficiaries have taken loan for contributing own share. About one-fifth of the beneficiaries contribute their share by selling their assets. However, almost similar number of beneficiaries have given cash for eco-development investment.

Table 13. 2 : Different ways of 25 per cent contribution according to social category

Various modes	*SC (n=83)*	*ST (n=152)*	*GEN (n=142)*	*Total (n=377)*
Sale of own asset	8.43	33.55	16.20	19.36
Loan	33.73	19.74	28.17	26.79
Own asset+ interest	8.43	4.60	1.41	4.24
Cash + interest	14.46	11.84	20.42	15.65
Cash	27.71	19.08	28.17	24.40
Cash +asset	2.41	8.55	1.41	5.84
Kin	4.82	2.63	4.22	3.71

About one-third of ST beneficiaries had to sell their own asset for contribution whereas a similar percentage of SC beneficiaries had to take loan. Beneficiaries of general category have mostly given cash amount for own contribution towards assets created. However, some had taken loan for contribution.

It is also revealed that more than 40 per cent of daily labourers and firewood sellers had to take loan for their own contribution (Table 13.3). Another one-fifth of firewood sellers and daily labourers had sold their own asset. Small, marginal cultivators contribute their share either by selling own asset or by cash. As expected more than half of the people of white colour jobs, rickshaw or van pullers had contributed their share by cash.

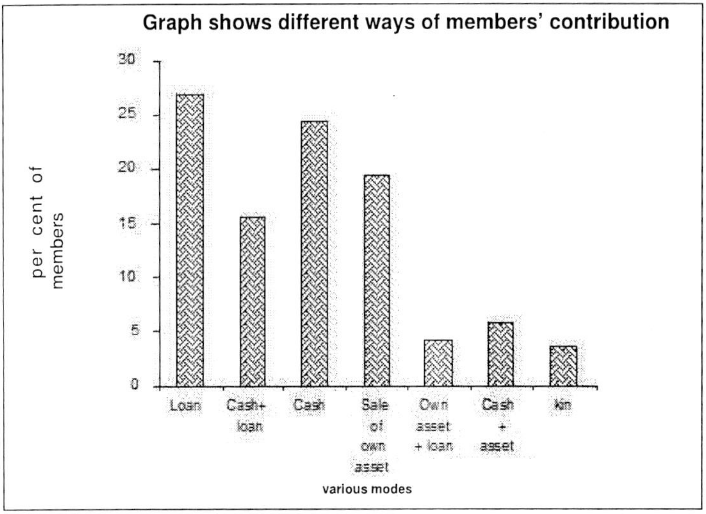

Table 13.3 : Different ways of contribution on the basis of occupational status

Occupation	*n*	*Sale of own asset*	*Loan*	*Own asset + interest*	*Cash + interest*	*Cash*	*Cash+ asset*	*Kin*
Daily labourers	69	18.84	42.03	8.70	7.23	13.04	7.25	2.90
Cultivators	148	25.68	18.24	4.05	11.49	27.70	6.76	6.08
Firewood sellers	55	20.00	40.00	3.64	2.18	7.27	3.64	3.64
Small business	64	9.37	31.25	3.12	26.56	25.00	3.12	1.56
Others*	41	12.20	9.76	-	17.07	53.66	2.44	4.88

* Workers at forest Department, private service, rickshaw / van pulling etc.

More than 40 per cent of landless beneficiaries had to take loan from money lenders with high interest to contribute their own share towards investments (see Graph). On the other hand, a fair percentage of land owners had given either cash or by selling own household asset. Interestingly about half of the landless SC beneficiaries had taken loan but the number of beneficiaries is somewhat less for ST landless category. About one-fourth of ST landless beneficiaries had to sell own asset for contribution of share in asset created.

Graph shows how landless villagers arrange own contribution

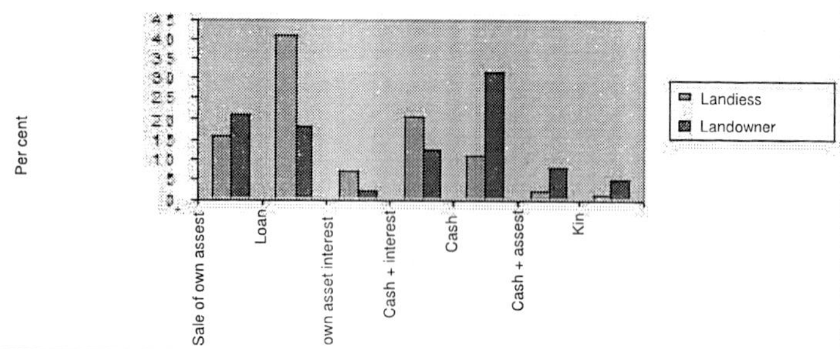

* Forest villagers got some amount of cultivable lands as per agreement with Forest Department.

It is revealed that landless daily labourers got less benefit in general in comparison to others, as they are not able to contribute 25 per cent share. It is revealed that marginal farmers, share croppers and landless people sold livestocks (like milch cow, pig, goat, etc), arecanut and bamboos took loans from kins in addition to credit with interest (popularly known as *hawalat*) to contribute 25 per cent share for eco-development investments.

Some members have taken money with high interest from moneylenders for 25 per cent share. But they had to wait for 5 to 10 months for assets after depositing 25 per cent share. As a result members had to pay increased interest to moneylenders. For this, they had to sell microplan investment for repayment. A classic case can be pointed in this regard.

Sarki Biswakarma, a landless member of Godamdabri EDC, deposited Rs, 2000 as 25 per cent contribution for piggery through daily labour and waited for 10 months. He has become frustrated and wants to get back the same money for utilization in rituals (*sradh*) of uncle. He has lost hope of getting alternative economic activities to be provided under IEDP. In fact delivery of microplan investments is constrained by organization systems and procedures like budgeting, time frames, procedure for approval, sanctioning fund disbursement as reported by David Mosse (2001). So, timely disbursement of money is absolutely necessary to save members from the circle of moneylenders existing in and around BTR.

It is also revealed that in some FPCs/EDCs, rich and powerful members invested a large amount of money for poor marginalized members who are incapable of contributing 25 per cent share in eco-development investment. As a result, rich members became protectors of poor marginalized people. They are taking maximum benefits for microplan investment depriving other less powerful members of the committee (e.g. Raimatang EDC). However, members opined that they got something instead of nothing.

Discussion

It is widely accepted that biodiversity is difficult to conserve in most parts of the world without consideration of local communities' needs and aspirations (Christensen, 2004). It is assumed that dependence on forest over resources by local communities can be reduced by improving income level. It will increase positive attitude towards forests as against continuous conflict between people and forest staff due to protectionist paradigm of management of forests. In India, ecodevelopment has been considered as a measure that increases positive attitudes towards conservation by providing alternative income generating activities. Eco-development investments under IEDP at Buxa Tiger Reserve along with other six tiger reserves across India are positive steps in this direction. This initiative has been undertaken to improve the condition of forest villagers occurred due to curtailment of forest access after declaration of Buxa region as protected area under Wildlife Protection Act, 1972. It is no denial that the framework of project design and implementation set out by the World Bank is a well conceived approach towards positive development of local people and forest health. To achieve eco-development objectives under the project several strategies ranging from eco-development investment through local institutions, PRA based micro-plan preparation as per local peoples' own wishes and interests based on local resources, to ensure that women, tribal, landless labourers and other disadvantaged and marginalized groups participate in the planning process and get benefits. Perhaps most important strategy of village eco-development is people's contribution.

Above analysis reveals that villagers selected diverse activities from community level activities like road improvement, farm forestry and poultry to large group level activities like agricultural development, renovation of ponds and fishery to individual activities like goatery, piggery, rice business etc. But what reveals is that most of the activities have failed. However, some individual activities were successful largely due to earlier experience of those particular activities. It is seen that villagers were forced to take some labour intensive activities like road improvement, renovation of water bodies, farm forestry or agricultural development as it creates maximum employment opportunity for the landless, poor, and marginalized as agricultural labourers. Further it will help poor, marginalised beneficiaries for 25 per cent contribution of eco-development investments. But these types of community or large scale activities were not chosen based on people's own immediate needs and wishes. What happened is that as 25 per cent of total investments have to be borne by the villagers themselves, some local powerful and elite members with the help of forest staff included those activities in the microplan. As a result, a large number of poor and disadvantaged, landless people did not participate in real terms during planning process as against the project strategy. Beneficiaries became the labourers not the owners in these activities like other employment generated rural development activities despite own contribution.

The study reveals that sense of belongingness or ownership of eco-development activities has not developed among most of the members as members still feel that eco-development activities at the community or large group level are not their own properties despite members' own contribution for investments.

Besides the landless, poor, marginalized, forest dependent people are the losers in the intervention programmes in several counts. Firstly, they got less benefit in general in comparison to others, as they are unable to contribute 25 per cent of share for investments. Secondly, those who had been able to get income generating activities after arranging cash for own contribution, most of the activities became loss making (e.g dairy activities). Thirdly, in some cases, to meet 25 per cent share either they had to sell own assets or take loans from moneylenders at higher rate. Distribution of funds was sometimes very late. As a result, they had to repay whole benefit to moneylenders by selling benefits, whatever benefits they got. Fourthly, a group of rich members have come into existence who are contributing 25 per cent share for poor members. They got maximum benefit by depriving poor members. However, poor members opined that they got something instead of nothing. So, these members got impoverished further as against the basic objectives of the project as observed in other conservation projects like ICDPs (Dove, 1993).

So the basic assumption of cost sharing for successful eco-development investments has little base as this intervention suggests. People's contribution fails to instill belongingness towards assets created under the project. Instead forest dependent, poor members sometimes had to take loans for contribution with high interest from money lenders. Delay in fund distribution on the part of project officials for eco-development investment was another major cause that pushed the members further in the trap of moneylenders causing impoverishment.

It is to be noted that cost sharing in investments is not sufficient to create ownership or belongingness towards asset created. It requires a genuine support, needs and aspiration. Opportunity should be given to poor and marginalized people to be a part of decision-making and action, to raise issues in meetings, to get respect and equal status etc. Though this approach was reiterated in the project document, on the implementation level the whole process became 'top down' approach instead of 'bottom up' approach.

Concluding Remarks

It is beyond doubt that most forest dependent people live under extreme poverty in developing countries. They are sustaining their livelihoods for generations using sustainable forest resources. Under protectionist paradigm of conservation initiatives, people became further marginalised and impoverished disregarding the basic rights of livelihoods of local people. Eco-development investments again contribute to poverty traps of already marginalised forest people. This is because of one-sided, paternalistic agenda of conservationists with poor understanding of the socio-economic status of the local people. The strategy of 25 per cent contribution as cost sharing for eco-development investments has become real burden for the poorest of the poor. This initiative further alienates local support for conservation activities as against project objectives.

To achieve greater success proper understanding of the local level situation and about the people and their social, economic, political as well as historical background is absolutely necessary. There should be genuine efforts, primarily on the part of forest officials with people's initiative for proper implementation of the activities of the future projects leading to active involvement of local forest dependent people to ensure positive interactions on biodiversity of the forest.

Acknowledgements

I want to express my gratitude to Professor Amiya Kumar Bagchi, Director of the Institute of Development Studies Kolkata for constant inspiration and help. I would like to express gratitude to Dr. Abhijit Guha for presenting the paper in his session at the Indian Anthropological Congress at Bhopal. I also express my gratitude Mr. Ravi Kant Sinha, Field Director, Buxa Tiger Reserve for logistic supports and constant help. I am grateful to Mr Y.T. Aden, DFD (West) and Mr. S.P. Yadav, DFD (East) of BTR for keen interest in evaluation and providing vehicular support during field work. I am thankful to all the staffs of concerned Ranges especially Amar Dey, Shyamal Chakroborty and Beats of BTR for co-operation. Last but not the least, I am thankful to the concerned villagers especially Niren Narjinery, Budhiar Rahaman, Banikanta Marak, Bikash Mitra, Rajkumar Nag, Haridhan Das, Shankar Burman, Bimal Narjinary who helped me a lot during data collection in the field.

REFERENCES

Adams, W.M. *Against Extinction: the story of conservation.* London, UK : Earth Scan Publications. 2004.

Amend, S. and Amend, T. Espacios sin habitantis? : Parques Nacionales de America del Sur. Editorial. *Nueva Sociedad,* Caracas. 1992.

Arjunan, M., Holmes, C., Puyaravaud J.P. and Davidar, P. Do development initiatives influence local attitudes toward conservation ? : a case study from the Kalakad Mundanthurai Tiger Reserve, India. *Journal of Environmental Management* 79 : 188-197. 2006.

Arnold, J.E.M Clarifying the links between forests and poverty reduction. *International Forestry Review* 4(3) : 231-233. 2002.

Badola, R. People and protected areas in India. *Unasylva.* Vol.50. 1999.

Christensen, J. Win-win illusions,*Conservation in Practice,* 5 (1) : 12-19. 2000.

Das, B.K. Ecodevelopment in Practice at Buxa Tiger Reserve in West Bengal: Lessons from the field. In: *Levels of Human Existence: Issues and Challenges.* Edited by Abhijit Guha. INCAA Occasional papers 7. Jhargram, India. 2008.

Das, B.K. Role of NTFPs among forest villagers in a protected area of West Bengal. *Jr. of Hum. Ecol.* Vol. 18 No.2. 2005.

Das, B.K. Growth of Ethnic groups in forest villages of Buxa Tiger Reserve, West Bengal, *Indian Forester,* Vol. 131, No.4, Dehradun,2005.

Das, S.C., *Management plan for Buxa Tiger Reserve* (1999-2009). Dept. of Forests. Govt. of West Bengal. India. 1999.

Dove, M.R. A revisionist view of tropical deforestation and development. *Environmental Conservation* 20(1) : 17-25. 1993.

Hutton, J.M., Adams, W.M., and Murombedzi, J.C. Back to the barriers ? Changing narratives of biodiversity conservation. *Forum for Development Studies* 2: 341-370. 2005.

Kothari, A., Pandey, P., Singh, S. and Variava, D. *Management of National Parks and Sanctuaries in India: a status report.* New Delhi: Indian Institute of Public Administration. 1989.

McNeely, J.A. and K.R. Miller (eds) *National Park Conservation and Development: the Role of Protected Area in Sustaining Society.* Washington DC: Smithsonian Institution Press. 1984.

McNeely, J.A., K.R. Miller, W.V. Reid, Mittermeir, R.A. and Werner, T.B. *Conserving the World's Biological Diversity.* Gland, Switzerland: IUCN; WRI, CI, WWF-US and the World Bank, Washington D.C. 1990.

Mosse, D. 'People's knowledge', participation and patronage: Operations and Representations in Rural Development. In: *Participation: The New Tyranny?.* Edited by Bill Cooke and Uma Kothari, Zed Books, London, New York. 2001.

Pabla, H.S., Pandey, S. and R. Badola *Guidelines for Eco-development Planning.* Wildlife Institute of India, Dehra Dun. 1995.

Panwar, H.S. *Eco-development : an integrated approach to sustainable development for people and protected areas in India.* Paper presented in the iv World Congress on National Parks and Protected Areas, Carcas, Venezueala, 10-21 February, 1992.

Saberwal, V. Pastoral Politics : Gaddi grazing, Degradation and biodiversity conservation in Himachal Pradesh, India. *Conservation Biology,* 10(3). 1996.

Sayer, J, Campbell B., Petheram, L., Aldrich M, Ruiz Perez M., and others, Assesing environment and development outcomes in conservation landscapes. *Biodiversity and conservation* 16: 2677-2694. 2007.

Schmidt-Soltau, K. The cost of rainforest conservation: local responses towards integrated conservation and development projects in Cameroon. *Journal of Contemporary African Studies.* 22(1) : 93-117. 2004.

Shah, A. Management of protected areas : exploring an alternative in Gir. *Economic and Political Weekly.* vol: XLII, Nos. 27 &28. pp. 2923-2930. 2007.

Sinha, R.K. and B.K. Das *The Buxa Case Study,* Paper presented in World Park Congress, Durban, South Africa. 2003.

Tiger Task Force *Joining the Dots,* Report of the Project Tiger Task Force. WWW.projectiger.nic.in. 2005.

Wells, M.P., McShane. T.O., Dublin, H.T., O' Conner. S., & Redford, K. The future of integrated conservation and development projects: building on what works. In : *Getting Biodiversity Projects to work: towards more effective conservation and development*, ed. T McShane and M. Wells, pp.397-422. New York, USA : Columbia University Press. 2004.

Wells, M. and Brandon, K. *People and Parks: Linking Protected Area Management with local communities*. World Bank /WWF/USAID, World Bank, Washington. 1992.

World Bank, *Staff Appraisal Report*. India Eco Development Project. 1996.

14

Community Based Mangrove Restoration as Instruments of Conserving Marine Biodiversity and the Protected Areas

An Exploratory Analysis from Gujarat

P.K. Viswanathan

Introduction

Mangroves are salt-tolerant woody plants that form low-diversity forests with complex food webs and ecosystem dynamics (Macnae, 1968; Tomlinson, 1986). On a global scale, mangrove vegetation covers roughly 170,000 square kilometres of the earth's surface (Spalding *et al.*, 1997, Valiela *et al.*, 2001). Research on mangroves and the supporting ecosystems reveal the multiple functions of mangroves in the conservation of biodiversity, livelihood security, etc. Preliminary evidence from the 12 Indian Ocean countries affected by the 2004 Asian Tsunami suggests that those coastal areas that had dense and healthy mangrove forests and other substantial vegetative cover suffered fewer losses and less damage to property than those areas in which mangroves had been degraded or converted to other land use (EJF, 2005; Kathiresan and Rajendran, 2005; UNEP, 2005; Vermaat and Thampanya, 2006; Wetlands International, 2005; Barbier, 2008).

There are more, yet emerging empirical evidences supporting that mangroves provide multitudes of ecosystem services which are particularly valuable in the context of emerging climate change risks. That mangroves provides multiple benefits and ecosystem services are widely appreciated especially in the Asian context. While a large number of studies dwell on the socio-economic and ecological significance of mangroves (Amarasinghe *et al.*, 2002; Islam and Haque, 2004; Iftekhar and Islam 2004; Islam and Wahab, 2005; Reitenbeek, 1994; Adger *et al.*, 2001; Barbier, 2006; Hoq, 2007; Walters *et al.*, 2008); another set of studies discuss their benefits in terms of coastal protection from Tsunami, tropical cyclones, reduction of intensity of sea waves, stabilisation of coastlines, etc. (Mazda *et al.*, 2007; Alongi, 2008; Thampanya *et al.*, 2006; Kathiresan, 2003; Cochard *et al.*, 2008; Das, 2007, 2009). By and large, several of these studies have tried valuing mangrove ecosystems in terms of assessing the total economic value (TEV) developed by Barbier (1993; 1994). A study by Conservation International on Coral Reefs, Mangroves and Seagrass compiles the results of a large set of economic valuation studies on coral reefs and related ecosystems around the world, with a focus on five important ecosystem functions/goods, services and benefits, viz.: (a) Biodiversity conservation; (b) Tourism Potential; (c) Fisheries benefits; (d) Coastal protection benefits; and (e) Carbon sequestration potential (Conservation International, 2008). A large number of studies also examine the effectiveness of different mangrove restoration/management regimes: community based management *vs.* state management as well as public-private management (Malakoff, 2008; Suwannodom *et al.*, 1998; Kovacs, 2000; Glaser, 2003; Zorini *et al.*, 2004; Webb and Shivakoti, 2008).

Against this background, this chapter analyses the potential role of community based mangrove restoration (CBMR) activities as effective instruments of sustainable biodiversity conservation and the protection of coastal ecosystems, including marine protected areas in the coastal state of Gujarat. The chapter is organized into four sections including the introduction. In section 2, we discuss the potential threats facing the coastal environments and the mangrove ecosystems especially in the marine protected areas in Gujarat with specific reference to the Marine National Park, Jamnagar. Section 3 explores the prospects of CBMR as an effective instrument for conservation of coastal ecosystems. This section largely draws from the empirical analysis of the multifunctionality and benefits of mangroves and their restoration impacts as revealed by the coastal communities in the Gulfs of Kutch and Khambhat in Gujarat. Section 4 concludes the chapter with brief discussion on the policy as well as institutional imperatives for legitimising the community based mangrove restoration activities as critical instruments of sustainable biodiversity conservation in the coastal environments, including the marine protected areas (MPAs).

The data/information and findings as discussed in this chapter are drawn from two recent studies undertaken by the author on the impacts of industrialisation on the marine protected area (Viswanathan and Parikh, 2010) and the socio-economic and environmental impacts of mangrove restoration in Gujarat (Viswanathan *et al.*, 2011).

Threats of Industrial Expansion on the Coastal Ecosystems, Livelihoods, Marine Protected Areas and Biodiversity in Gujarat

The significance of protecting the coastal ecosystems, livelihoods and marine biodiversity in Gujarat stems from the larger concerns arising from the development dilemma caused by the unbridled pace of industrialisation taking place along the coasts of Gujarat. The dilemma is pertaining to protecting the coastal environments, the ecosystems including the marine protected areas (MPAs) from the ruthless industrial expansion underway in the state especially since the launching of economic reforms. The longest coastline stretching 1600 km has always been a triggering factor behind the industrial growth dynamism in the state. The availability of coastal waters, easy road and water transportation facilities and the facilities for disposal of industrial wastes and effluents also act as the triggering factors behind the industrial expansion along the coasts in Gujarat.

More recently, the coastline between Jamnagar and Salaya off the Gulf of Kutch has also emerged as the prime location for industrial development. Many mega industries have already been set up in the region. Prominent ones include Integrated Petrochemical Refinery at Sikka (RPL) and Vadinar (Essar, IOC); Thermal Power Project, Cement Factory & Fertilizer Factory at Sikka. In addition, the coastal regions also have a long tradition of port-led development activities, like ship building/repairing, ship breaking, bunkering facility, training ships, marine ship building parks (probable stretches), ship recycling, logistics and services, etc.

The Ecosystems Surrounding the MPAs in Jamnagar

Jamnagar district is located along the coasts of the Gulf of Kutch in Gujarat state. More than 30 per cent of the total geographical area of the district is covered by water bodies, including coastal wetlands. The district is also rich in terms of coastal (marine) and mineral resources. The district has rich deposits of organic minerals, such as bauxite and inorganic minerals, such as limestone, gypsum, silica and quartz. The 355 km long coastline in the district accounts for about 22 per cent of the total coastal length of the state. Jamnagar is also famous for its brass products and parts, (bandhani) tie dyed fabric, and handicrafts, petrochemicals industries, and production of salt. Besides, coastal district provides the base for 9 ports, including intermediate and minor ports.

Jamnagar has two of the important biodiversity hotspots, viz., the Marine Sanctuary (MS) and the Marine National Park (MNP). These two MPAs were established in 1980 and 1982 respectively, under the provision of the Wildlife (Protection) Act, 1972. The main purpose of these two eco-systems is to protect the marine flora and fauna in the area. A complex coral reef ecosystem coupled with extensive mangroves dominates the landscape of the shallow water of the MNP areas. The mangroves of the Gulf of Kutch are of unique ecological and economic importance.

Intertidal zones along with 42 islands in Jamnagar district have also been included in the marine protected areas. With a total area of 162.89 sq. km the MNP is also known for its species diversity, as there are more than 37 varieties of hard and soft corals, 70 species of sponges, 150-200 species of fishes, 27 species of prawns, 30 species of crabs, 94 species of water birds, 3 species of sea mammals, 78 species of terrestrial birds, 108 species of brown, green and red algae, etc. In view of these, the International Union for Conservation of Nature (IUCN) has declared the MNP as Category-II area in the list of important National Parks of the world. Since 1991, coral reefs and mangroves in the region have additionally been accorded the highest degree of protection under the 1991 Coastal Regulation Zone (CRZ) Notification (Biswas, 2009). Obviously, coral reefs and mangroves have a high ecological significance, because, both increase shore stability, offer protection against tidal surges and act as the breeding grounds of a host of fishes, crustaceans, algae and other forms of marine life.

Since the protected areas are constituted under the Wild Life

Protection Act (1972), the management of the area is under the jurisdiction of the state's Forest Department. Jamnagar District has an area of 665.9 sq. km mangrove cover, predominantly of scrubby and sparse type. The MNP areas are also rich in terms of their fishery wealth. In 2005-06, the average value of the marine fish landed in Jamnagar was over 70 per cent higher than the average value of catch for Gujarat. During 2005-06, at 66,489 tonnes, Jamnagar contributed 10 per cent of the total marine fish production in the State (Biswas, 2009).

Thus, being a rich repository of ecological wealth, there is no wonder that the coastline of the state, including the MPAs of Jamnagar have become the prime zones of industrial growth and economic dynamism due mainly to the resource intensive industrialisation policies followed by the state in the post-reforms era as observed. At the same time, the unrestrained expansion of industries surrounding the protected areas causes serious threats to the marine ecosystems and the protected environments.

By and large, some of the major threats affecting the ecosystems of MPAs include destruction of mangroves, oil spills, toxic waste and reclamation, etc., which got intensified in recent years with the establishment of oil refineries closer to the MNP in Jamnagar. Besides, the sustenance of the marine ecosystem is also threatened by the existence of salt industries; chemicals, cement and fertiliser manufacturing industries, oil and petroleum refineries, sub-sea oil pipelines, etc. While land diversion for salt industries has caused destruction of mangrove forests surrounding the MNP, the loss and degradation of coral reefs has been primarily caused by effluent discharge from toxic and highly polluting industries, oil spills and leaks, etc. Reportedly, the marine waters have also been polluted by garbage and sewage disposals, including municipal wastes. The infrastructure development activities, such as development of ports and industries, such as oil/petroleum refineries, cement, fertiliser, salt pans, mining of bauxite, limestone, dredging, shipping and related activities, etc have also become serious threats to the marine ecosystem and the protected areas (Viswanathan and Parikh, 2010).

Impacts of Industrial Pollution on the MPAs

Availability of reliable data is an issue while analysing the industrial impacts on the coastal ecosystems and MPAs. Lack of sampling networks and ill-defined sampling and analysis procedures also adds to the problem of inconsistency (TERI, 2002). As such, except the routine inventory of hazardous wastes and water quality assessments by the individual units as per CPCB norms, there are no realistic data/ information on industrial pollution and environmental impacts that are available for public scrutiny. The data pertaining to pollution and water quality parameters gathered by the individual industries as part of the Environmental Impact Assessment (EIA) process are not very much revealing in most cases, as such data are often used by the industries for getting environmental clearance from the CPCB or the respective state pollution control boards (PCBs). Thus while there is no dearth of data as almost all industries (polluting and non-polluting) have to carrying out periodical monitoring to fulfil environmental compliance procedures, their reliability and quality is always contested, when it comes to reporting of data on the critical environmental parameters. The efforts of individual researchers to resolve some of these data problems are also very much limited by their coverage and sensitivity of the information gathered and presented.

Nevertheless, in what follows, we briefly discuss the major threats affecting the ecological health of the marine protected environments as well as the livelihood supporting resources, including fisheries, of the areas surrounding the PAs in Jamnagar. The criticality of protecting the marine ecosystems and the PAs emerge from the fact that the MNP area stretches to seven of the ten talukas in Jamnagar district, viz. boundary of Dwarka, Kalyanpur, Khambhaliya, Lalpur, Jamnagar, Dhrol and Jodiya. In 2008, these seven talukas accounted for 67 per cent of the SSI units, 73 per cent of investments and 85 per cent of the industrial employment in the SSI sector in Jamnagar district. Similarly, almost 93 per cent of the medium and large scale industries in Jamnagar are located in talukas, surrounding the MNP, which together accounted for 98 per cent of investments and 57 per cent of the employment. Some of the industries, which are high profile and highly detrimental to marine ecosystems and environment, include: (a) Petroleum and Petrochemicals, (b) Chemical industries, (c) Cement manufacturing, (d) Fertilizers, (e) Salt works, (f) Thermal power generation, (g) Ports and jetties, and (h) Ship-breaking industry (Viswanathan and Parikh, 2010).

The highly diversified industrial structure with the mix and proliferation of micro, small, medium and large enterprises along with the increasing pace of urbanization and rising population densities, have all contributed to the growing incidence of environmental degradation, including air pollution along the coastlines of Gujarat, especially, Jamnagar. In view of the highly polluting nature of industries, the Ministry of Environment and Forests (MoEF) has already developed standards for regulating emissions for these industries. Majority of these industries belong to the 'red category' by their pollution impacts and processes as per norms of the CPCB (GOI, 2009).

The categorization of industries based on pollution status indicate that of the 729 registered large, medium, small and micro industries in Jamnagar, 66 per cent of the units are highly polluting (Red), followed by medium polluting (Orange) industries during 2009. Further, the inventory of hazardous waste generated by the industries in Jamnagar district shows that almost 99 per cent of the wastes were generated by heavily polluting (Red) industries and the share of Landfillable wastes was almost half of the total hazardous wastes. An analysis of the composition of wastes across industries indicates that small scale industries generate the largest quantity of landfill wastes (82%). This indicates the severity of the problem affecting the protected areas and surroundings as a large number of the small-scale industries dump their wastes around the PAs, as they do not have secured landfill sites for dumping their wastes, unlike the large and medium scale industries (Viswanathan and Parikh, 2010).

Degradation of marine ecosystems occur due to discharge of wastes into the sea causing damage to living resources, hazards to human health, hindrance to fishery and deterioration of quality of seawaters. Marine pollution is associated with the changes in the physical, chemical and biological conditions of seawater. The major sources of marine pollution in the case of the PAs in Jamnagar include: (a) operational and accidental discharge of pollutants from ships; (b) Oil spills due to faulty handling of Single Buoy Moorings (SBM) operation in the Gulf of Kutch; (c) Maritime accidents due to collision, fire, explosion or grounding which results in the release of oil, either from the ship or from the cargo tank; and (d) Intentional discharges of oil or oily waste from the pumping of bilges or de-ballasting cargo tanks or from tank washing. Besides, anthropogenic activities such as discharge of industrial and municipal sewage, land use, tourism, maritime transport, offshore oil exploration and production, dumping at sea have also been identified as causing degradation of the PA environment. Disposal of sewage, industrial effluents and agricultural wastes cause major chunk of pollutants entering the sea water in the MNP. While pesticides and Insecticides are used in agriculture, large volumes of synthetic detergents are consumed for washing and cleaning purposes. About 25 per cent of these chemicals and synthetic detergents find their way into the marine environments (Viswanathan and Parikh, 2010).

The present development scenario in the Gulf of Kutch (GoK) including the MNP is a complex one, as it is surrounded by several industries, like 21 salt work units, major polluting industries, such as Tata Chemicals and Associated Cement Company at Mithapur, Digvijay Cement Factory and Unit of Gujarat State Fertilizer Corporation at Sikka, Salaya-Mathura oil pipeline, Crude oil terminal of Indian Oil Corporation at Vadinar, Reliance Petroleum and ESSAR Oil Refineries at Moti Khavdi and Jam-Khambhaliya respectively, and the proposed Vadinar-Bina Pipeline of Bharat Petroleum on the Saurashtra coast, the sub-sea pipeline of Bharat-Oman Petroleum near Narara Bet, the proposed Kandla-Karnali oil pipeline, the Vadinar-Kandla undersea pipeline and Sanghi Cement Company on the Kachchh coast. It may be noted that the Gulf area is being aggressively developed as oil importing base because of its proximity to the oil exporting countries of the Middle East. Further, to facilitate unloading of oil from Very Large Crude Carrier (VLCC), seven Single Buoy Moorings (SBM) have been planned to be anchored along the southern shore of the Gulf of which four are already in place – one off Narara Bet, two off Vadinar, one off Sikka and two more under planning.

All these activities are either close to or inside the 411 km^2 area of the MNP, which has been established to protect and preserve the fragile ecosystem, particularly the coral reefs of the Gulf of Kutch. Seventy per cent of India's total crude import is reportedly taking place through the Gulf of Kutch; its oil traffic in 2007 was estimated to be about 84 million tonnes. As of now, import of 40 Million Tone Per Annum (MTPA) of crude oil has been cleared through the SBMs in the Gulf, which will be gradually raised to 80-110 MTPA. Each SBM can be expected to release a maximum of 300 barrels (41 Tonnes) of oil to the sea per year during operation. This would mean that the Gulf will receive around 300 tonnes of oil per year during operation of the 7 SBMs (Vethamony, *et al.*, 2007).

The increased import of crude oil has been due to the increase in refining capacity due to the setting up of the two major refineries, viz. the Reliance and the Essar in Jamnagar.

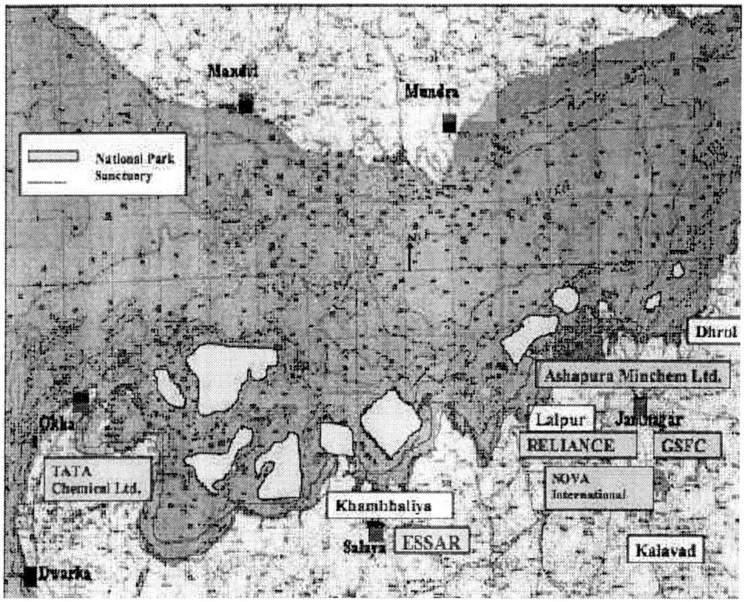

Map 14.1: Location of Major Polluting Industries around the MNP area in Jamnagar

The potential impacts of industrial expansion and related activities on the MNP and the surrounding environments may be visualized at three levels, viz., (a) impact on the biodiversity supported by the marine ecosystem; (b) the impacts on the farm lands and water bodies, especially, groundwater; and (c) the impacts on the livelihoods of coastal community and livestock integrated support systems. The impacts as caused by the discharge of industrial and domestic wastes on the biodiversity are experienced in terms of loss/ degradation of mangrove cover and coral reefs supported by the ecosystem.

Decline and Degradation of Coastal Ecosystems

One of the major impacts of the industrial expansion activities on the coastal areas, including the MPAs has been the decline in mangroves and the coral reefs. Besides the toxic chemicals and effluents that are let into the coastal waters, cooling water from thermal power plants and nuclear installations also cause adverse effects on the marine fauna.

It has been reported that the various development activities and industrial expansion along the coastal areas of Gujarat have caused severe depletion of its mangrove cover between the 1960s and 1980s (Hirway and Goswami, 2004). The decline was dramatic in the MNP/MS areas as the mangrove cover had declined from 138.5 sq. km in 1975 to just 33.4 sq. km in 1985 (Fig. 14.1).

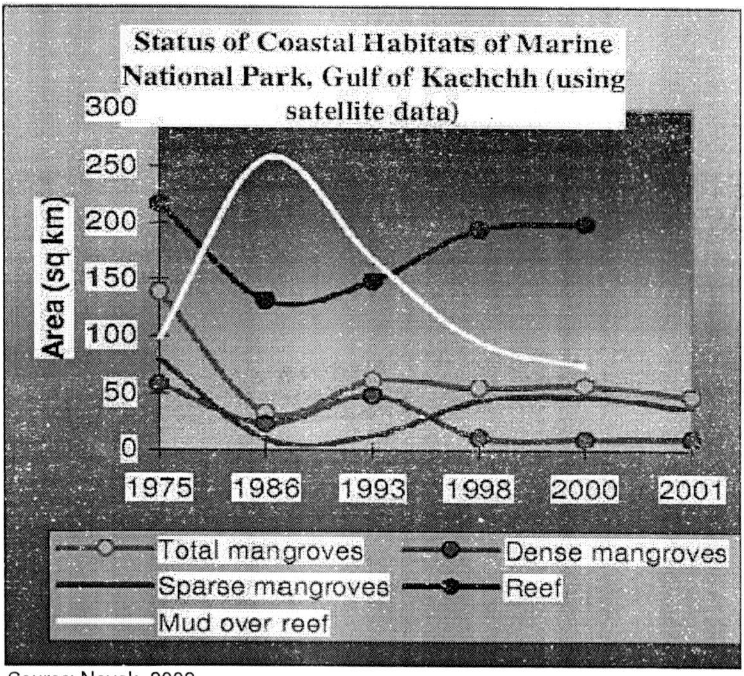

Source: Nayak, 2002.

Fig.14. 1: Trends in Mangroves cover and coral reefs in the Gulf of Kutch, covering Marine National Park, Jamnagar

Decline in mangrove cover has been caused by the diversion of mangrove lands for establishment of industries, decreased freshwater discharge into mangrove areas due to the damming of rivers, port-related activities, aquaculture, mining, expansion of salt industries, marine oil pollution, gathering of fodder and fuelwood, and reduced natural regeneration (Singh, 2006; Hirway and Goswami, 2004). Mangrove species such as Rhizophora, Ceriops and Aegiceros, which are reported to have once existed in the region, are now rare, while the species Bruguiera is extinct (Stanley, 2002). Mangroves have virtually disappeared from the Gulf of Khambhat as well. Between 1960 and 1993, the decrease in mangroves cover was about 96 per cent in the Gulf of Khambhat. On the other hand, the Gulf of Kutch containing the MNP reported a 73 per cent decline of mangrove cover between 1975 and 1982 (Viswanathan and Parikh, 2010).

Similarly, another study (Nair, 2002) reports that the total reef area in the Gulf of Kutch decreased from 217 sq. km in 1975 to 123 sq. km in 1986, causing a net loss of 43%. During this period, coral reef cover within the Core Areas of the MNP/MS declined by 54%. The study also states that, reefs presumed to have died, actually lie buried under mud, indicating that heavy silt load caused damage to the corals. Coral dredging by a cement company located closer to the MNP is held to be largely responsible for the heavy siltation (Biswas, 2009). Though a ban on coral mining between 1985 and 1991 by MNP authorities had resulted in an increase in corals in the Core Areas of the MNP/MS (Singh, 2006), satellite data has revealed the opposite with coral ecosystems facing stress due to industrialization and port-building (Nayak, 2002).

Of late, there was an increase in mangrove cover in Gujarat since the early 1990s from 397 sq. km (1991) to 960 sq. km (2003) and further to 1046 sq. km (2009) due to the massive mangrove restoration programme initiated under the India Canada Environment Facility (ICEF) and the subsequent state initiatives through the Gujarat Ecology Commission (GEC). However, despite the recent increase in mangrove cover stimulated by the restoration efforts by various agencies in Gujarat, the success of these efforts are largely thwarted by the parallel industrial activities, such as salt works, mining and quarrying, ports and jetties, ship building and breaking, which are always in conflict with the larger goals of conservation of the coastal ecosystems and the MNP. This concern is also strengthened by the fact that the decisions about type and location of industries are taken without adequate consideration to the impacts on the ecosystems and the environment of the MPAs. All these will pose serious threats to the potential future benefits that might accrue from conserving the MNP/MS as distinct entities from many angles, including its immense potential for development of eco-tourism (Viswanathan and Parikh, 2010).

Oil Spill threats for MNP and the Marine Ecosystems

The MNP area and the marine ecosystems are constantly under the threat of oil spill. With more than 2,000 ships landing annually on the major port at Kandla and intermediary ports, like Adani, Okha and Salaya, nearly 50 per cent India's crude oil imports (98.88 million tonnes during April-November 2009) are unloaded in the fragile zones of the MPAs. The annual average import of crude oil through the Kandla and other intermediary ports has been 28-32 million tonnes during the last decade, reaching 45.54 million tonnes during 2008-09. It may be noted that the carrying capacity of the Gulf of Kutch is most over loaded in terms of movement of ships with containers of POL as well as commodities, such as finished fertilisers, raw-fertilisers, coal, foodgrains, iron ore and various other products. All these activities are causing serious threat to the marine environment and ecosystems due to the frequent movement of containers and ships along with the threats caused by oil spills.

Asia's largest oil refinery is located at Jamnagar in the Gulf of Kutch. Considering the quantity of oil handled/transported, the area is most vulnerable for oil spills (Indian Coastguard). A few minor incidences of oil spill have occurred in the past. The Marine National Park (MNP), within three km of Vadinar, is likely to suffer from great damage from crude oil spills, according to senior State forest officials[1]. The Forest Department in agreement with the Union Ministry of Environment and Forests (MOEF) had even denied the State Government permission to run a crude pipeline through the Gulf on its way to Bina in Madhya Pradesh by the Bharat Oman Refinery (Joshi, 1998).

Impact of Soda Ash and Salt works Industries

Jamnagar has been a major source of salt production in Gujarat for about the last 60 years or so. The two MNP Talukas, viz. Jamnagar and

Khambhaliya together account for about 35 per cent of the total salt production area (24409 ha) in Jamnagar district. While a major salt works factory operated by Tata Chemicals Limited (TCL) uses salt pans in the Okha Rann region and other areas of north Okha mandal, smaller salt works are dispersed throughout Jamnagar coasts, inside or close to the MPAs. An area of 103.25 sq. km of mangrove forests is leased out to 21 salt industries, especially in the vicinity of the MNPS[2]. The abundant availability of limestone and common salt, materials required for the production of soda ash, has led to the establishment of giant soda ash plants along the coast at Mithapur, Sutrapada and Porbandar (Viswanathan and Parikh, 2010).

A study by Zingde (1993) observed that the TCL plant at Mithapur produces around 18 million litres per day (MLD) of highly alkaline process waste. The wastewater contains about 150 gm/l of suspended solids and 25 mg/l of ammonia cal nitrogen. This is released through marshy lands above the high tide line in the marine sanctuary area. Due to its high density, the milky white effluent does not mix well with sea water but instead spreads along inter-tidal areas or settles in heaps along the shore. The white colour of the effluent is due to high levels of suspended solids: calcium carbonate, calcium sulphate, magnesium hydroxide and silica. The raw effluent was reported to be toxic and even at 20 per cent concentration, fish did not survive in it for more than 15 minutes (Zingde, 1993).

The effluent-carrying pipelines from the Mithapur plants were laid years before the declaration of the MNPS. In the present decade, two devastating accidents have taken place within a three-year period. On 2 June, 2001, a salt brine pipeline running through the MNP, from a TCL factory at Samlasar to its Padli and Mithapur salt works, burst open, spilling thousands of tonnes of effluent into the PAs. A case was registered against the company under the WLPA and two engineers of the company placed temporarily under arrest ("Toxic destruction"; Down to Earth, 15 July, 2001). Within three years of the salt brine spill, there was yet another accident in October 2003. This time, a TCL slurry pond burst, releasing 300,000 tonnes of calcium chloride into the PAs. Over 1,500 mangrove plants were damaged. The Gujarat State Pollution Control Board ordered the closure of the company's soda ash manufacturing plant ("Four held in Tata Chemicals leakage case"; *Times*

News Network; 25 October, 2003). However, less than a week later, the company (that had dodged responsibility for clean production for 15 years), was allowed to reopen its plant on the mere promise that it would clean up the slurry waste and comply with safety measures in future.

Though the TCL claims that it has state of the art technology for waste management and secured landfill site within the premises of the plant, there are apprehensions as regards the management of voluminous effluents and solid wastes by the plant. In June 2008, an investigation that examined files pertaining to TCL's consent application at the Gujarat Pollution Control Board's head office in Gandhinagar found that the effluents were being discharged right into the MNPS after some preliminary treatment. According to the investigators, TCL managed to secure a permit citing a 1987 stay order from the Gujarat High Court on grounds that the unit had come up before the Park was notified ('Scorching Salt', Down to Earth, 15 June, 2008). An analysis of the water consumption pattern of Tata Chemicals indicate that the plant consumed about 166 million kilo litres of water during 2009 and major share of this water is drawn from the sea waters (51%), followed by surface water-lakes (35%) surrounding the plant area and ground water (12%). Interestingly, such a huge withdrawal of sea water by the TCL is against the provisions of the Wild Life (Protection) Act, 1972, which clearly states that no wildlife produce, including water, can be used for commercial purpose.

A study by the DOD-ICMAM Project Directorate in 2002 estimated that salt pans discharge about 2.95 million kilolitres of bittern annually. Bittern is a highly concentrated form of sea water obtained in the final stage of salt production, when salt is crystallized. The bittern discharged and the negative water balance of the Gulf result in increased salinity of sea water and soil (DOD-ICMAM, 2002). Bittern is also toxic for mangroves. Between 1975 and 1982, the mangrove cover in the State decreased from 733.53 sq. km to 177.31 sq. km, a 76 per cent decline along with a corresponding increase in the area occupied by salt pans from 4.81 sq. km to 49.13 sq. km.

Impact of Cement Industry

Although several cement companies operate in the coastal talukas of

Jamnagar, the Digvijay Cement Co. (DCC) is the closest to the MNP area. Until 1982, DCC was dredging materials from an area of 648 ha in the Gulf of Kutch for cement production. The area was leased out by the State Government and included six coral reef islands, namely, Pirotan, Kalvan, Jindra, Dhani, Dera and Goose. These islands now fall under the MNP area. Sustained coral mining, at the rate of about 0.5 MTPA by the company, caused major destruction to coral reefs (Singh, 2006). The 1994 MNPS management plan points out that due to the extensive dredging, mud and suspended particles continue to settle on coral reefs and such deposits are lethal for corals. Today, although the company cannot dredge within the MNPAs, it continues to extract raw materials from areas in the immediate vicinity, thus increasing the overall environmental burden in the Gulf of Kutch.

In the last 10 years, the loss of about 64 sq. km of reef area has been reported within the National Park due to heavy sediment loads, mostly caused by the cement plant (Singh, 2006). A report by the Bombay Natural History Society also supports this finding by observing that during the past three decades, rampant extraction of corals and sand by the cement industry has left deep scars on the fragile ecosystem of MNP and has caused substantial destruction leading to increased turbidity. This has also been pointed out as the main reason for the sharp decline in marine life and at places like Narara and Pirotan the environmental and ecosystem damages are beyond repair (BNHS, undated).

Impact of Thermal Plants

A 240 MW capacity, coal-based power station run by the Gujarat State Electricity Board (GSEB) operates closer to the MNPAs. The power station uses massive fly ash ponds extending over thousands of acres for fly ash disposal. A report by the GEER Foundation points out that these fly ash ponds are associated with frequent overflows during the rainy season, which contributes to the degradation of marine life. At the Sikka port, the bulk transport of coal for the thermal power plant also poses a threat to marine life (DOD-ICMAM, 2002). Significantly, several new thermal power stations are coming up in the region. Essar Power Holdings Limited plans to set up a 1,200-MW power plant in

Jamnagar, based on coal imported from Indonesia and South Africa (The *Financial Express*, 2007). The Reliance Group was also planning to develop a 500-MW coke-based power plant in addition to its existing captive power generation units at Jamnagar. One of the major threats to the MNP due to the power plants would come from dumping of ash and discharge of wastes/effluents from the power stations.

It is reported that a part of the MNP and the Sanctuary will be regularised under the state government owned Western Gujarat Electricity Company (WGEC)/Paschim Gujarat Vij Company Limited (PGVCL). The water cooling system — intake and outlet of a 240 MW power plant was functioning on two hectares of the Sanctuary since 1982. Now the Gujarat Wildlife Advisory Board (WAB) has recommended the Central Government to hand over the said piece of land to the WGEC. The WAB has termed its decision as a formal step towards land regularization even as the Fisheries College under the Junagadh Agriculture University reports that the bio-diversity at the MNP has been seriously damaged by industrial pollution. It is reported that the power plant and the nearby petrochemical units of Reliance and Essar release effluents and oily waters, impacting the biodiversity of the MNP. Even if the land belonged to the thermal power plant from the very beginning, the decision on its regularisation goes against the WPA, which lays down that "there should be no activity within five kilometers of the Park" (Dave, 2008).

Impact of Ports and Jetties

There are many environmental problems associated with increased port development and maritime activity, including tanker spills and accidents, sediment deposition on the mangroves and corals due to deep-sea dredging activities, causing the death of marine mammals, like dolphins, porpoise and dugong (also see Singh, 2003). The accelerated development of ports and harbours will also greatly increase the vulnerability of the fishing communities, as that would restrict their fishing grounds and depletion in the fish catch.

There was significant growth in the commodity traffic in all the major ports in the Gulf of Kutch. Obviously, this might have adversely affected the marine environment due to the disturbances caused by the increased traffic and the loading/unloading of the commodities, particularly, oil and other highly toxic substances, which needs detailed empirical investigation as regards the sensitivity of the MNP/MS and their ecosystems to these commodities.

Impact of Ship Breaking Industry

Ship breaking is a major activity along the West Coast of India especially in Gujarat. Ship breaking industry creates numerous hazards for the coastal and marine environments. Sachana in Jamnagar coast is the second-largest ship breaking unit in Gujarat. Of the 15 ship breaking plots in the industrial yard at Sachana granted by the Gujarat Maritime Board (GMB) in areas adjoining the PAs; three are already operational. Between 1992 and 2001, 71 ships were broken there. The ship breakers on an average dismantle a ship of about 10000–13000 tones in a day or two. Consequently, a considerable level of sediment and seawater contamination is envisaged at the intertidal zone along the coast including the MNP areas in the Gulf of Kutch (Gujarat Maritime Board, 2003). It has been estimated that ship-breaking activity produces around 4000 tonnes of solid waste per annum. These wastes are disposed of on seashores and cause health and environmental hazards to terrestrial and marine environments (CPCB, 2001).

A large number of dangerous pollutants including toxic waste, oil, polychlorinated bi phenyls and heavy metals are released into the marine waters and seabed. While most of the oil is removed before a ship is scrapped, sand used to mop up the remaining oil is thrown in to the sea. High concentration of oil and grease are found in the coastal waters, choking marine life. Among these contaminants, heavy metals and petroleum hydrocarbons are considered as the most serious pollutants due to their toxicity and tenacity (UNESCO, 2004). It has been reported that any scrap from ship breaking activity that does not have sale value is simply dumped in the protected zone. Engine oil and other non-degradable toxic compounds flow into the waters of the PAs in the Gulf of Kutch from where tides wash them into neighbouring creeks and mangrove swamps. Consequently, mangroves in the region get degraded beyond regeneration. There are also reports that oil spills from the breaking of ships at the Ship Breaking Yard in Sachana have also adversely impacted the marine life and the eco-system.

Impact of Urban/Municipal Waste on the MPAs

Besides the various impacts caused by industrial and infrastructure development activities as described above, the MNP/MS areas and ecosystems are also threatened by the growing problem of urban (municipal) wastes. In most cities of Gujarat, including Jamnagar, the underground drainage (UGD) system comprises sewer pipes that collect domestic waste water, that are also connected to storm water drains. In so far as the MPAs are concerned, the growing quantity of solid wastes becomes problematic as a significant proportion of the solid particles are discharged through the municipal drains which find their way to the coastal waters. The GPCB estimates reveal that about 124 litres/capita per day of untreated sewage water is discharged into the Gulf of Kutch through the municipal drains. Based on the estimated urban population of Jamnagar, i.e. 5.06 lakhs, the total discharge of untreated waste water into the Gulf of Kutch may be estimated at 62.69 million litres per day (MLD) and 22881.85 million litres per annum (Viswanathan and Parikh, 2010). According to the GPCB officials, the quantity of industrial effluents discharged into the marine waters is quite insignificant when compared to the urban effluents that are discharged into the city sewerage that finally reaches the coastal waters (GPCB: personal communication).

Discharge of Industrial Effluents and Extraction of Coastal Fresh Waters

The severity of the discharge of sewage water into the coastal waters surrounding the MPAs becomes a major cause for concern also because of the contamination of the effluents discharged by majority of the small industrial units located in the industrial estate in Shankar Tekri as well as Mithapur, Lalpur, Jam Khambhalia, etc. As per GPCB Jamnagar authorities, there are about 150 small scale polluting industries in Jamnagar, a vast majority of which do not have own facilities for waste disposal or effluent treatment. Despite the large concentration of industries, Jamnagar does not have infrastructure facilities, such as TSDF and CETP. In the absence of such facilities, the industries dispose their solid wastes in the landfill sites either in Rajkot or Bharuch, which also involves huge transportation costs. Majority of them discharge their effluents into the municipal drains which find their ways into the coastal waters near the MNP/MS areas. Reportedly, on an average, these industrial units generate about 200-250 litres of effluents per day (37500 litres/day) which is about 12.5 million litres per annum. All these effluents are also discharged into the coastal waters with or without primary treatment. It may further be noted that due to the laxity of industries in terms of proper treatment for reuse of the waters, almost 60-70 per cent of the fresh seawater consumed by the industries are discharged into the sea, adversely affecting the marine ecosystems in the PAs (Viswanathan and Parikh, 2010).

Livelihood Issues Surrounding MPAs

Primarily, the damages caused to the marine ecosystems and the PAs by various industries as discussed above, also affect the surrounding coastal communities, like fishermen, farmers and farm and non-farm workers. There are several reports of increasing livelihood security issues faced by fishermen and farmer communities in particular in the villages surrounding the MNP/Sanctuary areas in Jamnagar. In fact, fishing in Jamnagar has been part of a well-developed, traditional coastal economy. The district has 17 fish landing centres. About 10.8 per cent of Gujarat's fishing families reside in 23 fishing villages along the coasts of Jamnagar, including the MNP areas. The fishing population in Jamnagar is 31,910 with 6,459 fishing families, which is nearly 10 per cent of Gujarat's total fisher population.

The rapid degradation of coastal wetlands, such as mangroves and swamps, has affected fishermen in a significant manner. A report states that coastal wetland degradation has led to the loss of fish species diversity in the Gulf of Kutch. This region, which adjoins the MNP/MS at the head or closed end of the Gulf of Kutch, has an estimated 9,000 active fishermen who use traditional fishing practices. The destruction of natural hydrological patterns, the depletion of mangroves and other coastal vegetation, and continued apathy towards marginal fishermen have seriously jeopardized the livelihoods of traditional fishers (SEAP, 2003). There was notable decrease in fish catch particularly in sites, like Sikka and Vadinar which are closer to the MNP/MS areas from 8876 tonnes during 2002-03 to 6264 tonnes during 2005-06.

Besides fishermen being adversely affected of by the environmental damages caused by the industries, the fish processing industry by itself causes pollution to the marine environments. In this regard, a study by CPCB reports that about 14 fish processing units are located in the surrounding regions of Mangrol, Porbander and Dwarka, which are closer to the MNP areas. These fish processing units cause pollution to the MNPs, as fish processing in two stages generates large volumes of wastewater which is being discharged into the sea directly or indirectly (CPCB, 2003).

Thus, it emerges from the foregoing analysis that the industrial expansion taking place around the MPA/MS in Jamnagar in Gujarat has been causing serious threats to the biodiversity and the ecosystems supported by the MPAs. The biodiversity surrounding the MPAs had once been enriched by the natural mangrove forests and the coral reefs, which also had been important sources of livelihoods for the coastal communities, including fisher households.

The issues as discussed above bring out the imperative of protecting the MPAs, their biodiversity and ecosystems for the future. However, while the legitimacy of the need for conserving the protected environments such as the MNP/MS is conspicuous, it also opens up two pertinent questions that call for immediate attention. First, what could be the nature and type of interventions needed for conserving the coastal ecosystems and marine biodiversity? Second, can we, and if at all, how we could achieve reasonable amount of success in creating better outcomes in stakeholder participation in conserving the MPAs? Both these questions need serious thoughts in the current context when the issue of conservation of ecosystems and marine environments is at stake, despite there is a common consensus the world over about the importance of conservation and its long term implications on sustainability of coastal ecosystems.

Community based Mangrove Restoration as Instruments for Ecosystem Conservation

In this regard, this section explores the relevance and feasibility of the community based model of mangrove restoration as an effective instrument of conservation of coastal ecosystems and marine biodiversity in the context of India. The basis of such a proposition mainly draws from the evidences of community based mangrove restoration (CBMR) underway in the coastal areas of Gujarat.

It has been observed that a major initiative for development and restoration of mangrove plantations has received worldwide attention since 2005 following the devastating Asian Tsunami that struck the Indian Ocean on 26 December, 2004. The occurrence of the catastrophe caused a wide realization that the presence of mangrove forests might have mitigated a significant scale of the economic damages and loss of lives and properties caused by the disaster. Thus, following the 2004 Tsunami, there have been enormous attention given for rapid expansion of mangroves in the Indian Ocean region in particular, supported by national governments, international agencies and the NGOs, that are attempting to replant and rehabilitate mangrove ecosystems as "natural barriers" to future tsunamis and other tropical storms (Barbier, 2008).

As a result, today, mangroves are considered to be one of the most important nursery ground for various fishery resources with immense potential to support the livelihoods of dependent communities and protect the coastal environments from tidal attacks. Mangroves are also seen highly important in the current context as they are proven to be highly productive ecosystems with multiple socio-economic, environmental benefits and ecosystem functions. In the wild, mangrove plantations serve as protection for fish, crabs, oysters, lobsters and shrimp. Their roots provide attachment surfaces for marine organisms such as colourful sponges and oysters. Moreover, mangrove forests are considered as carbon sinks as they filter out pollution, stabilize sediments, hold nutrients, protect the shoreline from erosion and provide food, nesting and nursery areas for many animals, including at least 220 fish species, 24 reptiles and amphibian species, 18 mammal species and 200 bird species (Viswanathan *et al.*, 2011).

An inventory of the existing mangrove plantations indicate that mangroves of South and Southeast Asia are the world's most extensive and diverse mangrove systems comprising 41.4 per cent of the global mangroves (Spalding, 1997). Indian mangroves make up 3.1 per cent of the total global cover and are distributed along all the maritime states, except the union territory of Lakshadweep, covering an area of about 4639 sq. km along the 7,500 km long Indian coastline. As at the global level, the post-tsunami period also marked significant rise in area under mangroves in India as well. For instance, between 2001 and 2009, the area under mangroves in India had increased from 4482 sq. km to 4639 sq. km, with significant growth reported mainly from states, such as Gujarat, Maharashtra, West Bengal and Orissa (Table 14.1). Though West Bengal has the largest area under mangroves, the area expansion was most spectacular in Gujarat, as it increased by almost 15 per cent from 911 sq. km to 1046 sq. km during the last decade.

Table 14.1: Trends in growth of area under mangroves in India, 1991 to 2009 (Sq km)

States	*1991*	*1995*	*2001*	*2005*	*2009*	*% share*
1. Andhra Pradesh	399	383	333	354	353	7.6
2. Gujarat	397	689	911	991	1046	22.5
3. Maharashtra	113	155	118	186	186	4.0
4. Orissa	195	195	219	217	221	4.8
5. West Bengal	2119	2119	2081	2136	2152	46.4
6. A & N Islands	971	966	789	635	615	13.3
Total	4244	4533	4482	4581	4639	100.0

Note : The six states together occupy more than 98 per cent of the total mangroves area and the rest is grown in states, such as Tamil Nadu, Kerala, Goa and Karnataka.
Source: FSI Report, 2009.

It may be noted that the highest expansion in mangrove area as achieved by Gujarat has been mainly contributed by the Restoration of Mangroves (REMAG) project implemented by the Gujarat Ecology Commission (GEC) during 2002-2007 with financial support from the India Canada Environment Facility (ICEF). The REMAG project aims at development of mangrove plantations in the gulfs of Kutch and Khambhat, outside the conventional forest areas, i.e. in the wastelands provided by the government of Gujarat. As the original project came to a close by 2007, the Gujarat Ecology Commission has taken over the task of mangrove restoration activities in the state with a major thrust on public-private partnership (PPP) based management/ governance regime. Map 14.2 shows the district wise locations where mangrove plantations are carried out under the PPP initiatives.

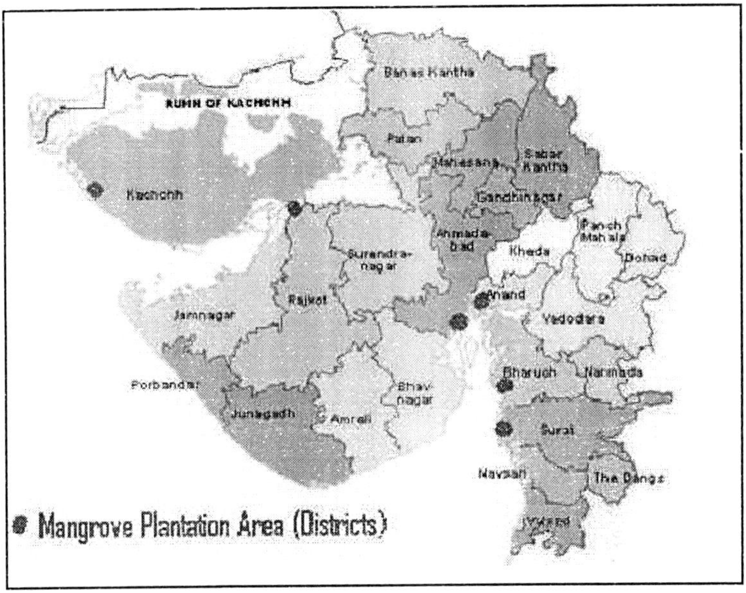

Map 14.2: Locations of Mangrove planted areas in Gujarat

Under the extended REMAG programme, investments by private sector companies/industries have also been encouraged with a commitment to cherish community participation in the mangrove development/restoration efforts. Accordingly, the PPP driven community based mangrove regeneration activities accounted for 30 per cent of the mangrove planted area in the state. Out of the total area of mangroves planted, 56 per cent are located in the Gulfs of Kutch (27%) and Khambhat (29%), while the South Gujarat coast accounts for 44 per cent of the area.

Based on the information available up to March 2010, the mangrove plantations developed by various private sector companies have been almost 26 per cent, which form the second largest category after the ICEF and the Government of Gujarat in the state sector (Table 14.2). Among the various private sector companies, the largest mangrove area belongs to Adani (28%), followed by Pipapav Shipyard (23.4%), Shell Hazira (14%) and NIKO (12%).

Table 14.2: Distribution of Mangrove plantations by various agencies in Gujarat, 2010

	Type of Implementing Agency	*Area-Ha*	*per cent share*
A.	**State sector agencies**		
1.	Gujarat Heavy Chemicals Limited (GHCL)	50	0.81
2.	Gujarat Maritime Board (GMB)	120	1.95
3.	Gujarat Mineral Development Corporation (GMDC)	170	2.76
4.	GSPC Pipapav Power Company (GPPC)	10	0.16
5.	India Canada Environment Facility (ICEF)	4101	66.51
6.	Ministry of Environment and Forests (MoEF)	300	4.87
7.	Government of Gujarat (GoG)	1415	22.95
	Sub-Total	6166 (74.1)	100.00
B.	**Private sector agencies**		
1.	ABG Shipyard	50	2.31
2.	ADANI	600	27.78
3.	Ambuja Cement	150	6.94
4.	Anjan Cement	25	1.16
5.	Bayer	10	0.46
6.	Essar	200	9.26
7.	NIKO Resources India Ltd.	250	11.57
8.	Petronet LNG	50	2.31
9.	Pipavav Shipyard	505	23.38
10.	Shell Hazira	300	13.89
11.	Ultatech	20	0.93
	Sub-Total	2160 (25.9)	100.00
	Grand Total	8326 (100.0)	

Note: Figures in parentheses indicate the percentages in the total area.
Source: Estimated from data provided by GEC, Gandhinagar, March 2010.

As per the community based PPP model, GEC acts as the Nodal Agency with key responsibility of preparation of project management plan, financial management and imparting trainings on both technical and social aspects to the project implementation partners (PIPs) and the community based organisations (CBOs) for smooth implementation of the project. The PIPs play the role of facilitators for community mobilization, formation and registration of Community Based Organizations (CBOs), helping the community in micro-planning and implementation of the project activities. The physical implementation of the project at the grass root level is carried out by the CBOs. This includes, activities like preparation of micro-plans, undertaking activities like seed collection, nursery development, plantation, land development etc., protection of the plantations through social fencing, formation and amendment of bylaws for the utilization of the corpus funds, benefit sharing and conflict resolution (Viswanathan, *et al.*, 2011).

The entire mangrove development and restoration activities promoted by the GEC in Gujarat are being carried out through 22 CBOs spread across eight districts. Of the total mangrove planted area (8326 ha) operated by the CBOs, Surat district has the largest share (40%), followed by Kutch (16%), Bhavnagar (15%), Rajkot (10%), Bharuch (8%) and Ahmedabad (6%).

For empirical analysis of the socio-economic outcomes or communal benefits of the mangrove restoration activities, a stakeholder survey has been undertaken during 2010 in seven villages, *viz.*, Lakki, Ashira Vandh, Nada, Kantiyajal, Dandi, Karanj and Tada Talav, spread over six talukas from four districts, viz., Kutch Bharuch, Surat and Anand. A total of 227 households were selected at random for the survey. The villages selected are diverse in terms of growth of plantations and their beneficial outcomes. Also, villages are seen to be distinct in terms of concentration of communities with uniform activity status (like fisheries, agriculture, livestock, etc.).

The analytical framework used tried to understand the dynamic interface between economy, society, ecology and the environment. It signifies that the ongoing CBMR activities interact with the economy, society, ecology and the environment. The mangrove development/ restoration activities are a joint outcome of participation between the state, the private sector and the local communities as the three important stakeholders. In the first instance, mangroves provide various economic benefits, say firewood, fodder for cattle, etc. Second, mangroves offer ecological functions in terms of enhancing the fish stock in the surrounding MPAs where mangroves grow as well as other coastal resources. From the environmental angle, mangroves protect the coastal environments from heavy tides, winds, sea level rise, etc. The human/ livestock interactions with the mangroves may prove to be beneficial as well as detrimental for the success or demise of the mangrove ecosystems, which calls for proper planning and policies leading to effective institutional and environmental governance regime for the sustainable management of mangrove eco-systems (Viswanathan *et al.*, 2011).

The empirical surveys undertaken in the seven study villages in Gujarat demonstrate significant socio-economic gains and environmental benefits as realised by the communities within a shorter span of 6-7 years of the CBMR activities. Table 14.3 provides a comprehensive view of the major benefits as reported by the mangrove based communities across the seven villages.

It is evident from Table 14.3 that the household dependence on mangroves for various benefits has been quite significant across the villages (34%) with highest dependence in Dandi (55%) and the lowest at Ashirawandh (25%). While fishermen communities are present in all the villages, the highest proportion of fisher households has been found in Karanj (67%), Nada (41.5%) and Dandi (40%) villages. Households also report having farm lands closer to the mangrove restoration cites (53%) which could not be cultivated earlier due to coastal cyclones.

An important benefit realised by the households from development of mangrove plantations has been increase in employment and wage earnings. While all households were benefited by the employment opportunities created by development and maintenance of mangrove plantations, the percentage of women households getting such opportunities has been quite significant in all the villages, except Karanj. On an average, each household received wage employment for 134 days per annum during the seven year period, with Ashirawandh reporting the highest employment to the tune of 243 days, followed by Lakki (188 days) and Tadatalav (185 days). The resultant gain in wage earnings has been as high as Rs. 14,820 per annum in Ashirawandh, followed by Rs. 12,577 in Lakki and Rs. 10,327 in Tadatalav.

Majority of the households tend to extract mangroves for various uses (46%), which ranged from 94 per cent in Ashirawandh to 88 per cent in Lakki, 72 in Tadatalav and 56 per cent in Nada. Compared to male household members, more proportions of women have been engaged in mangrove extraction for various uses.

Among the various uses for which mangroves are extracted, fodder and fuel uses are the prominent ones, with highest extraction of mangroves reported for fodder use for cattle. Reportedly, this provided

Table 14.3: Socio-Economic and Environmental Benefits of Community Based Mangrove Restoration in Gujarat, 2002 to 2007

	Descriptives	*Lakki*	*Ashirawandh*	*Karanj**	*Dandi*	*Nada*	*Kantiyajal*	*Tadatalav*	*All villages*
1.	Household dependence on mangroves (%)	27.6	25.2	35.2	54.8	28.4	35.1	33.6	34.1
2.	Presence of fishermen communities (%)	29.4	16.7	66.7	40.4	41.5	18.0	10.3	29.5
3.	Land close to mangrove sites (%)	25.0	42.9	0	0	66.7	80.0	36.4	52.5
4.	Women household members getting employment (%)	52.2	63.0	0	60.3	45.1	55.9	51.5	53.9
5.	Annual average employment generated per household during 2002-07 (No.)	188	243	0	67	103	85	185	134
6.	Annual average earnings from mangroves work (Rs.)	12577	14820	0	4728	6822	3954	10327	8735
7.	Households extracting mangroves for various uses (%)	88.2	94.4	0	21.3	56.1	22	71.8	45.8
8.	Women extracting mangroves (%)	26.7	76.5	0	90.0	52.2	27.3	85.7	62.5
9.	Mangroves extraction for fodder (%)	100.0	100.0	0	10.0	56.5	90.9	92.9	64.3
10.	Mangroves extraction for fuel (%)		0	0	90.0	43.5	9.1	7.1	35.7
11.	Percent gain in fishery income after mangroves	32.8	50.1	31.3	17.2	73.0	19.1	13.5	31.5
12.	Households own livestock (%)	82.4	94.4	13.3	0.0	26.8	30.0	71.8	38.3
13.	Mangroves reduced salinity ingression in crop lands (%)	58.8	44.4	0.0	68.1	68.3	76.9	71.4	55.4
14.	Mangroves reduced the crop damage due to winds (%)	82.4	55.6	0	19.1	53.7	68.0	71.8	50.1
15.	Households reporting seriousness of coastal cyclones (%)	94.1	100.0	73.3	51.1	87.8	72.0	97.4	78.9
16.	Households reporting reduced effects of coastal cyclones after mangrove plantation	82.4	83.3	25.0	66.0	85.4	78.0	94.9	73.6

Source: Viswanathan *et al.*, 2011.

two immediate benefits to the communities, viz., (a) helping them avoid purchase of fodder from the market; and (b) an increase in milk production as mangrove leaves were available in plenty to be fed upon to the livestock, especially in Ashirawandh, Lakki and Tadatalav. Besides, a large number of households have also reported about the multiple benefits realised, in the form of extraction of mangrove leaves (49%), fuelwood (24%), collection of seeds (23%) and wood planks (4%). Similarly, mangroves have benefited the fishermen communities in terms of an increase in fish catch from surrounding mangrove areas, which resulted in an increase in income from fishery. The income gains reported has been very high for fishers in Nada (73%) and Ashirawandh (50%) with other villagers also reporting significant income gains.

As observed, the environmental benefits realised by the households have been several. For instance, the villagers had been suffering from frequent coastal cyclones, which affect their farm lands causing damage to the crops. Similarly, salinity ingress in farm lands has also been a major problem reported by the villagers. An overwhelming majority of the communities reported that mangroves have reduced the salinity ingression in crop lands and thus saving crops from being lost. Further, the coastal cyclones always cause serious damages to the houses and other immovable properties of the households, which have now been protected by the mangrove plantations. Thus, from the above, it is evident that the CBMR activities have been highly rewarding in terms of its socio-economic impacts and environmental conservation benefits.

Besides the socio-economic and environmental benefits as discussed above, the mangroves also provided several intangible benefits, especially, protection of coastal ecosystems and the biodiversity. This was further evident from the detailed biological assessment undertaken to examine the vegetative growth and biodiversity dimensions of mangrove plantations in the study villages. The assessment brought about the diversity of the study villages in terms of presence of invertebrates, mobile fauna and other species. Among the villages, Lakki, Ashirawandh and Kantiyajal have reported the highest species richness supported by the mangrove ecosystem. The mangrove areas have been found to be quite rich in terms of other species, such as mudskippers, crabs, bivalve, gastropods, fish, and habitat for other species. As mangroves areas have achieved good growth over the past few years, they also found to be providing habitat for birds and marine reptiles, like snakes. An assessment of the biodiversity surrounding the mangrove plantations revealed interesting insights of the rich biodiversity as presented in Table 14.4.

Table 14.4: Status of biodiversity observed in the mangrove restoration villages

		Tadatalav	*Lakki*	*Ashirawandh*	*Karanj*	*Dandi*	*Nada*	*Kantiyajal*
1.	Crustacean							
	(a) Crabs	++	++++	+++	+++	++	++	++++
	(b) Prawns	++	+++	++	++	+	+	++
2.	Molluscan							
	(a) Gastropods	++	++++	+++	+++	+++	+++	++++
	(b) Bivalves	++	+++	++	++	+	+	+++
	Snake	+	-	-	-	-	-	+
	Birds	-	++	+	-	-	-	++
	Mudskipper	+++	++++	++++	++++	+++	++++	+++
	Other Fish	++	+++	++	++	++	++	+++

Note: - Absent, + Satisfactory, ++ Good, +++ Excellent, ++++ Quite rich.
Source: Viswanathan *et al.*, 2011.

Policy Issues and Institutional Imperatives

From the foregoing analysis, it emerges that the increasing expansion of industries along the coastal areas, including MPAs have caused increasing burden on the environment and ecosystems. It also emerges that the CBMR can be considered as an important instrument having significant potential for helping the regional economies to evolve policies and action oriented strategies for protecting the ecosystems and the MPAs in the larger Indian context. However, although stakeholder participation plays an important role in rehabilitation, conservation and management of mangroves, economic benefits to the different stakeholders to be derived from the planted mangroves and the newly established lands seem to be necessary in order to determine the sustainability of the programmes and their long-term impacts on biodiversity conservation. Since mangrove conservation requires long-term maintenance, the expectations of the stakeholders in terms of both short-term and long-term economic benefits from mangrove restoration and regeneration should be addressed systematically.

At the same time, how far the CBMR activities could be successful in protecting the ecosystems and the MPAs remains a moot question. This could be a potential area for research in the context of Gujarat in particular, where private industries and companies are in the forefront of claiming prime lands, including lands in the coastal fringes for setting up of industries, as discussed already. A vast majority of these industries/ companies are also expected to maintain greenbelts in their industrial premises as a measure of environmental protection. Invariably, mangroves are the most popular species being used by most of these industries for establishing the green belts.

In this regard, one of the major challenges especially in the specific context of the MPAs in Gujarat is to determine how the private and state sector industrial entities can be held primarily responsible for the serious casualties that have impaired the marine ecosystems and biodiversity? It needs serious thinking along with concerted actions as to how the private and state sector entities could join together in developing certain long term strategies for conserving the ecosystems and biodiversity of the MPAs. It then requires scaling up of the CBMR activities to cover more areas which need to be designated for expansion of mangrove plantations.

It also call for evolving long-term policies and institutional intermediations for carrying forward the development of new mangrove plantations as well as conservation/ restoration of the existing plantations. In this connection, it is important to consider that the local communities and the CBOs need to be more strengthened in terms of increased awareness, skill development, capacity building, etc so as to enable them to conserve/ restore the mangrove ecosystems for the future. Though a majority of the communities (91%) do feel that growing mangroves is important for protecting the coastal systems and livelihoods from the adverse effects of cyclones, soil erosion, etc., they still lack the motivation and incentives to conserve the resources on a sustainable basis. This is an important challenge, which needs to be addressed through policies and interventions for creating motivations for conservation and restoration. The fact that growth of mangrove plantations is adversely affected by industrial pollution as well as garbage deposited into the coastal waters has been identified as a serious environmental issue by the communities. Given this, it may be made mandatory that the coastal industries set apart certain amount of their financial resources for mitigating the environmental/ecosystem damages caused by their actions as well as for capacity building among the local communities to help conserve the environments, including the MPAs.

Finally, sustainable CBMR activities essentially call for more efforts for creating opportunities for collective action among the multiple stakeholders, like line state departments under various government portfolios, the local communities, private firms and industries who are increasingly investing in mangrove plantations, NGOs, local administration units, like the village Panchayats. This requires more frequent interactions among these stakeholders towards identifying more innovations and action plans for sustainable development and restoration of mangrove plantations in the villages. Needless to say that all these innovations and action plans should be targeted towards strengthening the capabilities of the local communities and sustaining their livelihoods without compromising on the broader goals of sustainable management of mangrove ecosystems.

FOOT NOTES

1. Reportedly, a Forest Official observed that "disposal of waste and spillage that will finally go into the Gulf while handling huge quantity of crude oil at Vadinar and other points, would certainly increase the level of pollution in the MNP. Forest officials hold that "the Gulf should be left alone, as too many projects have crowded it. Spillage from ships takes place when the imported crude oil is unloaded at the ports along the Gulf as also to the Single Buoy Mooring (SBM) set up by the Indian Oil Corporation in the sea off the Vadinar coast. The SBM poses a 'great threat' to the MNP, as it handles millions of tonnes of crude oil per year in a terminal within the sea itself. Minor spills that took place in the terminal in the past, caused extensive damage to mangroves and the marine life. The crude oil evacuated from ships to the SBM is pumped to the Mathura and Koyali refineries" (Joshi, 1998).
2. From the available data, it appears that 20 out of the 21 leases granted to salt manufacturers in mangrove areas adjoining the MNPS expired by the year 2005. Since the leases are granted or extended by the Forest Department, clarification on the current status of these leases was sought from the Principal Secretary of the Forest Department in Gujarat. It was informed that the current situation is yet unknown.

REFERENCES

Adger, W.N., P. M. Kelly and N.H. Tri,: Costs and benefits of mangrove conservation and restoration. In: Turner, R.K., Bateman, I.J., Adger, W.N. (Eds.), *Economics of Coastal and Water Resources: Valuing Environmental Functions.* Kluwer Academic Publishers, Dordrecht, The Netherlands, pp. 259–279. 2001.

Alongi, D.M. : "Mangrove forests: resilience, protection from tsunamis, and responses to global climate change", *Estuarine, Coastal and Shelf Science,* 76: 1-13. 2008.

Amarasinghe, U.S., M.D. Amarasinghe, and C. Nissanka : Investigation of the Negombo estuary (Sri Lanka) brush park fishery, with an emphasis on community-based management. *Fisheries Management and Ecology* 9 (1), pp. 41-56. 2002.

Barbier, E.B. : "Valuing Tropical Wetland Benefits: Economic Methodologies and Applications", *Geographical Journal,* Part 1, 59 (March.), pp. 22-32. 1993.

Barbier, E.B. : "Valuing Environmental Functions: Tropical Wetlands", *Land Economics,* 70(2), pp. 155-173. 1994.

Barbier, E.B. : Natural barriers to natural disasters: replanting mangroves after the tsunami, *Frontiers Ecol. Environ.* 4, pp. 124–131. 2006.

Barbier, E.B. : In the wake of tsunami: Lessons learned from the household decision to replant mangroves in Thailand. *Resource and Energy Economics,* Elsevier, vol. 30(2), pp. 229-249. 2008.

Biswas, Nilanjana : *The Gulf of Kutch Marine National Park and Sanctuary: A Case Study,* International Collective in Support of Fishworkers (ICSF), Chennai, 46p. 2009.

Cochard, R., Ranamukharachchi, S.L., Shivakoti, G., Shipin, O. & Edwards, P.J. : The 2004 tsunami in Aceh and Southern Thailand: a review on coastal ecosystems, wave hazards and vulnerability, *Perspectives in Plant Ecology, Evolution and Systematics,* 10: 3-40. 2008.

Conservation International : *Economic Values of Coral Reefs, Mangroves, and Seagrasses: A Global Compilation,* Center for Applied Biodiversity Science, Conservation International, Arlington, VA, USA, 23p. 2008.

CPCB : *Report of the High Powered Committee on Management of Hazardous Wastes,* Central Pollution Control Board, New Delhi. 2001.

CPCB : Environmental Information System, Central Pollution Control Board Annual Report 2002-03, Chapter VI — Present State of Environment, Environmental Problems and Counter Measures, Central Pollution Control Board, New Delhi. *http://cpcbenvis.nic.in/ar2003/ar2-3ch6.htm* (accessed on 18 July 2010). 2003.

Das, Saudamini : 'Storm protection values of mangroves in coastal Orissa', in P. Kumar and B. Sudhakara Reddy (eds.), *Ecology and Human Well-Being,* New Delhi: Sage Publications, pp. 197-212. 2007.

Das, Saudamini : 'Can Mangroves Minimize Property Loss during Big Storms? An Analysis of House Damage due to the Super Cyclone in Orissa', SANDEE Working Paper No. 42-09, (July), 36 p. 2009.

Dave, Hiral : "Power plant to come up on Jamnagar Marine Park land", *The Indian Express*, September 4, 2008.

DOD-ICMAM : Geographical Information System for Gulf of Kutch, Government of India, Department of Ocean Development, Integrated Coastal Marine Area Management (ICMAM) Project Directorate, Chennai. 2002.

EJF : *Did the Loss of Mangrove Forests Exacerbate the Impact of the Tsunami?*, Environmental Justice Foundation, London. 2005.

FSI : *India State of Forest Report* Ministry of Environment & Forests, Govt. of India. 2009.

Glaser, M. : Interrelations between mangrove ecosystem, local economy and social sustainability in Caet´e Estuary, North Brazil, *Wetland Ecol. Management,* 11, p.p.265–272. 2003.

GOI : *State of Environment Report, India-2009,* Environmental Information System (ENVIS), Ministry of Environment and Forests, 179p. 2009.

Hirway, I. and S. Goswami : *Valuation of Coastal Resources: The Case of Mangroves in Gujarat,* Academic Foundation, New Delhi, p.170. 2007.

Hoq, M.E. : An analysis of fisheries exploitation and management practices in Sundarbans mangrove ecosystem, Bangladesh. *Ocean & Coastal Management* 50 (5-6), pp. 411-427. 2007.

http://www.expressindia.com/latest-news/power-plant-to-come-up-on-jamnagar-marine-park-land/357160/ (accessed on 22 July 2010)

http://www.icsf.net/icsf2006/uploads/resources/usefulDocs/docs/english/%3C1238387193203%3EReport-Gujarat-MPA_final_march09_kg.pdf (accessed on 4 June 2010).

http://www.moef.gov.in, http://envfor.nic.in (accessed on 20 June 2010).

Iftekhar, M.S. and M.R. Islam : Degeneration of Bangladesh Sundarbans mangroves: a management issue. *The International Forestry Review* 6 (2), pp. 123-135. 2004.

Islam, M.S. and M.A. Wahab : A review on the present status and management of mangrove wetland habitat resources in Bangladesh with emphasis on mangrove fisheries and aquaculture. *Hydrobiologia,* 542, pp. 165–190. 2005.

Islam, M.S. and M. Haque : The mangrove-based coastal and near shore fisheries of Bangladesh: ecology, exploitation and management. *Reviews in Fish Biology and Fisheries* 14, pp. 153–180. 2004.

Joshi, Deep : "Oil spills threaten Gujarat Marine Park", *The Indian Express,* Thursday, September 17, 1998, *http://www.indianexpress.com/ie/daily/19980917/26050054.html* (accessed on 20 July 2010). 1998.

Kathiresan, K. : Global policies and institution, Biodiversity in mangrove ecosystems, pp. 317-332, In: K. Kathiresan & A.N. Subramanian (eds.) UNU -UNESCO International Training Course on Biodiversity in Mangrove Ecosystems, Course Manual, Annamalai University, India. 2003.

Kathiresan, K. and N. Rajendran : Coastal mangrove forests mitigated tsunami, *Estuarine Coastal and Shelf Science.* 65(3), pp. 601–606. 2005.

Kovacs, J.M. : Perceptions of environmental change in a tropical coastal wetland, *Land Degradation and Development,* 11, pp. 209–220. 2000.

Macnae, W : A general account of fauna and flora of mangrove swamps and forests in the Indo-West Pacific region, *Advances in Marine Biology*, 6:73-270. 1968.

Malakoff, D. Massive mangrove restoration backfires, *Science Now* [http://news.sciencemag.org/sciencenow/2008/07/15-01.html, accessed on 25 August 2010] 2008.

Mazda, Y., E. Wolanski, P.V. Ridd, (Eds.) : The Role of Physical Processes in Mangrove Environments, *Manual for the Preservation and Utilization of Mangrove Ecosystems,* Terrapub, Tokyo. 2007.

Nair, V. : *Status of the Flora and Fauna of Gulf of Kutch, India*; National Institute of Oceanography; Goa. 2002.

Nayak, Shailesh : Use of satellite data in coastal mapping, *Indian Cartographer,* 22; 147-156. 2002.

Reitenbeek, H.J. : Modelling economy-ecology linkages in mangroves: economic evidence for promoting conservation in Bintuni Bay, Indonesia. *Ecological Economics*; 10(3): pp. 233-247. 1994.

SEAP : *Environmental Action Plan for Gujarat – Problems, Causes and Solutions; State Environment Action Programme,* Gujarat Ecology Commission, Vadodara (Unpublished). 2003.

Singh, H.S. : Sea Mammals in Marine Protected Area in the Gulf of Kachchh, Gujarat State, India, *Indian Journal of Marine Sciences,* 32(3): 258-262 (September). 2003.

Singh, R.B : "Critical Problems of Coastal Ecosystem in India", *Indian Cartographer.* 2006.

Spalding, M.F.; F. Blasco C.D. Field : World Mangrove Atlas, International Society for Mangrove Ecosystems. 1997.

Stanley, O.D. : Proceedings of the National Seminar on Creeks, Estuaries and Mangroves – Pollution and Conservation, 28th to 30th November, 2002, Thane. Quadros, G. ed. 2002; 78-83. 2002.

Suwannodom, S., S. Siriboon and N. Paphavasit : *An approach to rehabilitate mangrove forests in Thailand,* In: *Proceeding of the fifth International conference on remote sensing for Marine and coastal environment,* San Diego, California, 5-7 October, 1998, Vol. II, pp. 241-247. 1998.

Thampanya, U., J.E., Vermaat S. Sinsakul and N. Panapitukkul, : "Coastal erosion and mangrove progradation of Southern Thailand", *Estuarine, Coastal and Shelf Science* 68: 75-85. 2006.

Tomlinson, P.B. : *The Botany of Mangroves, Cambridge Tropical Biology Series,* Cambridge, University Press, USA. 1986.

UNEP : After the Tsunami: Rapid Environmental Assessment Report, United Nations Environment Program (UNEP), Nairobi. 140 p. 2005.

UNESCO : Impacts and challenges of a large coastal industry, Alang-Sosiya Ship-

Breaking Yard, Gujarat, India, Coastal region and small island papers 17, United Nations Educational, Scientific and Cultural Organization, Paris, 65 pp. 2004.

Valiela, I., J.L. Bowen and J.K. York : Mangrove forests: one of the world's threatened major tropical environments. *Bioscience* 51(10), pp. 807–815. 2001.

Vermaat, J.E. and U. Thampanya : Mangroves mitigate tsunami damage: a further response, *Estuarine, Coastal and Shelf Science*, 69, pp. 1–3. 2006.

Viswanathan, P.K. and Jyoti Parikh : *Impact of industrialisation and related Activities on marine protected areas: A Case Study of Marine National Park, Jamnagar District in Gujarat*, Report submitted to IRADe, New Delhi, July 2010, pages: vi+103. 2010.

Viswanathan, P.K.; Kinjal D. Pathak and Ila Mehta : *Socio-Economic and Ecological Benefits of Mangrove Plantation: A Study of Community Based Mangrove Restoration Activities in Gujarat,* Gujarat Ecology Commission (GEC), Government of Gujarat, Gandhinagar, Ahmedabad, 164p. *www.gec.gov.in/pdf/GIDR%2520Report.pdf* 2011.

Walters, B.B., P. Ronnback, J.M. Kovacs, B. Crona, S.A. Hussain, R. Badola, J.H. Primavera, E. Barbier and F. Dahdouh-Guebas : Ethnobiology socio-economics and management of mangrove forests: A review, *Aquatic Botany*, 89, pp. 220–236. 2008.

Webb, E.L. and G. Shivakoti, (Eds.) : *Decentralization, Forest and Rural Communities: Policy Outcomes in South and Southeast Asia*, Sage Publishers, New Delhi. 2008.

Wetlands International : The Asian tsunami–the people and their wetlands, *Newsletter of Wetlands International*, April, No. 13, 6-7. 2005.

Zingde, M.D. : Studies on impact of release of liquid industrial waste from soda ash industry in the near shore water of North Gujarat; NIO, Environmental Impact on Aquatic and Terrestrial Habitats; 9-30. 1993.

Zorini, L.O., C. Contini, N. Jiddawi, J. Ochiewo, J. Shunula and S. Cannicci : *Participatory appraisal for potential community-based mangrove management in East Africa*, Wetlands Ecol Management, 12, pp. 87–102. 2004.

Annexure

Major Issues evolved from the Conference on 'Potential of Diverse Biodiversity Conservation Approaches and Livelihood Concerns in India'

Ajit Banerjee

We summarize hereafter the proceedings of the question and answer sessions that followed each presentation. Participants raised questions about the contents presented, wanted clarification and offered critical comments to which the speakers responded.

As some of these questions were repeated in different presentations we decided not to write on separately on each of these question and answer sessions after every presentation but to make a summary of those so that the readers can appreciate the problems the subject of the conference face and how different participants assess them. Some comments indicate how the problems need to be further studied or overcome.

The questions and answers can be broadly divided into the following issues. We will treat them each separately incorporating the major comments and their responses by other participants.

The issues are :

1. Potential of community management replacing state management of wild life reserves.
2. Potential of forest improving the livelihood of the people primarily forest dependent, based mainly on Non Timber Forest Produces (NTFPs).
3. Potential of culling to reduce straying of wild animals to the countryside when the number of animals exceeds the carrying capacity of the reserve.

4. Human population increase resulting in degradation of forests and wild life due to overuse.
5. Eco-tourism.
6. Neo-liberal approaches to biodiversity conservation.
7. Potential of landscape management of wild life instead of the present method of inclusive management.

1. Potential of community management replacing state management of Wildlife reserves

A number of participants indicated that state management of wild life reserves in India had been ineffective. The shortfalls include confrontation with the forest dependent local people living in or in the fringes of reserves, failure of constant endeavour to keep the local people away from using the forest for their subsistence, high cost of staff maintenance and causing hurt to forest quality and disturbance of animals due to over-sponsorship of eco-tourism to earn revenue for specific reserves, and lack of capacity to contain mafias and increasing list of endangered species with visible signs of decrease of population of some key species such as tigers.

On the contrary, some argued that there are examples in India such as community management of about 1 million hactare of forests in Orissa, community managed forests of Himachal Pradesh and of Uttarakhand and Joint Forest Management (JFM) in many states have shown comparative efficacy of community participation. They further argued, therefore, that state managed forest should be gradually transferred to local people for management. This will do away with high cost of reserve protection, substantial improvement to keep track of mafia and illegal operations as hundreds of village eyes will be at it and their confrontation with FD will reduce.

The arguments were vigorously opposed by others especially participants of State forest departments (SFDs). They contended that FD is being always made scapegoats for whatever ills the forests face. In the context of rising population pressure, large number of forest dependent people, acute poverty and unemployment in the forest fringe villages; they believe SFDs have done very well in securing the forests of the country. The community management evidences of Orissa, Himachal Pradesh etc. are really very small and their performance is not so good as has been painted. FD had been the savior in many cases which are not mentioned. One recent example is that of Forest Rights Act (FRA). In the Act, the forest department has no role but the departments which were to implement it fell back on the FD to assist them, in fact, carry out the major parts of implementation as the FD was found to be the only office capable of handling it. Transfer of forests and wild life reserves to community would create chaos and disaster.

As a counter argument, the participants were told that they are not advocating the change in one-go but a gradual transfer over a period. They understand that this will take quite a bit of advance action such as training, change of acts and rules etc. We can also see the progress of the management and development work of the forests being transferred presently to individuals and communities by FRA.

2. Potential of forest improving the livelihood of people primarily dependent based mainly on Non-Timber Forest Produces (NTFPs)

Quite a few participants believe that earning from forest by the fringe people motivate them to participate in forest management. FD and many others including some NGOs try to assist the people to add value to the NTFPs and improve their income. One question raised very emphatically in the proceedings whether we want the forest dependent people to continue to lead forest dependent deprived life for ever instead of we trying to give them alternative occupation for a more secure and better quality livelihood.

The question was not thoroughly discussed but comments were made that migration of rural and forest fringe people to urban and semi- urban areas is going on and the likelihood that finally forest dependence will go away when poverty in the country significantly reduces. This will take quite sometime, at least a few decades, and therefore, forest policy should continue to be people-oriented in respect of providing forest services to the people including incentives of collection of forest produces from some parts of the reserves as well. In addition there should be investment to improve forest productivity including those of NTFPs so that dependent people can earn additional income.

3. Potential of culling to reduce straying of wild animals to the countryside when the number of animals exceeds the carrying capacity of the reserve.

Culling of animals was another topic that was contested in the meeting by participants. It was introduced by a few authors and supported by some others that straying of animals from the reserves to the neighbourhood causing loss of property and life is increasing. Example of tiger in Sunderbans, elephant damage in different forest of India, pig and deer damages of agricultural crops in villages are examples. Straying may be due to various reasons but one of the chief causes is the lack of sufficient food for the animals within the reserve for the animal population. In some cases, it is not forest degradation that has caused the mismatch but increase of population in certain reserves due to good protection. This is particularly true for elephants in some reserves, deer and pigs in others. The proponents of culling proposed that after a thorough study, culling of animals should be allowed to keep specific animal population number down in such reserves subject to carrying capacity of the reserve. They also said that culling will add to the revenue that can go as investment and protection of the animals and vegetation in the reserve.

While the proposal was found be logical, some suggestions to avoid it came from others. One suggestion was that we can move some of the excess numbers to other reserves which are suffering from low population. However, transfer is very expensive and causes a lot of tortuous animal mortality. The second suggestion was that the reserve size could be suitably increased.

The record of culling in international experience was quoted to focus on the problems of culling. For example, elephant culling done for Africa with a target of 90,000 elephants ended up with killing of 300,000 elephants. In Indonesia 1500 crocodiles were allowed to be culled but because of the poor control of law 3000 were killed. There is, however, contrary example. In Australia 200,000 kangaroos were to be culled and the decision was strictly followed.

Culling has also an ethical aspect that cannot be ignored in India. This statement, however, was counteracted by indicating that we attend to ethics when larger animals are involved. We do not bother when small life forms are destructed to keep human beings in healthier state.

4. Human population increase creating pressure on the forest and wild- life

During the question-answer sessions quite often mention was made of rise in population in the country including the population of the forest dependent people. It was also mentioned that although the per cent of poverty is on the decline but the absolute number of poor people is on the increase whose forest activities affect adversely the forest quality. Specific case study for example in Sunderbans of West Bengal was cited. This is, however, true for the most of the forest areas of the country.

There was however, another opinion which indicated that population increase need not necessarily be the cause of degradation. A specific case study of Sunderbans also indicated that a welfare scheme over ten years created a situation where the people in response to the scheme vowed that they will protect the forest area and in fact the state of the forest over the ten years has dramatically improved. Similarly, Midnapore forest in 1970 was in a very bad state but with the peoples' participation and forest protection, the forest rehabilitated by 2000 although in 30 years, namely during the period of 1970-2000 the population have increased by not less than 200 per cent.

It is not a question of population increase singularly that adversely affect forest and wild life. It is the attitude of the people and their degree of forest stakeholding that influences forest protection and conservation.

5. Ecotourism

Eco-tourism was discussed in the question-answer session. It was mentioned that ecotourism has come to stay and is expected to continue to increase its dimension over time. It is seen that generally some of the reserves get a name because of the frequency of locating some important and large animals such as tigers, elephants, lions, specific birds as found in Bharatpur and so on. Ecotourism thus is an instrument by which people get more and more exposed to our ecological heritage. It also earns revenue for the government that make some of the reserves better funded. Eco-tourism, therefore, should be encouraged.

The contrary thought was that large frequency of visitors to the reserve areas greatly disturbs wild life in their abode and it may also create problems of breeding. The visitors' in India generally do not follow the rules and regulations that should be maintained during such visits. For example, once a tiger is located in a tiger reserve more than 25 cars with hundreds of riders will crowd the place sometimes not too distant from the animal concerned.

There was some consensus amongst the participants, namely that eco-tourism should go on with certain restrictions such as of limited number of visitors at a time and in a restricted space and no visit to the core area. The visitors should also be given a briefing about do's and don'ts in the reserve before they are allowed entry into the reserve.

6. Neo-liberal approaches to biodiversity conservation

Proponents of this approach argued that patterns of use natural resources (including conservation) are best determined by market processes implying that private resources can be traded in market without intervention of any other intermediary. In consequence producers will bid prices of the produces so that alternative uses that degrade the environment will not be attractive to producers. One example quoted was that of elephant trophy hunting and ivory sales where elephants are conserved but not utilized. They became serious pest to local live and livelihood in Africa. However, if the elephants are utilized for regulated hunting and ivory sales there, then the local people will protect and manage them and thus reduce damage of properties.

On the contrary, others argued that this approach is problematic in Indian context where marginalised tribals mostly inhabit in most diverse region as they are incapable to market forces. Further neo-liberalization constitutes to shift towards privatization of management to community management that is found to have superior conservation attainments to state management.

7. Potential of landscape management of wildlife instead of the present method of inclusive management

A number of papers advocated that the present system of having wild life reserves such as national parks, sanctuaries, specific animal reserves such as tiger project, elephant project etc. should be under landscape management. This would mean that the wild life will not be restricted over a localized forest space but allowed freedom of movement outside forest as well such as in agriculture, horticulture areas and even over inhabited rural areas. They pointed out that the reason for advocating change is that the present management system is imperfect. These include the forests outside the wildlife reserves (in India 25 per cent of the total forest, 75 per cent outside of it) are also the habitat of many animals but do not get enough attention. Secondly, when in a particular reserve, any specific animal exceeds that of the carrying capacity of the reserve, the animals stray into the neighbouring areas and damage crops and life creating man-animal conflict. Thirdly, there is a chance of (example, lions of Gujarat) of inbreeding making the animals vulnerable to pathological attacks.

In response it was pointed out that landscape idea is theoretically good but practically difficult to implement. Even straying of animals from reserve into the neighbouring areas creates large damage to property life etc. So allowing animals to stray anytime and even inhabit such areas would create more damage.

Secondly, supervision of 25 per cent of forest which are now declared as reserves of some category is expensive but making intensive supervision of the whole area of 100 per cent will be financially prohibitive.

Thirdly, inbreeding can be technically managed by bringing in fresh outside animals from time to time to diversify the DNA stock. As a counter argument it was suggested by some participants that landscape management would make the people habituated to the norm and will not be affected as of now by sudden attack by stray animals migrating from the reserve. Another counter-argument was that it was not necessary for staff to increase *pro rata* as the proposed system will dramatically change from wild life inclusive management to open management which will not need staff supervision as local people will be involved then in this task as a part of their daily chores.

One specific case study presentation claiming landscape management was on Gir lions. Although the analysis showed that the lions often stray out of the reserve on to the village areas they are in fact captured and returned to the reserve. The author pointed out that the local people assist in recapture and are not hostile to lions. This particular case study is still, however, not a clear-cut case of landscape management.

Index